50 Canadians Who Changed the World

50 Canadians
Who Changed the World

Ken McGoogan

HarperCollins*PublishersLtd*

HarperCollins Publishers Ltd
2 Bloor Street East, 20th Floor
Toronto, Ontario, Canada
M4W 1A8

www.harpercollins.ca

Library and Archives Canada Cataloguing in Publication
information is available upon request.

ISBN 978-1-44340-930-8

Printed in the United States of America
RRD 9 8 7 6 5 4 3 2 1

To Sheena, my fellow traveller
And to Carlin, Keriann, Travis, Sylwia, James, and Veronica
Long may we run . . .

Contents

IN THE BEGINNING

In the beginning, the Dominion Institute conducted the mother of all Canadian surveys. The poll proved notable not for its sample size or methodology, but for what it revealed: our ignorance. The institute asked 1,000 Canadians to identify iconic figures from photographs. Almost 90 percent could name Terry Fox and Céline Dion, and 75 percent knew Wayne Gretzky and Pierre Elliott Trudeau. But from there the scores plummeted. The year was 2009. Less than half the respondents recognized Michaëlle Jean, then serving as Canada's Governor General. And only 19 percent could name Tommy Douglas, who, five years before, had been voted the greatest-ever Canadian.

Given a chance, most Canadians could probably identify Margaret Atwood, Farley Mowat, and David Suzuki. But judging from that mother of all surveys, few would be able to name the small-town busker who reinvented the circus, the aspiring comic-book artist who transformed Hollywood movies, or the convent school girl, child of a broken marriage, who ended up bringing war criminals to justice. And what of the militant humanitarian who leads the fight against AIDS, the feminist tackling the global water crisis, or the electrical engineer who sparked a communications revolution?

All of these transformative figures were born in the twentieth century. They have changed or are changing the world. In recent years, our citizens have led United Nations programs and commissions,

1

spearheaded research into life on other planets, and turned up on lists of the world's most influential people. Canadians have written hundreds of books that have reached millions of people in scores of languages. We have won Booker Prizes, Grammy Awards, Oscars, literally hundreds of international awards for everything from architecture to human rights. The typical Canadian responds, "Well, if these people are great, how come we know nothing about them?"

Some say it's because our schools don't teach Canadian history. That is part of the problem, certainly. But the vast majority of the world-beaters in this book are alive today. They are not historical but contemporary figures. Why don't we know these people and what they have accomplished?

Three reasons spring to mind. First, we live in denial. The late pianist Oscar Peterson, who turns up later in this book, put it this way: "How can he play any good? He comes from here! He's a Canadian!" Second, we shrink from blowing our own horns. Fiction writer Alice Munro, who also appears in *50 Canadians*, recalls being taught never to "call attention" to herself. She titled one of her books *Who Do You Think You Are?* Third, we revel in self-deprecation. When we fill in the blanks, we remain "as Canadian as possible under the circumstances." We love Will Ferguson's title: *Why I Hate Canadians*. We laugh at ourselves to ensure that nobody beats us to it.

Denial, inhibition, self-deprecation. Together, they betray our national inferiority complex, a condition fostered by both our colonial past and our American present. As a political entity, Canada sprang from France and Great Britain, which boast written histories extending back over centuries. Looking at that, Canadians feel like toddlers in a world of adults. At the same time, we live next door to the world's only superpower, a Godzilla nation with ten times our population and a commensurate ability to project a national narrative. Pierre Elliott Trudeau likened Canada to a mouse that sleeps with an elephant: "No matter how friendly and even-tempered is the beast, if I can call it that, one is affected by every twitch and grunt." We feel small. We feel marginal. We apologize and poke fun at ourselves.

A decade ago, in *While Canada Slept: How We Lost Our Place in the World*, Andrew Cohen wrote that while once Canada "punched above its weight internationally," it no longer does so. The country has cut spending on humanitarian aid and global intelligence gathering, while conducting "pinch-penny diplomacy and foreign policy on the cheap." Canada is trading on a reputation built two generations ago, he writes—"a reputation we no longer deserve."

If we compare Canada with other countries, nation to nation, state to state, then Cohen has a case. But what if we look at individuals? As soon as we turn from the state to the private citizen, we discover a universe filled with Canadian world-beaters. Judging from the evidence laid out in this book, Canadians are changing the world in far greater numbers than we have any right to expect. As individuals, we are still punching above our weight.

Why should this be so? The answer is Canadian pluralism. As I wrote in *How the Scots Invented Canada*, ours is a kaleidoscopic nation. Here we find French Canadians, Scottish Canadians, Chinese Canadians, Jamaican Canadians, Polish Canadians, Irish Canadians, Vietnamese Canadians, the list goes on. Here, too, we find myriad Aboriginal peoples: Inuit, Mohawk, Mi'kmaq, Cree, Dene, Blackfoot, Haida. Cutting across these ethnicities, we discover regional and local identities: Newfoundlanders, Atlantic Canadians, Québécois, Torontonians, Manitobans, Albertans, British Columbians.

Most developed countries tolerate plural identities. But what they struggle to accommodate, Canada embraces and proclaims. This is partly the result of necessity: ours is a country of minorities. But it derives also from historical timing. The original thirteen colonies of the United States of America adopted a constitution in 1787.

Inevitably, that document reflected eighteenth-century ideas about the nation state: one nation, one state, one national identity. As a result, the United States became proudly one and indivisible, and it fought a civil war to stay that way. Citizens of the United States have a single, overriding identity: they are Americans.

Canada, by comparison, did not even begin to emerge as a state until late in the nineteenth century. The country reached a political milestone in 1867 with Confederation. But even then Canada remained subject to the British North America Act, a document that Britain could repeal at any time. Only in 1982, under Pierre Elliott Trudeau, did this country gain control of its own constitution. By then, Canada was too complex to fit into an eighteenth-century constitutional mould. Trudeau recognized that the country had become pluralistic: regional, multicultural, multiracial, multinational.

He realized that, as a pluralistic state, Canada could become "a brilliant prototype" for the civilization of tomorrow. He convinced Canadians to reject the ethnocentric model (one nation, one state) championed by Québécois nationalists—and adopted in the 1700s by Americans—and recognize that freedom is most secure when two or more nations co-exist within a single state. This pluralistic vision, rendered into reality by the Canadian Charter of Rights and Freedoms, makes Canada unique among developed nations. That reality means individuals have room to grow, no matter their roots, no matter their complexities. It explains why so many Canadians have changed the world.

It also explains why, instead of arguing ideas, I decided to focus on individuals. That, I reasoned, is where the stories are. I quickly discovered a multitude of extraordinary individuals—far too many. And so I adopted two basic criteria. First, because I hoped to paint a portrait of contemporary, cutting-edge Canada, I confined my selections to Canadians born in the twentieth century. This meant excluding remarkable figures from an earlier era, but opened up space for those changing the world today. Second, I wanted to focus on Canadians who have made a difference globally. This ruled out people who have worked miracles here at home but have had little impact in the great wide world.

A third criterion emerged as I wrote. If you want to build an Olympic team, you don't choose all sprinters, all swimmers, or all hockey players. You seek to achieve a balance. Guided by the argument implied in the title, I organized my individuals into six broadly inclusive groups. Three of them include those who act directly on the external world: activists, humanitarians, and scientists and inventors. Two comprise individuals who work indirectly, from the inside out, and change the world by transforming others: artists and performers. The sixth group consists of visionaries who, working both directly and indirectly, guide us into the future. And now an order evolved.

I. Activists vigorously advocate causes or decry political or social situations. Here we discover an Ontario farm boy providing Keynesian economic advice to American presidents, an Inuit woman linking climate change to human rights, and a spirited Muslim calling for an Islamic Reformation.

II. Visionaries discern possible futures and lead us into them. Consider the media guru who anticipated the global village, the bicycling matron who transformed our idea of the city, and the architect who creates buildings that reflect his Aboriginal heritage.

III. Artists change the way we perceive the world and keep us honest. Here we include painters, writers, and filmmakers, among them a Japanese Canadian paving the way for minorities, a transnational filmmaker investigating identity, and a playful inventor who built a universe of trivia.

IV. Humanitarians strive to alleviate suffering. Examples include the former Governor General who brings hope to Haiti, the Hollywood star taking on Parkinson's disease, and the globe-trotting doctor who does most of her work in war zones.

V. Performers, among them actors, musicians, and athletes, showcase what pluralism can accomplish. They broaden and intensify experience while fostering tolerance and opening new channels of communication. Examples: an eccentric pianist changed the way we hear classical music; a Mohawk actor kicked down Hollywood doors for Aboriginal peoples; a nightingale sings French Canada to the world.

VI. Scientists and inventors extend our knowledge of the physical world and improve our daily lives. Here we encounter a Nobel Prize winner who pointed the way to lasers, an immigrant geneticist battling rare diseases, and a female astrophysicist leading the search for life on other planets.

Do these categories overlap? Absolutely. Margaret Atwood is an activist and an artist, Michael J. Fox a humanitarian and a performer, and David Suzuki a scientist and an activist. But no organizational scheme could precisely encompass the complexity of the individuals chronicled here. Not only that, but in a few instances, a transformative Canadian accomplishment involved more than one individual: stem cell research, for example, or the development of the graphic novel. Complexities notwithstanding, we begin each of the book's six parts with a notable exemplar, subsequently profiled, and encounter the others roughly in birth order (exceptions arising by virtue of date of impact).

Researching the book proved instructive. If you arrange the Canadians included here chronologically by date of birth, for example, the percentage of women increases as we move deeper into the twentieth century. But of course: women did not become "persons" in Canada until 1929. How could "non-persons" hope to change the world? The gradual emergence of women reflects the evolution of the country. In the end, women turn up in every category and comprise almost 40 percent of our total.

Canada famously has more geography than history. The second-largest country in the world, after Russia, it is bigger than India, China, or the United States, all of which have far larger populations. The country's distances might be expected to spawn achievements in communications. Sure enough, in this field we find such figures as Marshall McLuhan, Don Tapscott, and Mike Lazaridis. Canada also boasts three coastlines, numerous wilderness areas, and a striking reach into the High Arctic. So we should not be surprised to discover environmentalists scattered through our six categories, among them Farley Mowat, Margaret Atwood, Maude Barlow, Sheila Watt-Cloutier, and David Suzuki.

What about our vaunted humanitarianism? Our respect for civil liberties? These traditions thrive in such figures as Stephen Lewis, Roméo Dallaire, Louise Arbour, Michaëlle Jean, Irshad Manji, Samantha Nutt, K'naan Warsame, and Craig Kielburger. And our commitment to freedom of expression has called forth a dazzling array of creative artists and performers, from Jay Silverheels and Alice Munro through Oscar Peterson, Leonard Cohen, and Joni Mitchell.

Inevitably, *50 Canadians Who Changed the World* reflects my values, my judgments, my vision of Canada. If my views or assessments prove challenging, debatable, or provocative, so much the better. If this paean sounds so immodest as to be almost un-Canadian, I do not apologize. These individuals changed the world. Many started with unusual gifts. All discovered possibilities where others saw none. They set objectives, they made commitments, they applied themselves with energy and discipline. They overcame barriers, they travelled distances, they created legacies. They leave us not just astonished, but humbled and inspired, proud to be Canadian, and happy to be alive.

Part I

Activists

They act directly to effect social and political change

The headline read, "Aga Khan hails Canada for getting pluralism right." The *Toronto Star* article, published on October 15, 2010, quoted the spiritual leader of fourteen million Shia Ismaili Muslims as praising Canada for allowing citizens to keep their personal identities as they become Canadian. "What the Canadian experience suggests to me is that honouring one's own identity need not mean rejecting others." The Aga Khan marvelled that 44 percent of Canadians are of neither French nor British descent. "We might talk not just about the ideal of harmony—the sounding of a single chord—but also about counterpoint," he added. "In counterpoint, each voice follows a separate musical line, but always as part of a single work of art, with a sense both of independence and belonging."

The Aga Khan's words would have been music to the ears of Prime Minister Pierre Elliott Trudeau, who voiced the same idea with a tide-turning speech during the 1980 Quebec referendum campaign. Speaking at a massive rally in Montreal, Trudeau responded to separatist leader, René Lévesque, who had suggested that the prime minister was not truly a Quebecer because his "Elliott side" had gained the upper hand. Trudeau was not *"pur laine."* In *Just Watch Me: The Life of Pierre Elliott Trudeau, 1968–2000*, biographer John English devotes several pages to Trudeau's response, which he made at the Paul Sauvé Arena.

English notes that Trudeau's "voice broke with emotion"—unusual in itself—"as he responded to Lévesque's reported remarks about his mother's name." Trudeau denounced the taunt as showing contempt for all those Quebecers who had a drop of foreign blood in their veins. His emotional defence of his own pluralistic heritage, French and Scottish, became "the story of the speech," English writes. For Trudeau himself, whose motto was "reason over passion," the address was "surely too personal—too close to his own memories of his struggles with identity and his relationship with his past."

Pierre Elliott Trudeau was world-renowned as an intellectual. But as he showed when responding to the nationalist provocation, he was also, and perhaps primarily, a political activist. He vigorously advocated pluralism, and he acted to make it a Canadian reality. Viewed from a global perspective, Trudeau turned Canada into a beacon of pluralism. Judging from the words of the Aga Khan, he changed the world.

To Trudeau, we shall return. As a globally transformative Canadian activist, he does not stand alone. Here in Part I, we meet at least one other activist politician. But we also encounter a military man who halted a genocide, and five women who battle war criminals, water crises, climate change, religious fundamentalism, and disaster capitalism. Canadian suffragist Nellie McClung was born too early for inclusion in this book. But she sounded a chord that would resonate with Canada's twentieth-century activists when she said, "Never explain, never retract, never apologize. Just get the thing done and let them howl."

1

TOMMY DOUGLAS

A folksy preacher brings socialized medicine to North America

When he was ten years old, Tommy Clement Douglas lay in a Winnipeg hospital bed, hoping that doctors would find a way to fix his aching leg. For months, the boy had been limping in pain as a result of a knee injury that had got infected and turned into osteo-myelitis. He had undergone one medical procedure after another. He did not know it, but doctors had told his parents that, short of a wildly expensive operation, they could do no more. To end the boy's pain, they would have to cut off his leg at the knee.

Such was the prognosis when an orthopedic surgeon, Dr. R.H. Smith, led a group of medical students through the children's ward. Possibly the specialist had got wind of the situation: suffering child, hard-working but poor immigrant family. He stopped, chatted with the boy, and flipped through the chart at the foot of his bed, reading the history of failed procedures. The case intrigued him. Later that day, the surgeon told Tommy's parents that he would undertake a difficult experimental surgery for free if they would allow him to use the operation as a training exercise.

As an adult, Tommy Douglas would describe this moment as a turning point in his life. The procedure worked better than anyone had dared to hope. Before long, he was hiking, running, playing soccer, and even boxing his way to a provincial championship. "If I hadn't been so fortunate as to have this doctor offer me his services gratis," Douglas said later, "I would probably have lost my leg. I felt that no boy should have to depend either for his leg or his life upon the ability of his parents to raise enough money to bring a first-class surgeon to his bedside. And I think it was out of this experience, not at the moment consciously, but through the years, I came to believe that health services ought not to have a price-tag on them, and that people should be able to get whatever health services they required irrespective of their individual capacity to pay." These beliefs, passionately held, eloquently expressed, would make Tommy Douglas a groundbreaking politician beloved across the country.

Proof came in 2004, when the Canadian Broadcasting Corporation invited the people of Canada to choose the greatest Canadian of all time. After six months of voting by email, letter, and website, the network aired a first show revealing the bottom forty of the top fifty contenders. Then it presented a series of documentary profiles of the top ten, with a different celebrity championing each finalist. Five of the finalists turn up in this book, including the top three. The winner, and the recipient of more than 1.1 million votes, was this diminutive, Scottish-born politician who spent much of his career in Saskatchewan.

Why did Canadians, who voted from coast to coast to coast, name Tommy Douglas the greatest Canadian of all time? Certainly, as premier of Saskatchewan for seventeen years, he had led the first socialist government in North America, and made it work. Certainly, he had orchestrated the formation of the federal New Democratic Party and led it for a decade. But really, Douglas was chosen because he brought universal public health care to Canada, an accomplishment that sparks astonishment around the globe even today. Tommy Douglas changed the world by establishing socialized medicine within a capitalistic North America.

Douglas had been born into a family of ironworkers in Falkirk, south central Scotland, on October 20, 1904. At age six, he moved with his parents to Winnipeg, Manitoba. Four years later, he underwent the surgery that saved his leg. Later that year, when his reservist father went to fight in the First World War, his mother brought Douglas and his sisters back to Scotland to be near family. When the War finally ended, the reunited Douglases returned to Winnipeg, arriving just in time to catch the violent suppression of the 1919 General Strike.

From a downtown rooftop, as an appalled fifteen-year-old, Tommy Douglas witnessed the clubbing and shooting of striking workers. By then he had quit school and begun working as a printer's apprentice. Now he took up boxing and trained at the One Big Union Jim [sic]. In 1922, at 135 pounds (61 kilograms), he fought for the lightweight championship of Manitoba. After a six-round fight during which he suffered a broken nose and lost several teeth, Douglas emerged victorious. The following year, he defended the title successfully. He was a scrapper.

From his Scottish father, Douglas had learned to appreciate the egalitarian poetry of Robert Burns, to savour the historical narratives of Sir Walter Scott, and to admire the fortitude of Robert the Bruce, who had fought his way through six defeats to final victory. He became active in the church, the Boy Scouts, and then the Cameron Highlanders, and on parade days he would don a kilt and play clarinet in the marching band. At twenty, having decided to become a church minister, Douglas resumed his education at Brandon College in Manitoba, which was run by Ontario Baptists. There, during the next six years, he emerged as a natural leader. He also embraced the social gospel movement, which insisted that Christianity should be more a social religion than one focused on the great hereafter. In 1930, he married Irma Dempsey. Their daughter, Shirley Douglas, would marry actor Donald Sutherland and give birth to another actor, Kiefer Sutherland.

Ordained as a Baptist minister, Tommy Douglas moved to Saskatchewan, where the Great Depression began taking a heavy toll. As minister at Calvary Baptist Church in the town of Weyburn, Douglas got a good look at unemployment, poverty, and despair. That experience galvanized him. He organized a local wing of the Independent Labour Party. This soon evolved into the Farmer Labour Party, which fought for unemployment insurance, universal pensions, and public health care.

In July 1932, with the Depression ongoing, Douglas attended a four-province founding convention of the Co-operative Commonwealth Federation (CCF), an alliance of western labour parties that became Canada's first nationwide socialist party. Two years later, while honing the folksy speaking style he had begun developing as a preacher, Douglas ran in a provincial election and lost. But in 1935, encouraged by a friend, he ran federally for the CCF. This time, at age thirty-one, he got elected.

During two terms as a Member of Parliament, Douglas forged a reputation as a witty, informed debater. He championed the underprivileged and frequently took controversial stands. He was renowned for his folksy stories. He wrote a fable called "The Cream Separator," an extended anecdote, based on an observation by the scholar Lewis Mumford. It describes how capitalism provides cream to the elite, whole milk to the middle classes, and a watery blue residue to workers and farmers. Douglas would insist "that the time has come in this land of ours for the worker and the primary producer to get their hands on the regulator of the machine so that it begins to produce homogenized milk in which everybody will get a little cream."

Douglas made a similar argument with his version of "Mouseland," in which mice, voting to choose their leaders, keep alternating between black cats and white cats. When finally one mouse suggests that they select one of their own as leader, he is denounced as a Bolshevik and thrown into jail. Douglas would say you can lock up a mouse or a man, but you can't lock up an idea. Today, an animated version of "Mouseland," using Douglas's narration and introduced by his actor grandson Kiefer Sutherland, is available online.

In 1939, when the Second World War broke out, Douglas volunteered for overseas service. A medical examination kept him in Canada: it identified a leg problem that was probably related to that boyhood operation. When the war ended, Douglas argued in a radio broadcast that "if we can produce in such abundance in order to destroy our enemies, we can produce in equal abundance in order to provide food, clothing, and shelter for our children."

Believing he could accomplish more at the provincial level, Douglas resigned his seat in Parliament to contest the Saskatchewan election as leader of the CCF. He ran on the slogan "Humanity First" and won. For the next seventeen years, he governed his adopted province as the most socially revolutionary premier Canada has ever seen. He introduced an old-age pension plan that covered medical, hospital, and dental services. He transformed the education system and installed a medical school at the University of Saskatchewan. He paid off the provincial debt and rebuilt the physical infrastructure, improving everything from roads to sewage pipes. Douglas introduced Canada's first publicly owned automobile insurance plan and created Crown corporations that competed in the private sector. He also became the first head of any Canadian government, federal or provincial, to advocate a constitutional bill of rights.

In 1961, after introducing universal medicare legislation in Saskatchewan, Douglas resigned as premier to help create, and then to lead, the federal New Democratic Party (NDP). The NDP brought together the CCF (backed by farmers) and the Canadian Labour Congress (unionized workers). As the first leader, Douglas proved an outstanding spokesman for democratic socialism. Yet in 1962, he failed to win his own seat, largely because of a backlash, led by the medical profession, against the implementation of medicare. This provincial program, which he had designed and introduced, prompted doctors in Saskatchewan to strike. Eventually they backed down and, in Saskatchewan, medicare was born.

Within a decade, despite jurisdictional overlap between national and provincial levels of government, that province's health care model had become entrenched across the country, with the federal government contributing to a national program that remains the envy of the world. In December 2012, *Globe and Mail* columnist Jeffrey Simpson put it this way: "Say what you like about medicare today, its arrival in Saskatchewan in 1962 and its extension across Canada in 1972 was one of the most consequential developments in 20th-century Canada." In his 2007 film documentary *Sicko*, the American political activist Michael Moore hails Tommy Douglas while decrying the fact that almost fifty million Americans have no health insurance coverage, and many who thought they had it have been denied care.

By the time he retired from politics in 1976, Tommy Douglas had kicked open several doors. He had led the first socialist government in North America and made it work. Then, by leading the NDP for a decade, he had moved democratic socialism into the political mainstream. Finally, he had become the father of medicare, a system of universal health care that, although it undoubtedly needs updating, is rightly viewed as one of the most advanced in the world. Analyzed and admired by Americans who support "Obamacare," or the introduction of affordable health insurance for all citizens, the program even today provides a measure of what can be achieved within the context of a capitalist economic system.

2

John Kenneth Galbraith

An Ontario farm boy advises American presidents

American Republicans could see him coming a mile away, and not just because he stood six foot eight in his socks. On his first morning in Massachusetts, where at age twenty-five John Kenneth Galbraith had arrived to teach economics at Harvard University, his just-met Republican landladies told him to find other accommodation. The previous evening, this lanky Canadian farm boy had voiced his unabashedly liberal views while championing the "New Deal" being rolled out by President Franklin Delano Roosevelt. The year was 1934. The Great Depression had arrived to stay. Thirteen million Americans were out of work, one-quarter of the workforce, and some said twenty million. The young ex-farmer from Ontario had spent the summer in Washington, working for the Agricultural Adjustment Administration, one of Roosevelt's initiatives. That first evening in Cambridge, he must have spoken with some passion, because the Boston Brahmin homeowners could not abide his continuing presence in their house.

Galbraith took refuge among the Boston Irish, whom he would later remember fondly. He proceeded to become a thorn in the side of Republicans, and arguably the most influential economist of the century. Before he was done, Galbraith would publish 1,100 articles and four dozen books. Those works would sell seven million copies in thirty-odd languages. Galbraith would receive fifty honorary degrees. He would serve as adviser to three American presidents and become American ambassador to India. During the Second World War, he would rule the economy as "czar" of consumer price controls. He would become president of the American Economic Association and of the American Academy of Arts and Letters. Through it all, as he liked to say, he sought "to comfort the afflicted and afflict the comfortable."

Ken Galbraith, as he preferred to be called, was born in 1908 in Iona Station, a hamlet in southwestern Ontario. He grew up Scottish Protestant on a 50-acre family farm where his father raised cattle. In a wry memoir called *The Scotch*, Galbraith would later paint a vivid picture of "the uncompromising Calvinism of our upbringing." The local school "was a plain rectangular structure of white brick and consisted of one small room together with a very small entry where we hung our coats on hooks and stowed our lunch boxes on a shelf above." Here Galbraith learned to read and write—mostly, he suggests, despite his teachers. As for the Baptist church he attended, "it contained nothing, literally nothing, but square oaken pews and a plain wooden pulpit. Church doctrine forbade a choir, organ—in fact music of any kind. The singing of Psalms was allowed."

Galbraith found the austerity hard to bear and the sermons worse. Yet he would become so clearly a product of his early environment—independent, duty-driven, overachieving—that in retrospect he serves as a poster boy for Scottish Canadian Protestantism, minus the religious faith and somewhat in the spirit of Robbie Burns. Galbraith attended high school in the town of Dutton. Later, he would sprinkle his elegantly written works with humorous anecdotes. His favourite from his school days finds the young farm boy leaning against a fence outside his home, chatting with an attractive female neighbour. Out in the pasture, a big white bull mounts a willing cow. The young man reddens, kicks at the dirt, and stammers, "I think it would be fun to try that." According to Galbraith, the visitor doesn't miss a beat: "Well, go ahead," she says. "It's your cow."

Galbraith's parents were politically active. His mother died in 1923, but his father, a "man of standing" in the community, remained a leading Liberal Party activist until his death in the late 1930s. After high school, Galbraith attended the Ontario Agricultural College (OAC, now the University of Guelph). Here he discovered and honed a talent for storytelling, co-founded a campus newspaper, and ended up writing a weekly column for two small-town papers. During his senior year at OAC, Galbraith travelled to Chicago for the International Livestock Exhibition. This trip, which included visits to agricultural facilities at several American universities, opened his eyes to the great wide world. That summer, he landed a research job interviewing farming families about the devastating effects of the Great Depression. The experience convinced him that something had gone wrong with agricultural markets.

In 1931, having won a fellowship to study agricultural economics at the University of California, Galbraith travelled to Berkeley with a family friend. There he hit his intellectual stride, bashing through courses on economic theory, research methods, agricultural policy, the history of economic thought, money and banking, and public finance. He emerged as an outstanding student. At Berkeley, Galbraith encountered the progressive work of Richard Ely and Thorstein Veblen, who in the name of fairness and equity challenged the prevailing neoclassical thinking that free markets could solve any economic problem. For his doctoral thesis, and while teaching part-time, Galbraith wrote a public-finance study of county expenditures in California. Early in 1934, nearing graduation, he attended a meeting of the American Economic Association. There he learned that the economics department at Harvard University was seeking to add a junior staff member for a year. He landed the job, travelled to Massachusetts, and, after being rejected by the Brahmin landladies, eased into an association with Harvard that, briefly interrupted, would last four decades. Three of those would see him serving as the world's most influential economist.

Early on at Harvard, Galbraith found a mentor—economist John D. Black—who shunted important research projects his way, including some that involved him in New Deal programs. In 1937, Galbraith spent a fellowship year at Cambridge University in England. There, he absorbed the groundbreaking work of John Maynard Keynes, who challenged free-market orthodoxies and advocated government intervention—fiscal and monetary action—to reduce the devastating effects of recessions and depressions. Galbraith had already written five long papers about the workings of Roosevelt's New Deal, which focused on relief, recovery, and reform. Now, he co-authored a book, *Modern Competition and Business Policy*, arguing that the government should establish a commission to promote economic recovery.

In 1940, during the Second World War, Galbraith went to work for the New Deal government of President Franklin Delano Roosevelt. He became deputy head, or "price czar," at the Office of Price Administration, a virtually invisible position of such power that later he would joke that the rest of his career had been all downhill. He mobilized the public to accept wage and price guidelines and fostered rapid growth through the war years. Afterwards, he helped lead strategic bombing surveys and, on behalf of America, advised administrations in Germany and Japan.

Galbraith taught for a year at Princeton University. Then, from 1943 to 1948, he served as editor of *Fortune* magazine, a position that allowed him to popularize the work of John Maynard Keynes. In 1949, he returned to Harvard as a professor. While attached to that university (he would become professor emeritus in 1975), Galbraith forged a multifaceted career as an economist, public intellectual, and political adviser. In *John Kenneth Galbraith: His Life, His Politics, His Economics*, biographer Richard Parker shows how Galbraith drew on his writerly gifts and his formidable grasp of economic theory and practice to produce a stream of highly readable books. In *American Capitalism: The Concept of Countervailing Power* (1952), Galbraith identified unions and lobby groups as constituting a "countervailing power" that would restrict the worst excesses of big business.

Two years later, he followed up with *The Great Crash, 1929*, an analysis of the financial disaster that launched the Great Depression. Against all the odds, that book became a bestseller. It is laced with his trademark sardonic humour and remains in print even today. With *The Affluent Society* (1958), Galbraith produced another block-buster. Lambasting "conventional wisdom," he argued that post-war America should use taxation to fund highways, health, and education. He proved relentless, elaborating his arguments through such books as *The New Industrial State, Economics and the Public Purpose*, and *A Short History of Financial Euphoria*.

While he studied and wrote, and having already served President Roosevelt, Galbraith worked as an adviser to presidents John F. Kennedy and Lyndon B. Johnson. With Kennedy, in particular, he became close friends. Later, he would describe how, on arriving in Kennedy's office one morning, the president asked him what he thought of an article that had just appeared in *The New York Times*. Galbraith said he liked it well enough, but added, "I don't see why they had to call me arrogant." Kennedy responded, "I don't see why not. Everybody else does."

Galbraith had long since acquired American citizenship, and in 1961, Kennedy appointed him ambassador to India. In that country, he worked closely with Prime Minister Jawaharlal Nehru. He criti-cized Britain's passivity during the 1947 partition of India, helped establish a computer science department at a leading technological institution, and paved the way for First Lady Jacqueline Kennedy to visit India and Pakistan on diplomatic missions. Galbraith received the Presidential Medal of Freedom twice—once each from Harry S. Truman and Bill Clinton. His other honours include the Order of Canada, the Padma Vibhushan, India's second-highest civilian award, and fifty honorary degrees from around the world.

The election of Republican president Richard Nixon in 1969 saw him excluded from the corridors of power. Galbraith wrote more non-fiction books. He presented a BBC series on economics, and even produced a few novels, notably *A Tenured Professor*. During the 1980s and '90s, when neo-conservatives were in the ascendant, celebrating free markets and decrying government regulation, Ken Galbraith fell out of fashion. After all, this was the man who, in his 1986 book *The Good Society: The Humane Agenda*, had written, "The basic need is to accept the principle that a more equitable distribution of income must be a fundamental tenet of modern public policy in the good society, and to this end progressive taxation is central." As for his naysayers: "The modern conservative is engaged in one of man's oldest exercises in moral philosophy: that is, the search for a superior moral justification for selfishness."

In 2006, when Parker's biography of Galbraith appeared, William Greider reviewed the book in *The Nation*. He predicted that Galbraith's works would eventually come back into vogue: "When the right's rigid ideology falters and breaks down, sooner perhaps than people imagine, Americans will need an explanation for what went wrong. They can read Galbraith." Two years later, Lehman Brothers declared bankruptcy. The ensuing financial crisis spawned economic problems that are still unfolding throughout the developed world. And those who looked back discovered that, in his efforts to comfort the afflicted and afflict the comfortable, Ken Galbraith changed the world: he sowed the seeds of twenty-first-century resistance to increasing inequality.

3

PIERRE ELLIOTT TRUDEAU

An intellectual prime minister creates a pluralistic beacon

"Of course my name is Pierre Elliott Trudeau," the Canadian prime minister declared at the Montreal rally introduced on page 11. "Yes, Elliott was my mother's name. It was the name borne by the Elliotts who came to Canada more than 200 years ago. It is the name of the Elliotts who, more than 100 years ago, settled in Saint-Gabriel-de-Brandon, where you can still see their graves in the cemetery. That is what the Elliotts are. My name is a Quebec name, but my name is a Canadian name also, and that's the story of my name."

The prime minister was speaking in May 1980 during the run-up to the first, hotly contested provincial referendum on whether Quebec should separate from Canada. Separatist leader René Lévesque had suggested that Trudeau was not really a Quebecer because he was part Scottish. Trudeau responded with uncharacteristic passion. Journalist Ian MacDonald, often critical of the prime minister, later called the speech "the emotional and intellectual coup de grâce of the referendum campaign."

Pierre Elliott Trudeau was bent on vindicating the notion of plural identity. His mother, Grace Elliott, had been raised by her widower father—a Scottish Canadian of United Empire Loyalist stock. She married Charles-Émile Trudeau, a French Canadian lawyer and entrepreneur who became wealthy when he sold a chain of gas stations to Imperial Oil. Born in 1919, Trudeau grew up speaking French to his father and English to his mother. When he was fifteen, his father died of pneumonia. Trudeau helped his mother through the crisis, and continued to live with her through his twenties and thirties. In his early forties, he escorted her to parties and concerts, and even took her on a holiday to Europe, where he drove her around on the back of his motorcycle.

An athletic loner, young Trudeau was a canoeist, a skier, an accomplished diver. He was a fearless traveller who, decades before it became fashionable, went backpacking not just around Europe but through Cuba, China, and the Middle East. He was an intellectual who honed his arguments and debating skills at Collège Jean-de-Brébeuf, Harvard, the Sorbonne, and the London School of Economics. Having become a tough-minded political philosopher who enjoyed a rough-and-tumble debate, Trudeau jumped into the public arena when, as a thirty-year-old lawyer, he actively supported unionized workers during an Asbestos strike that marked a turning point in Quebec social history. Through the 1950s, he wrote articles and founded a magazine, *Cité Libre,* that lambasted the reactionary politics of Quebec premier Maurice Duplessis.

By 1965, he was teaching constitutional law at the Université de Montréal when, with two Quebec allies, he agreed to run in the federal election as a Liberal. Elected in Mount Royal, Trudeau served as parliamentary secretary to Prime Minister Lester Pearson. Then he became minister of justice. Casting about for the toughest challenge he could find, Trudeau liberalized divorce laws. He legalized contraception, abortion, and lotteries, and decriminalized homosexuality, famously declaring, "The state has no place in the bedrooms of the nation."

In 1968, after Pearson stepped down, the charismatic Trudeau was chosen Liberal party leader. He called a federal election and found himself riding a wave of popularity that came to be called

"Trudeaumania." The evening before the election, while attending the Saint-Jean-Baptiste parade in Montreal, a Quebec nationalist celebration, he faced down a ragtag band of separatist rioters who threw rocks and bottles in his direction. The next day, newspapers ran with a variation on a single headline: "Trudeau defies Quebec separatists." He won enough seats in the House of Commons to form a majority government, the first in six years, and became prime minister of Canada.

At this time, almost seven decades into the twentieth century, Canada did not control its own constitution. The country was still governed under the British North America Act of 1867, according to which legal authority over Canadian affairs rested with Great Britain. This explains why, for example, Canadian women had been forced to appeal to the British Privy Council in 1929 to gain recognition as "persons." In the 1960s, Canadian thinkers and politicians—among them Donald Creighton, George Grant, and John Diefenbaker—still envisioned a Canada with a single identity. They thought the country could become a modern nation-state built on the European model of the eighteenth century, the model that had given rise to the United States of America. In their view, the state of Canada should consist of only one nation or people.

In 1967, during a Progressive Conservative leadership convention, Diefenbaker entered the race at the last minute expressly to fight the party's "Deux Nations" policy. He could not countenance the idea that "Canada is composed of two founding peoples with historic rights who have been joined by people from many lands." He argued that this gave special status to Canadians of English or French descent, and relegated all others to "a secondary position." Diefenbaker insisted, and here Trudeau agreed, that citizenship should not be dependent "on race or colour, blood counts or origin." The problem was that "Dief the Chief" took a narrow view of citizenship: one nation, one

identity. And he never glimpsed the possibility
postmodern: the notion that a Canadian citizen
one identity, and be, for example, both a Canadi
or both a Canadian and a Québécois.

Pierre Elliott Trudeau recognized that the Ca
in the second half of the twentieth century was
into the eighteenth-century mould. He saw the co
bilingual, multicultural, regional, multinational. 1
that, as a pluralistic state, Canada could become "a
for the moulding of tomorrow's civilization." He urged Canadians to
reject the old ethnocentric model (one nation, one state) championed
by Québécois nationalists, and recognize that freedom is most secure
when nations coexist within a single state. "I've always believed in
the superiority of a multinational society," Trudeau would observe
late in life. "There are very few countries left where people are all of
the same ethnic stock. Even if you wanted to say that of Canada, it's
just not true."

In October 1971, driven to answer the challenge of ethnocentric
Quebec nationalism—"*Le Québec aux Québécois*"—Pierre Elliott
Trudeau told the House of Commons that "there cannot be one cultural policy for Canadians of British and French origin, another for
the original peoples, and yet a third for all others. For although there
are two official languages, there is no official culture, nor does any
ethnic group take precedence over any other. No citizen or group
of citizens is other than Canadian, and all should be treated fairly."
Trudeau noted that "adherence to one's ethnic group is influenced
not so much by one's origin or mother tongue as by one's sense of
belonging to the group." And then he articulated "a policy of multiculturalism within a bilingual framework" as a means of assuring
the cultural freedom of Canadians. "Such a policy should help to
break down discriminatory attitudes and cultural jealousies. National

unity, if it is to mean anything in the deeply personal sense, must be founded on confidence in one's own individual identity; out of this can grow respect for that of others and a willingness to share ideas, attitudes and assumptions. A vigorous policy of multiculturalism will help create this initial confidence."

This initiative won wide support in the House of Commons. Robert Stanfield, leader of the Progressive Conservative opposition, applauded the move towards "preserving and enhancing the many cultural traditions which exist within our country." He emphasized that the initiative "in no way constitutes an attack on the basic duality of our country," and chided the Liberal government only for being slow to recognize Canada's diversity. David Lewis, leader of the New Democratic Party, urged Canadians to take pride in "having been founded by two distinctive groups having two distinctive languages well known throughout the world," and also in having "in Canada representatives of almost all the cultures in the world." The diversity of cultures across the land, he added, "is a source of our greatness as a people." Even Réal Caouette, the Québécois leader of the Social Credit Party, declared himself in complete agreement. Caouette noted that he had repeatedly declared "that we have one Canadian nation, and not two, three or ten, that we have two official languages, English and French, and that we have a multiplicity of cultures which are the wealth of our country."

Federal politicians proved supportive. But in Quebec, the pluralistic vision of Pierre Elliott Trudeau ran into fierce opposition. Quebec nationalists wanted to separate from Canada and create what Trudeau repudiated as a reactionary, ethnocentric state. This clash of visions would play itself out over the next decade. The story has been told many times, notably in a three-part TV documentary called *The Champions*, which focuses on the struggle between Trudeau and nationalist leader René Lévesque. In 1980, while serving as premier of Quebec, Lévesque launched a provincial referendum seeking a mandate to negotiate independence from Canada. One turning point came when women mounted a rally in support of the federalist option. But even more crucial was Trudeau's emotional speech at the Paul Sauvé Arena: "My name is a Quebec name, but my name is a Canadian name also."

On referendum night, after winning the contest with almost 60 percent of the vote, Trudeau made explicit his pluralist sense of identity, when he declared, "Never have I felt so proud to be a Quebecer and Canadian." This statement implied, obviously, that other individuals could be Ontarian, Nova Scotian, Albertan, or whatever, while also being Canadian. And that was the vision that drove Trudeau to bring home the Canadian constitution. During the referendum campaign, Trudeau had promised that such a result would lead to a renewal of federalism. Now, in the face of mounting opposition, he set out to create a Canadian constitution with a charter of individual rights and freedoms and a domestic amending formula—a constitution that, for the first time, could be amended without the consent of Great Britain. To that end, he met behind closed doors with the ten provincial premiers.

Ultimately, thanks to adroit political manoeuvring, Trudeau gained the support of nine out of ten provinces (Quebec excepted); he himself, as an elected politician from Quebec, gave the process cross-country legitimacy. His Canadian Charter of Rights and Freedoms, amended after fractious consultations, reflected the "rights revolution" then unfolding in Western democracies. In addition to individual equality rights, the Charter provided language rights for French Canadians, legal equality for women, and treaty rights for Aboriginal peoples. Also, under Equality Rights, the constitution enshrined pluralism as a Canadian value by insisting that every individual "has the right to the equal protection and equal benefit of the law without discrimination and, in particular, without discrimination based on race, national or ethnic origin, colour, religion, sex, age or mental or physical disability."

Trudeau had to compromise in several areas, most notably by including a "notwithstanding clause" that would permit provinces to "opt out" of Supreme Court judgments they deemed unacceptable. But as Trudeau said later, "Better a Charter which is flawed than no Charter which is perfect." The constitutional wrangling was not ended. It would resurface in debates over the Meech Lake (1987) and Charlottetown (1992) accords, both of which would be defeated, and it would lead to a second Quebec referendum (1995), when federalists turned back Quebec nationalists by a narrow margin, winning just 51 percent of the popular vote.

Pierre Elliott Trudeau has been criticized for suspending civil liberties in 1970, when, after the politically motivated murder of a Quebec cabinet minister, he introduced the War Measures Act. Challenged by a TV journalist, who demanded to know how far he would go, Trudeau responded, "Just watch me," and then sent troops into the streets of Montreal. A decade later, he was accused of alienating western Canada when he launched a National Energy Program to regulate the oil and gas industry. These and other criticisms have some merit. But they do not alter the fact that on April 17, 1982, with Queen Elizabeth II, Pierre Elliott Trudeau signed the Constitution Act at an outdoor ceremony in Ottawa.

That was when Canada came of age as an independent nation. Only then did Great Britain cede the right to change the document serving as the Canadian constitution. Only then did the Supreme Court of Canada become the final authority over decisions affecting Canadians, with individual rights taking precedence over legislative rulings. And only then, with the enshrining of equality rights, and thanks to Pierre Elliott Trudeau, did Canada become a global beacon of diversity and pluralism.

4

ROMÉO DALLAIRE

A military man makes war on genocide

He arrived in Rwanda, Africa, to lead a United Nations peacekeeping mission. By the side of the road, he spotted an old woman
lying alone, pain and despair etched into every line of her face. She
weighed no more than a few dozen pounds. She lay in the ruins of
her former shelter, which had been stripped of its tarp and ransacked
of possessions. He realized that, in the grim reality of this refugee
camp, she had been given up for dead, her meagre belongings shared
out among her neighbours. When he asked, an aid worker shook her
head and told him that the old woman would not last the night. She
would die alone, like an animal, with nobody to hold or comfort
her. Faced with such misery, he thought that now, in August 1993, at
least he had seen the worst.

In fact, Roméo Dallaire had seen nothing like it. An old woman
dying alone? During the next several months, as he would write
later, he would see such sights as would make hers look like a merci-
ful death. He would see men, women, and children slaughtered, and
realize they were a fraction of the 800,000 who died during 100 days
of bloody madness. He would try, and fail, to prevent what he would
later describe, quite rightly, as the worst genocide of the twentieth century. Eventually, Dallaire would change the world by setting in motion
an investigation that would call to account those responsible for that
genocide—an investigation that would stand as a rebuke and a sign-

post warning that this was a road that should never again be taken.

Roméo Dallaire was born on June 25, 1946, in Denekamp, Netherlands, where his Canadian father, also named Roméo Dallaire, was serving as a non-commissioned officer when the Second World War ended. His mother was a Dutch nurse, Catherine Vermaessen. He arrived in Canada with his parents as a six-month-old baby and grew up in east-end Montreal, where he mastered both French and English. At age seventeen, he joined the Canadian army, becoming a cadet at the Collège militaire royal de Saint-Jean. He graduated with a bachelor of science from the Royal Military College of Canada in 1970, and was commissioned into the Royal Regiment of Canadian Artillery.

Over the next two decades, he advanced steadily through the ranks. In 1989, promoted to brigadier general, he commanded both the Collège militaire royal de Saint-Jean and the 5th Canadian Mechanized Brigade Group. Four years later, he was named Force Commander of UNAMIR, the United Nations Assistance Mission for Rwanda. At that point, he would write later in *Shake Hands with the Devil,* he knew nothing about Rwanda.

Dallaire soon learned that Rwanda was a small East African country where ethnic tensions had sparked a low-grade civil war. Suddenly, his appointment made sense. He had grown up negotiating ethnic differences. A staunch federalist, he had lived through the Quiet Revolution, the rise of Quebec nationalism, and the first Quebec referendum (1980). In Rwanda, two peoples, Hutus and Tutsis, shared a history of sporadic violence. Hutus comprised 85 percent of the population, and most were moderates. But an extremist Hutu government had inspired a Tutsi rebellion.

In July 1993, the militants signed off on the Arusha Accords, a peace treaty orchestrated by the United States, France, and the Organization of African Unity. As commander of UNAMIR, Dallaire was assigned to ease the transition and to see that the minority Tutsis were given positions of power within the Hutu government. Soon enough, he realized that all was not well. He learned that government troops had begun checking identity cards that proclaimed individuals either Hutu or Tutsi—a procedure that, for him, evoked the Nazi era, when the identity cards of Jews were marked with a distinguishing "J."

Early in 1994, a French airplane arrived in Rwanda loaded with ammunition and weapons for the government's Rwandan Armed Forces (Forces Armées Rwandaises, or FAR). Through an informant, Dallaire learned that FAR intended to use these weapons to attack Tutsis after orchestrating the withdrawal of the best-trained and best-equipped troops in the country, a Belgian contingent. He sent a telegram to United Nations headquarters asking permission to seize these weapons. The United Nations denied that permission. Dallaire was not to seize the shipment. His mandate was to watch, wait, and assist.

The Belgians, having lost heart, went home. And, as Dallaire had warned, the violence began. Government forces rounded up Tutsis and slaughtered men, women, and children. He consolidated his few troops to provide safe zones in the capital city of Kigali. Observers claim he saved more than 32,000 lives. But he had nowhere near enough troops. He cried out for more. He estimated that, with another 5,500 troops, he could quell the violence. But the United Nations said no. The United States and France said no. He received no more troops.

The slaughter escalated. Dallaire called it what it was: a genocide—a deliberate, systematic attempt to destroy a particular ethnic, racial, or religious group. The massacre would continue for 100 days. Barbarous and brutally efficient, the Hutu extremists would kill at least 800,000 Tutsis. Some say the total exceeded one million.

The United Nations Security Council reversed itself and the French, former colonial masters, sent troops. Their presence enabled the remaining Tutsi forces—the Rwandan Patriotic Front (RPF)—to sweep into Kigali and end the genocide. By August 1994, RPF leader Paul Kagame had gained control of Rwanda, and he remains president of the country to this day.

Another Canadian who appears in this book, Louise Arbour, would lead a multilateral investigation through the International Criminal Tribunal for Rwanda. As a military man, Dallaire's mission was at an end. He departed Rwanda and, though in some ways that country would not let him go, earned several more promotions: Deputy Commander of Land Force Command, Commander of 1 Canadian Division, and then Commander of Land Force Quebec Area. Dallaire became Chief of Staff, Assistant Deputy Minister (Human Resources—Military), and Special Advisor to the Chief of Defence Staff.

Meanwhile, for six years, as he would later reveal, he suffered post-traumatic stress disorder and endured "an unrelenting regimen" of therapy and medication. In 2000, haunted still by some of the atrocities he had witnessed, Dallaire attempted suicide by combining alcohol with antidepressant medication, an almost lethal combination that left him comatose. He survived. He applied himself to writing a book about his experiences: *Shake Hands with the Devil.* It would be published in Canada in 2003 and win the Governor General's Literary Award for Non-Fiction. As the work neared completion, Dallaire's co-author, an experienced writer, committed suicide.

In 2004, at the International Criminal Tribunal for Rwanda, Dallaire testified against a Hutu colonel, Théoneste Bagosora, offering testimony critical to the outcome of the trial. Bagosora was convicted of the murder of ten Belgian peacekeepers. The judges held that this "formed part of the widespread and systematic attack" against the Tutsis, and so constituted genocide.

Dallaire was not yet done. Retired from the military, he was appointed to the Canadian Senate in 2005, where today he remains as a Liberal representing the province of Quebec. Meanwhile, he had inspired a documentary film, *Shake Hands with the Devil: The Journey of Roméo Dallaire*, which won a 2004 Sundance Film Festival Award. That year, too, PBS Frontline broadcast a documentary, *Ghosts of Rwanda*, in which Dallaire declared, "Rwanda will never ever leave me. It's in the pores of my body. My soul is in those hills, my spirit is with the spirits of all those people who were slaughtered and killed that I know of, and many that I didn't know."

Two feature films surfaced as well—*Hotel Rwanda*, starring Nick Nolte, and *Shake Hands with the Devil*, a Canadian production that was nominated for twelve Genie Awards and won one. Dallaire inspired songs by Jon Brooks, Andy McGaw, and Welshman James Dean Bradfield. The United States made him an Officer of the Legion of Merit, the highest military decoration available to foreigners, and he received the inaugural Aegis Trust Award from the United Kingdom.

With honours and appointments flowing, Dallaire could have retired. But at the dawn of the new millennium, he spoke at a conference on children in war zones, and his singular insights landed him an appointment as a special adviser to the Canadian government on war-affected children. Ten years later, he published a book on the subject: *They Fight Like Soldiers, They Die Like Children*. In it, he wrote, "In Rwanda, I saw child soldiers in action and met the adults who directed them, and I was unable to engage and to stop them, leaving me with a rage that remains unabated nearly two decades after the fact. Despite my efforts, I have not yet been able to significantly influence action against the use of child soldiers, let alone eradicate their use. But that has not deterred me from continuously seeking means and ways of attacking the problem—or from hoping one day to succeed."

5

LOUISE ARBOUR

A law reformer brings war criminals to justice

People scoffed when Canadian Justice Louise Arbour was touted as a candidate for a high-profile, international position at the United Nations. In 1987, while serving as vice-president of the Canadian Civil Liberties Association, Arbour had angered feminists by leading the battle to overturn Canada's rape shield law. She argued, successfully, that the law was unconstitutional, that questions about the past sexual history of alleged victims could be relevant, and that it would take "only one wrongful conviction for all the gains that women have made in this area to be lost."

Five years later, while serving on the Ontario Supreme Court, Arbour argued, controversially but successfully, that prisoners should have the right to vote. She also was part of a three-person panel that acquitted a Hungarian-born Canadian, Imre Finta, of war crimes during the Second World War. She argued that Nazi war crimes, by definition, "do not meet stringent domestic evidence rules." This led some members of the Canadian Jewish community to claim she was making Canada a safe haven for Nazis.

In 1996, therefore, when Arbour went to interview for a top international posting—notably with American officials including Madeleine Albright, the tough-minded chair of the United Nations Security Council—she arrived trailing controversy. Some bureaucrats felt she was out of her league. But Arbour and Albright hit it off. At age forty-nine, Canadian Justice Louise Arbour became chief prosecutor of the International Criminal Tribunals for the former Yugoslavia and Rwanda. Before she was done, she would change the world by prosecuting war crimes with an unprecedented vigour, so fostering the emergence of an international human rights culture.

The former Yugoslavia had been the site of a savage ten-year war, and Arbour had to investigate massacres, ethnic cleansings, and rape camps. In Rwanda, she was dealing with still worse atrocities and the genocide that Roméo Dallaire had sought to prevent. Yet over the next three years, almost incredibly, Arbour earned global recognition for her successes with both files. As a result of her work at the tribunals, rape was recognized under international law as possibly genocidal: a crime against humanity. Arbour was still chief prosecutor when the court upheld the first-ever conviction of a head of state, Jean Kambanda of Rwanda, for orchestrating genocide. But she is most honoured for her 1999 indictment of Yugoslav President Slobodan Milošević for war crimes, the first time a serving head of state was called to account before an international court.

Louise Arbour came from a broken family. Her parents owned a hotel chain but found themselves unhappily married. They sent their ten-year-old daughter—born in Montreal on February 10, 1947—to a private all-girls convent school and eventually divorced. At Collège Regina Assumpta, Louise Arbour became editor of the school magazine and gained a reputation for impertinence. After graduating in 1967, she enrolled at the Université de Montréal and turned to mastering English. Three years later, she graduated with a degree in civil law. She worked for two years as a law clerk for a Supreme Court justice while completing graduate studies at the University of Ottawa.

Called to the Bar of Quebec in 1971, Arbour became a research officer for the Law Reform Commission of Canada. She then taught at Osgoode Hall Law School, York University, moving from lecturer (1974) to associate professor (1977) to associate dean (1987). Meanwhile, she published articles prolifically, writing in both French and English. After serving as vice-president of the Canadian Civil Liberties Association, she was appointed to the Supreme Court of Ontario and then to the Ontario Court of Appeal, the first franco- phone to achieve that last milestone.

In 1995, Arbour was appointed to lead an investigation into the strip-searching—"cruel, inhuman, and degrading treatment"—of women prisoners by a male riot squad at Kingston, Ontario. Her unflinching assessment and denunciations to the Solicitor General of Canada culminated in a shakeup at Correctional Service of Canada. During this period, the United Nations had begun seeking a chief prosecutor to lead two major war crimes investigations. Arbour accepted the position in 1996.

Even before she officially took up her appointment, she trav- elled to the former Yugoslavia, which had spawned 90 paramilitary groups, 150 mass graves, and 900 prison camps. She visited Vukovar in Croatia, where an eighty-seven-day siege had ended with 2,000 killed, 800 missing, and 22,000 forced into exile. At the local hospi- tal, where some fighters had taken refuge, soldiers had rousted 280 people, including many wearing pajamas and relying on crutches and canes. They led them out into a farm field and beat and murdered them, throwing the bodies into a makeshift grave. Shocked and horri- fied, Arbour set out to amass the evidence she needed to lay charges.

At the Hague, home to the international court and her main base of operations, Arbour discovered that governments had arrested few detainees, none of them from the upper echelons. She targeted two Serbian ringleaders: Milan Kovačević, who established concentration camps in Bosnia where thousands of civilians were raped, tortured, and murdered; and Slavko Dokmanović, the man behind the Vukovar hos- pital slaughter. Until now, the tribunal had issued public indictments, alerting targeted figures to be on guard. Arbour began issuing secret indictments and using SWAT teams. The first person to be arrested on a sealed indictment was Dokmanović. Arbour's office put a great deal of effort into prosecuting him, she said later, "and it was only because the accused committed suicide shortly beforehand that no judgement could be delivered in that case."

In Rwanda, meanwhile, Arbour confronted horrific evidence of mutilations, burnings, and beheadings, with parents murdered in front of children and children raped in front of parents. But challenges included computers and phones that didn't work, shortages of court staff, and wretched housing accommodation for detainees. Arbour used the media to raise the profile of the tribunal, secured changes in personnel, and from Jean Kambanda, elicited the first admission of guilt for genocide committed by a head of state. The trial of one of Kambanda's henchmen, Jean-Paul Akayesu, was the first to define certain instances of rape as an act of genocide.

In 1999, towards the end of her term, Arbour gleaned information about yet another massacre of civilians in Kosovo and acted to end the tradition of impunity for war crimes. She issued the first-ever warrant for the arrest of an active head of state, charging President Slobodan Milošević with crimes against humanity. Some international observers criticized this action, claiming that she was undermining the chances for peace. But as one informed observer wrote, "her vigorous strategic quest to frame indictments for the campaigns of torture and massacre was sustained by her empathy for the powerless, the terrorized, the bereaved." In 2001, Slobodan Milošević was arrested and sent to face charges before the international court at the Hague. His five-year trial ended without a verdict in 2006, when he died of a heart attack after refusing to take prescribed medicines.

By that time, Louise Arbour had become one of the best-known judicial figures in the world. Her work had inspired an acclaimed

Canadian-German movie entitled *Hunt for Justice: The Louise Arbour Story*. Since completing her term as chief UN prosecutor, Arbour has served on the Supreme Court of Canada, as United Nations High Commissioner for Human Rights, and as president and chief executive officer of the International Crisis Group. Throughout her career, she has received thirty-nine honorary degrees (and counting). Her international medals and awards include the Franklin D. Roosevelt Freedom from Fear Award, the French Legion of Honour, and the North-South Prize of the Council of Europe.

Louise Arbour offered an especially cogent synopsis of what she stands for in 2005, when she received the Thomas J. Dodd Prize in International Justice and Human Rights. Speaking at the University of Connecticut, Arbour said that the Nuremberg trials, which followed the Second World War, led to the development, despite strenuous resistance, of an international legal system. Nuremberg gave rise to the two international tribunals she led, and they in turn spawned the International Criminal Court (ICC). "War crime trials are a natural extension of the idea of universal rights," Arbour said, "which is itself the cornerstone of rights-based democratic regimes. The ICC reflects the emerging power of an international human rights culture."

Arbour declared "the old strategy of peace without accountability" ineffective and outdated. The concept of fundamental human rights, she said, is being recognized and vindicated: "We are witnessing an irreversible globalization of human rights expectations, and a consequent growth in institutions necessary to remedy the grossest abuses of the most fundamental of these rights." The significance of this global transformation, to which Louise Arbour contributed so much, can hardly be overstated.

6

Maude Barlow

A feminist champion warns of a global water crisis

The earth is running out of fresh water. So says Maude Barlow, who has served as senior adviser on water to the president of the United Nations General Assembly. Already, because of pollution, climate change, and surging population growth, almost two billion people live in "water-stressed" regions of the planet. By 2025, two-thirds of the world's population "will face water scarcity." In her seventeenth book, *Blue Covenant: The Global Water Crisis and the Coming Battle for the Right to Water*, Barlow warns that by the mid-2020s, "desalination plants will ring the world's oceans, many of them run by [dangerous] nuclear power." Corporations will employ nanotechnology, manipulating matter on an atomic scale to "clean up sewage water and sell it to private utilities, which will in turn sell it back to us at a huge profit." The rich will drink bottled water while millions die as a result of water shortages.

Barlow, co-founder of the Blue Planet Project and chairperson of the Council of Canadians, is changing the world by attracting international attention to this threat to survival. She has been writing of a looming water crisis for more than a decade. In 2002, as co-author (with Tony Clarke) of *Blue Gold: The Fight to Stop the Corporate Theft of the World's Water*, Barlow warned that transnational corporations, having defined water as a human need and not a human right, were taking control of public water services, bent on treating water "like any other tradeable good," and using it to make a profit. During the past decade, as can be seen on any number of videos available online, Barlow has insisted repeatedly that the scarcity of fresh water is "the greatest human rights and ecological crisis of our time." She describes it as the "first face of climate change" and calls it very much a women's crisis, in that water shortages lead to increasing violence against women.

For Barlow, whose international honours include Sweden's Right Livelihood Award (the "Alternative Nobel") and the American EarthCare Award, the struggle to protect water from profit-hungry corporations is part of the international resistance to economic globalization. It is linked to climate change and the global depletion of resources. And it evolved out of the women's movement, which "slammed into my reality in the 1970s."

This latest initiative has still deeper roots, judging from a CBC-TV documentary broadcast in 2001. Called *Immovable Maude: The Life and Times of Maude Barlow*, that work traces the roots of her activism to the influence of her father, Bill McGrath, a Second World War veteran who became a crusading criminologist and founder of the Canadian Association for the Prevention of Crime, a non-governmental watchdog that both assisted government and, when necessary, battled it.

Born in Toronto on May 24, 1947, Barlow grew up mainly in Ottawa. In *The Fight of My Life: Confessions of an Unrepentant Canadian*, she describes how her parents bought "a turn-of-the-century, three-storey red-brick family home" in the Glebe, a tree-linked enclave of civil servants, doctors, and lawyers. A well-adjusted middle child, she did well at Glebe Collegiate, regularly attended the United Church, and developed a strong sense of propriety. As a teenager, she felt "totally bored with the whole thing, and dreamed of a different type of world." She also adored performing and set her sights on becoming an actress.

After taking a couple of roles at the Ottawa Little Theatre, she enrolled in drama at York University in Toronto, and in her first year won the lead female role in a major production (*Don Juan*). Then she fell in love. She married "a handsome literary scholar," Garnet Barlow, gave birth to two sons in quick succession, and dropped out of York to become a stay-at-home mother. Enter the women's movement. Barlow plunged into the work of Simone de Beauvoir, Germaine Greer, Gloria Steinem, and Betty Friedan, who were "laying out a whole new analysis of the oppression of women in our society" and exposing systemic flaws. Suddenly, having put "a new lens on a set of glasses," she saw the world differently. She became "really upset, really angry" at the way women were being treated—a feeling that would lead her to get a divorce.

In the early 1970s, Barlow had helped set up the first women's centre in Ottawa. In 1975, she co-founded Women's Associates Consulting, which sought to improve the status of women. She advocated social equity and pay equity and provided sensitivity training to organizations such as the Canadian Police Academy. Her son, Will, who became a police officer, would remember almost ruefully that "she was in your face, all the time." Barlow left consulting to run the Office of Equal Opportunity for the city of Ottawa, where she learned "how to go around power and build support." She became women's rights adviser to Prime Minister Pierre Elliott Trudeau. As she turned thirty, encouraged by leading Liberals and forgetting that "you have no power unless you have a constituency," she sought the high-profile Liberal nomination in Ottawa Centre—and eventually lost a hard-fought battle. Looking back, Barlow says that this public defeat was hard to take but taught her a lot. She emerged "wiser, tougher," and would never again seek elected office. Choosing influence over raw power, she would do her fighting from outside the political system.

In 1988, Barlow joined Mel Hurtig and the Council of Canadians in leading the battle against a watershed free trade agreement (FTA) between Canada and the United States. The corporate agenda carried the day. But when the smoke cleared, Barlow realized that the FTA was just one setback in a continuing struggle. She became chairperson of the Council of Canadians, resumed the international struggle against globalization, and began authoring and co-authoring books. These included *Parcel of Rogues: How Free Trade Is Failing Canada*, *Straight Through the Heart*, and *Take Back the Nation*. In seeking to protect Canada's social programs, Barlow built on the work she had done in the women's movement. As she writes in *The Fight of My Life*, "any threat to universal social programs is also a threat to the hard-earned equality gains women have made."

In the mid-1990s, she joined American environmentalist Jerry Mander in establishing the International Forum on Globalization. Broadening her outlook, she perceived more interconnections and became more internationalist in perspective. In 2001, with Tony Clarke, she wrote *Global Showdown: How the New Activists Are Fighting Global Corporate Rule*. This book argues that the mechanisms of trade liberalization—among them the World Trade Organization, the World Bank, and the International Monetary Fund—are "lining the pockets of corporate dictators," forcing cuts to social and environmental programs and widening the gap between rich and poor around the world.

The following year, again with Clarke, Barlow wrote *Blue Gold: The Fight to Stop the Corporate Theft of the World's Water*, warning that major producers of bottled water are buying up fresh water rights and drying up crucial supplies. In 2005, she published *Too Close for Comfort: Canada's Future within Fortress North America*, arguing that a civil society is emerging to challenge "the juggernaut of free-market fundamentalism that has broken the social fabric in countries around the world."

Two years later, with *Blue Covenant*, Maude Barlow turned again to water, charging that bottled water companies are thriving on the backs of the poor. Half the world's hospital beds, she writes, "are occupied by people with an easily preventable water-borne disease," and citing the World Health Organization in reporting that "contaminated water is implicated in 80 percent of all sickness and disease worldwide." For Barlow, the water crisis is just another face of globalization. She said it best more than a decade ago: "I just know that if I don't do something about it, I'll make myself sick."

7

SHEILA WATT-CLOUTIER

An Inuit activist links climate change to human rights

The headline read, "Inuit leader nominated for Nobel." The story, published in *The Globe and Mail* on February 2, 2007, began, "Former U.S. vice-president Al Gore and Canadian Inuit activist Sheila Watt-Cloutier, chosen as a nation builder by *The Globe and Mail* last year, have been nominated for the 2007 Nobel Peace Prize for their wide-reaching efforts to draw the world's attention to the dangers of global warming." Børge Brende, a Norwegian Member of Parliament and former minister of the environment, said he joined with a political opponent to nominate Gore and Watt-Cloutier: "A prerequisite for winning the Nobel Peace Prize is making a difference," he said. "Al Gore, like no other, has put climate change on the agenda. Mr. Gore uses his position to get politicians to understand, while Sheila [Watt-Cloutier] works from the ground up."

The story went on to describe Watt-Cloutier as the chair of the Inuit Circumpolar Conference (now the Inuit Circumpolar Council), an organization representing about 155,000 Inuit living in Canada, Alaska, Greenland, and Russia. It noted that she had worked on a range of social and environmental issues affecting the Inuit people, and that her many awards and honours included Norway's Sophie Prize, for drawing attention to the impact of climate change and pollution on the traditional lifestyles of the Arctic's indigenous people. Al Gore would win the Peace Prize that year, and share it with the

Intergovernmental Panel on Climate Change, a scientific body established by two United Nations organizations. Watt-Cloutier, honoured by the nomination, would keep working. While she did not win the Nobel, she received prestigious awards not just from Canada, but from Norway, the United Nations, Kenya, and the United States.

Sheila Watt-Cloutier was born December 2, 1953, in the Inuit town of Kuujjuaq in Nunavik, a region comprising the northern third of Quebec. Her mother was known throughout Nunavik as a healer and an interpreter, and her father was an RCMP officer. She spent her first ten years living traditionally: "I travelled only by dogsled for the first decade of my life," she said in a *Canadian Geographic* citation for lifetime achievement.

Later, on CBC Radio's *This I Believe,* she elaborated, "I bonded with the ice, snow, and cold during those journeys, just as I bonded with my family and community. At the end of a day of hunting and fishing there was always a delicious meal prepared from the land and the sea." When she was ten, her parents sent her away to school, first in Nova Scotia and then in Churchill, Manitoba. "I lost a large part of my language and culture and through my own family the chance to learn all the lessons that my rich traditional way of life would have taught me."

After studying psychology and sociology at McGill University in Montreal, Watt-Cloutier returned to the north and rebuilt her connection with her roots. In her early twenties, she worked as a translator for Ungava Hospital and sought to improve local health and education conditions. In 1991, she joined in reviewing the educational system and contributed to an influential report entitled *Silaturnimut: The Pathway to Wisdom,* and also to a youth awareness video, *Capturing Spirit: The Inuit Journey.* "The Inuit strength is our culture," she told *CG,* "and our young people need to stay in touch with tradition."

In 1995, Watt-Cloutier began two three-year-stints as corporate secretary of Makivik Corporation, and was deeply involved with the Inuit land claim under the James Bay and Northern Quebec Agreement. That same year, she was elected president of the Inuit Circumpolar Council (ICC) Canada. In this role, she served as the spokesperson for the Arctic Inuit in negotiating the Stockholm Convention, which banned the manufacture and use of persistent organic pollutants (POPs), which pollute the arctic food chain and are especially dangerous to the Inuit: "We live off the land and eat wild food," Watt-Cloutier explained. "Contaminants entering our environment were a sign of the intrusive effects of globalization."

During these years, Watt-Cloutier also suffered the loss of her beloved sister, and then several other family members. In her grief, she said later, she "came to see in a vivid way that all things are inter-connected. I came to know courage, tenacity, and commitment. I needed these character skills in order to survive my grief. As it turned out, I also needed them to strengthen and raise the volume of my own voice on the global stage."

In 2002, Watt-Cloutier was elected International Chair of the ICC. As such, she launched the world's first international legal action on climate change. On December 2005, she filed a 167-page petition to the Inter-American Commission on Human Rights (IACHR). Signed by sixty-two Inuit elders and hunters, it charged that unchecked emission of greenhouse gases from the United States had violated Inuit cultural and environmental rights as guaranteed by the American Declaration of the Rights and Duties of Man.

Watt-Cloutier changed the world by making climate change a human rights issue. In presenting the petition, she drew on an exhaustive *Arctic Climate Impact Assessment (ACIA)* prepared over four years by 300 scientists from fifteen countries. It attested that the Arctic is experiencing some of the most rapid climate change on earth. It predicted that the change will accelerate and produce major physical, ecological, social, and economic consequences, and that these will lead to worldwide global warming and rising sea levels. The ACIA warned that some marine species would face extinction, and that the disappearance of sea ice would disrupt and might destroy the Inuit's hunting and food-sharing culture.

Identifying the Inuit as "the early warning system for the entire planet," Watt-Cloutier put a human face on the facts, figures, and graphs. "Climate change affects every facet of Inuit life," she said. "We have a right to life, health, security, land use, subsistence and culture. These issues are the real politics of climate change." Watt-Cloutier served as chair of the ICC until 2006, and has continued her crusade on behalf of her people.

In March 2007, she addressed the IACHR at its first hearing on climate change and human rights. The following year, when *Time* magazine profiled her as one of a handful of "Heroes of the Environment," Watt-Cloutier said, "Most people can't relate to the science, to the economics, and to the technical aspects of climate change," she said. "But they can certainly connect to the human aspect." Her aim is to "move the issue from the head to the heart."

In 2009, while accepting an honorary doctor of laws from the University of Alberta, Watt-Cloutier added an historical perspective to climate change in the Arctic. She reviewed how the Inuit "have weathered the storm of modernization remarkably well, moving from an almost entirely traditional way of life to adopting 'modern' innovations all within the past sixty or seventy years." Rapid changes and traumas "deeply wounded and dispirited many," she said, "and translated into a 'collective pain' for families and communities. Substance abuse, health problems, and the loss of so many of our people to suicide have resulted." Through all this, the Inuit drew strength from "our land, our predictable environment and climate, and the wisdom our hunters and elders gained over millennia to help us adapt."

Now, however, climate change has made the environment unreliable and capricious: "Just as we start to come out the other side of the first wave of tumultuous change, there is yet a second wave coming at us. We face dangerously unpredictable weather, unpredictable conditions of our ice and snow, extreme erosion, and an invasion of new species. These changes threaten to erase the memory of who we are, where we have come from, and all that we wish to be."

This situation moved Watt-Cloutier to bring forward the 2005 petition linking climate change and human rights. "Our petition was more than a legal document," she said. "It was a gift, an act of generosity from a people at the top of the globe, uniquely positioned to witness its changes, to a world now divided and disconnected. It was the most caring act that I have ever brought forth in the protection of my cultural heritage and in the protection of the future of my eleven-year-old grandson."

Speaking to the young people in the audience, and through them to the next generation emerging globally, she urged them "to look to the Arctic as the early warning—late for us—to our world of the consequences of forgetting our deep connectedness, whether that connection be to nature, to our food sources, to our environment, or of course to each other. Your generation will be called upon to balance what is now moving quickly to a tipping point."

8

Irshad Manji

A spirited Muslim calls for an Islamic Reformation

Irshad Manji insists she is mellowing but shows no signs of piping down. "The reality is that Muslims have been far too silent," she said not long ago, "and continue to be silent when terrorism happens." In a television interview posted on her website, Manji cited the Muslim American soldier who in Fort Hood, Texas, murdered thirteen of his comrades while muttering "*Allahu Akbar*," or "God is great." She shook her head. "Moderate organizations in America said, 'No no. Don't misunderstand. Islam has nothing to do with this.'" She took a beat. "Really? Why is it then that he was uttering religious inspiration when he did that?"

That is the kind of politically incorrect question that Manji wants moderate Muslims to ask. "I say all this as a faithful Muslim," she added. "Somebody who recognizes that there is a real problem within my religion today." The globe-trotting Manji was in Edmonton promoting her third book, *Allah, Liberty and Love: The Courage to Reconcile Faith and Freedom*. A recent review by another female Muslim had rejected the book's "sweeping refutation of moderate Muslims." But Manji cited other terrorist attacks and urged "good-hearted Canadian liberals" to stop bending over backwards and to "hold the moderate Muslim accountable for speaking truth about how the religion is being used to foment these kinds of crimes."

Manji is changing the world by calling for an Islamic Reformation.

In Edmonton, she said people should challenge the moderates to rein-terpret those verses of the Koran that the extremists are using: "Just as Christians have had to undergo their liberal reformation, just as Jews have had to do the same, we Muslims must now step up to the plate. And that can't happen if all we're preaching to you is, 'Islam means peace, please, believe us.' That's not thinking. That's sloganeering."

Irshad Manji, famously hailed by *The New York Times* as "Osama bin Laden's worst nightmare," is a founding director of the Moral Courage Project at New York University, an initiative that aims to create leaders who "challenge political correctness, intellectual con-formity, and self-censorship." She received Oprah Winfrey's first annual Chutzpah Award for "audacity, nerve, boldness and convic-tion." *Ms.* magazine named her a "Feminist for the 21st Century," and the American Society for Muslim Advancement a "Muslim Leader of Tomorrow."

Manji elicited these kudos with her international bestseller *The Trouble with Islam: A Muslim's Call for Reform in Her Faith* (later reti-tled *The Trouble with Islam Today*). Since first appearing in 2003, that controversial work has been published in more than thirty languages. Some of these translations—Arabic, Persian, Urdu, Malay, and Indonesian—can be downloaded for free from Manji's website. The Arabic version has been downloaded more than 250,000 times. The book "is an open letter from me," Manji writes, "a Muslim voice of reform, to concerned citizens worldwide—Muslim and not. It's about why my faith community needs to come to terms with the diversity of ideas, beliefs and people in our universe, and why non-Muslims have a pivotal role in helping us get there."

Along the way, Manji lambastes "the inferior treatment of women in Islam" and the "Jew-bashing that so many Muslims persistently engage in." She deplores "literalist readings of the Koran" and calls for a return to "the lost traditions of critical thinking" that in Islam are known as *ijtihad*. Not sufficiently controversial? Manji judges allegations of "Israeli apartheid" to be woefully misguided, and notes that Israel has several Arab political parties, a free Arab press, and a policy of allowing Arabs to live and study alongside Jews. What's more, she argues that Jews have ancient roots stretching back to Israel, and so have a right to a Jewish state.

Irshad Manji is no newcomer to controversy. Born in Uganda in 1968 to parents of Egyptian and Gujarati descent, she immigrated to Canada with her family at age four during Idi Amin's infamous expulsion of Asians. In Richmond, British Columbia, a suburb of Vancouver, she attended both a secular school and an Islamic religious one. She excelled at the former but was expelled from the latter for asking too many questions. Manji graduated from high school as class valedictorian. Then, while studying Islam privately, she earned an honours degree in the history of ideas from the University of British Columbia, winning the Governor General's Medal as top humanities graduate. Along the way, she came out as openly lesbian.

Moving to Ontario, she worked as a legislative aide in Ottawa, a press secretary in the Ontario government, and a speechwriter for the leader of the New Democratic Party. In 1992, at age twenty-four, she became the youngest mainstream editorialist in Canada when she joined the editorial board of the *Ottawa Citizen*. Manji found she didn't fit and moved to television. She hosted several public affairs programs, one of which won a Gemini Award, and in the mid-1990s, on TVOntario's *Studio 2*, articulated liberal views in sometimes fierce debates with right-winger Michael Coren. In 1998, she conceived and hosted *Queer TV* on Toronto's Citytv, one of the world's first commercial TV programs to explore the lives of gays and lesbians. Syndicated through a San Francisco–based web portal, it circumvented state censorship and reached a global audience.

Meanwhile, in 1997, Manji published her first book, *Risking Utopia:*

On the Edge of a New Democracy. Already, she was kicking down walls, urging readers to break free of the old ideological straitjackets of identity politics, including those of socialism and feminism, and instead to assert individualism while building community. Naomi Klein, who was then writing a column for the *Toronto Star*, hailed *Risking Utopia* for moving bravely "from the safe certainties of extremism towards the tumultuous terrain of individuality, democracy and compassion. Canada just got bigger."

In 2002, as writer-in-residence at the University of Toronto's Hart House, Manji began writing *The Trouble with Islam.* She then founded Project Ijtihad, whose aim is to renew the Islamic tradition of dissent and debate. She became a visiting fellow at the International Security Studies program at Yale University and a senior fellow with the European Foundation for Democracy in Brussels.

Manji released a PBS documentary, *Faith Without Fear*, in 2007. In it, she explores Islamism in Yemen, Europe, and North America. The film also tells the story of her personal journey as a Muslim reformer, which has included dealing with death threats. The video was a finalist for a National Film Board Award and, in 2008, won gold at the New York Television Festival. That same year, Manji moved to New York to spearhead the Moral Courage Project. In the negative book review mentioned above, after declaring *Allah, Liberty and Love* a lost opportunity to clarify the issues facing contemporary Islam, the writer admitted that Manji's "dismissal of the moderate Muslim may be just the impetus needed to broaden this complex debate." To that, almost certainly, Manji herself would say, "Yes!"

9

NAOMI KLEIN

A global activist leads the charge against "disaster capitalism"

For Naomi Klein, inviting protestors to Wall Street was "a stroke of organizing genius." Speaking in October 2011 to hundreds of people gathered in the heart of the American financial district, the charismatic Klein hailed the movement known as Occupy Wall Street for metaphorically planting a flag at "the site of maximal abundance." This called attention to the fact, she said, that the global economic crisis "is not a scarcity problem, it's a distribution problem."

Klein, who is changing the world by leading the charge against "disaster capitalism," compared this expanding grassroots protest with movements that sprang up in the late 1990s, notably at the World Trade Organization summit in Seattle. She identified several things "today's activists are doing better than we did back then." Those early protests focused on transient summits, she said—the World Trade Organization, the International Monetary Fund, meetings of the G8 countries—and so themselves became transitory: headlines today, gone tomorrow. But today's protestors "have chosen a fixed target: Wall Street, a symbol of the corporate takeover of democracy."

Secondly, she said, protestors "have committed themselves to non-violence," which keeps media focus on the message rather than on broken windows and street fights. But the biggest difference, Klein said, "is that in 1999, we were taking on capitalism at the peak of a frenzied economic boom." The good times were rolling and "taking on an economic system based on greed was a tough sell, at least in rich countries." But now, she said, there are no rich countries, but "just a whole lot of rich people—people who got rich looting the public wealth and exhausting natural resources around the world."

Everyone can see, she added, "that the system is deeply unjust and careening out of control. Unfettered greed has trashed the global economy. And it is trashing the natural world as well." The new normal "is serial disaster: economic and ecological. These are the facts on the ground. They are so blatant, so obvious, that it is a lot easier to connect with the public than it was in 1999." The task of our time, she insisted, is to "build a decent, inclusive society" while respecting the real limits of what planet Earth can take.

Those who would dismiss Klein as utopian or out of touch might recall that two of her books—*No Logo* and *The Shock Doctrine*—have sold more than one million copies each, and have been translated into more than two dozen languages. Klein did not come out of nowhere. Born May 8, 1970, in Montreal, she is the daughter of politicized Jewish parents who had left the United States three years before in protest against the Vietnam War. As a teenager, rebelling against the very idea of activism, she became a consumerist, fashion-loving "mall rat." But then, after high school, she took a year off and got in touch with her roots. Her mother was a documentary filmmaker, active in the women's movement, whose works included the anti-pornography classic *Not a Love Story*. Her paternal grandfather had been fired after speaking out during the 1942 Disney animators' strike. Her father, a doctor who grew up steeped in ideas of social justice, was a member of Physicians for Social Responsibility.

In 1989, soon after entering the University of Toronto, she became a student activist. In an interview published in *Global Values 101*, edited by Kate Holbrook, Ann S. Kim, Brian Palmer, and Anna Portnoy, Klein describes how she studied philosophy and literature but got wrapped up in campus politics. She started writing for *The Varsity* and "ended up editing the paper." This led to a student internship at *The Globe and Mail*, and that newspaper kept her on. Working in the mainstream media frustrated Klein "because they were not interested in covering the issues I cared about." She began to write for *This Magazine*, where at twenty-four she became editor. While churning out opinion pieces on marketing, public space, and labour conditions, she realized "that these things were connected by a corporate ideology, but this was too big for an article. That is when I decided to write the book."

The book was *No Logo: Taking Aim at the Brand Bullies*. Klein dedicated it to her husband, Avi Lewis, a TV journalist and documentary filmmaker, and the son of activist Michele Landsberg and humanitarian Stephen Lewis, who surfaces later in this book. *No Logo* appeared in January 2000, soon after the Seattle protests against the World Trade Organization made international headlines. In it, Klein attacks brand-oriented consumer culture and multinational corporations, accusing many of them of running sweatshops and exploiting workers in the world's poorest countries. Hailed as a manifesto for the anti-corporate globalization movement—*The New York Times* called it "a movement Bible"—*No Logo* was translated into twenty-eight languages and sold more than one million copies. Overnight, Klein had emerged onto the world stage. Toronto-based *NOW* magazine put it this way: "Fiercely committed, totally brainy, and one of our most stellar exports, Naomi Klein has done more to bring leftist politics to a new generation than any other writer in the world."

Two years after *No Logo* appeared, Klein published *Fences and Windows: Dispatches from the Front Lines of the Globalization Debate*, a collection of articles and speeches, with all proceeds from the book going to activist organizations. In the foreword, she suggests that "anti-globalization" is a misnomer. And in *Global Values 101*, which appeared in 2006, she clarified further. In Latin America, she writes, nobody speaks of anti-globalization: "they are reacting to neo-liberalism; it is an anti-neoliberal movement." More specifically, people reject "privatization, deregulation, and downsizing." These policies are globally enacted and "enforced by international institutions like the International Monetary Fund and the World Bank— one size fits all, cookie-cutter models." The movement, she writes, "is actually rejecting neoliberalism or what the French call 'savage capitalism.' It is a response to global economic policy, not globalization. It is not the fact of being global that is the problem; it is the policies that are the problem and the fact that they are globally enforced."

Klein elaborated on these arguments in *The Shock Doctrine: The Rise of Disaster Capitalism*, published in 2007. Like *No Logo*, this book became a *New York Times* bestseller and was translated into more than two dozen languages. Booker Prize winner Arundhati Roy described *Shock Doctrine* as "a brilliant, brave and terrifying book. It's nothing less than the secret history of what we call the 'free market.' It should be compulsory reading."

Actor and filmmaker Tim Robbins hailed the work as "the most important and necessary book of her generation. . . . so revelatory a book that it could very well prove a catalyst, a watershed, a tipping point in the movement for economic and social justice." And Seymour M. Hersh, a Pulitzer Prize–winning American journalist, described Klein as "one of the most important new voices in journalism today, as this book makes clear. She has turned globalism inside out, and in so doing given all of us a new way of looking at our seemingly unending disaster in Iraq, and a new way of understanding why we got there."

In *Shock Doctrine*, Klein argues that exploitive economic powers implement devastating free-market policies by striking immediately after major disasters (political, military, economic, or natural). She traces "disaster capitalism" back to the free-market policies of Milton Friedman and the Chicago School of Economics, and cites numerous "shock therapy" transformations around the world, including that of New Orleans, where a viable public education system was wiped out after Hurricane Katrina.

In *The New York Times*, Joseph Stiglitz declared *The Shock Doctrine* an "ambitious look at the economic history of the last fifty years and the rise of free-market fundamentalism around the world," adding that Klein is "not an academic and cannot be judged as one." In the UK, a review in *The Guardian* calls the book "both timely and devastating," while in California, a piece in the *Los Angeles Times* finds that "Klein launches a highly polemical, and persuasive, assault on free-market fundamentalism."

While nationalistic in many ways, Klein has achieved international recognition. In 2009, from the University of Warwick in the United Kingdom, she received the inaugural Warwick Prize for Writing, an award worth more than $80,000. And *The New Yorker* describes her as "the most visible and influential figure on the American left— what Howard Zinn and Noam Chomsky were thirty years ago." At Occupy Wall Street in October 2011, Klein made good on this billing. "My concern about this movement," she said in an interview available online, "is that if it stays amorphous, then all of this energy here will just be used and channeled by people who have much more reformist demands, and who really aren't dreaming big. I think it's fine for people who just want to raise taxes on the rich, or just want to regulate the banks, to use the momentum and energy of this moment to try to push through their demands. But I don't think that should be all this movement is. I think this movement should be able to make much more radical demands than that."

Naomi Klein wants capitalist society to begin again. She wants a new collective narrative, a different forward action, a real-life, democratic saga that rejects exploitation and moves towards a more equitable and humane society. And she is doing everything in her power to make that epic a reality.

Part II

Visionaries

They discern possible futures and lead us into them

D on't check now, but your inbox is overflowing with emails. You can't keep up with Facebook, YouTube, and Twitter, not to mention blogs and online newspapers and magazines. On a giant TV screen in your living room, you can watch earthquakes, tsunamis, African coups, Middle Eastern revolutions, and whatever else, live and in colour and unfolding in real time.

But not to worry. James Gleick, a Pulitzer Prize finalist, assures us that "the exhaustion, the surfeit, the pressure of information have all been seen before." In a hefty tome called *The Information*, he writes, "Credit Marshall McLuhan for this insight—his most essential—in 1962: 'We are today as far into the electric age as the Elizabethans had advanced into the typographical and mechanical age. And we are experiencing the same confusions and indecisions which they had felt when living simultaneously in two contrasted forms of society and experience.'"

With that observation, published in 2011, Gleick joined a small army of thinkers who regard McLuhan as transformative, hailing him as a cutting-edge theorist who changed the world by anticipating "the global village." Nor did McLuhan stop there: he ushered us into that village and showed us around, patiently explaining that "the medium is the message."

How did Canadian-born Malcolm Gladwell put it? "The visionary starts with a clean sheet of paper, and re-imagines the world." That is obviously true of McLuhan. It is true, as well, of the others we encounter in Part II, among them a bicycling matron who changed the way we view cities, the architect who creates flowing buildings inspired by his Aboriginal heritage, and the Québécois busker who reinvented the circus. These visionary Canadians discerned possibilities where others saw none, and then helped to make them real.

10

Marshall McLuhan

A media guru awakens the global village

In 1977, director Woody Allen gave Marshall McLuhan a cameo role in his Oscar-winning movie *Annie Hall*. Sixteen years after that, in its first issue, *Wired* magazine proclaimed McLuhan its patron saint. By 1996, Glenn Willmott was arguing, in *McLuhan, or Modernism in Reverse*, that Canada's best-known English professor should be recognized as "the world's first postmodernist." And three years later still, when Paul Levinson published *Digital McLuhan*, he hailed the high-tech guru, two decades dead, as a guide to the Internet and the Information Millennium. So it goes. A post-secondary institution called the Toronto School of Communication Theory originated in the work of McLuhan, and continues to lead media studies around the world.

Marshall Herbert McLuhan was born in Edmonton in 1911 to parents of Scots-Irish background. From the age of three, he grew up in Winnipeg. His father worked as a life insurance salesman, and his mother, once a Baptist schoolteacher, became an elocutionist, an acclaimed public reader, and finally an actress. After high school, McLuhan attended the University of Manitoba, where he won a gold medal in arts and sciences. At twenty-three, he went to England to study English at the University of Cambridge. There, while working with I.A. Richards and F. R. Leavis, he came under the influence of the New Criticism, which emphasized close reading and the training of perception. He also discovered the work of G.K. Chesterton, which converted him to analogical thinking—as distinct from logical or dialectical—and also, in 1937, to Roman Catholicism. McLuhan embraced the writings of Teilhard de Chardin, a Catholic intellectual who argued that computers were creating "a nervous system for humanity" and "a single, organized, unbroken membrane over the earth."

Unable to land a job in Canada while working on his Cambridge doctorate (focusing on a little-known Elizabethan satirist), McLuhan taught English at Saint Louis University. In 1939, he married American actress Corinne Lewis and began a family that would grow to include six children. After receiving his Ph.D. in 1943, McLuhan taught for two years at Assumption College in Windsor, Ontario. Then, in 1946, he moved to the University of Toronto (U of T), where he remained for the rest of his career. Already, McLuhan had explored the social criticism of Lewis Mumford, who distinguished two stages of industrial civilization: the first, mechanical, based on steam power, and the second, organic, based on electricity. At U of T, McLuhan discovered the work of his older colleague Harold Adams Innis, widely recognized as one of North America's leading economic historians. In 1950, Innis brought out *Empire and Communications*, which explores how, throughout history, modes of communication have shaped civilizations.

The following year, McLuhan published *The Mechanical Bride: Folklore of Industrial Man*, comprising a number of short essays that could be read in any order. Using this "mosaic approach" to book-writing, as he called it, McLuhan moved away from conventional English studies to examine communications, starting with the effects of advertising. Decades later, he would credit Innis with providing the "extra boost" that turned him to this field. But where Innis and the American Mumford had come to communications through economic history, and naturally focused on how technologies shape societies, cultures, and civilizations, McLuhan approached the subject via English literature and criticism. He tended to emphasize sight and hearing—sensory perception. And he perceived communication technologies as extensions of the human body. The television camera, for example, extends or augments the human eye. He speculated that this augmentation influences the way we think more than any content the medium delivers.

This line of thought gave rise to two seminal works. In the first, *The Gutenberg Galaxy* (1962), McLuhan argued that the advent of the alphabet and the printing press drove people to think in a linear manner. This altered social organization and human interactions, because it gave rise to specialization and, eventually, the modern world. Question: If linear thinking "created individualism and nationalism in the sixteenth century," as he wrote, what would instantaneous communications accomplish? McLuhan predicted that "electronic interdependence" would bring an end to print culture, with its emphasis on individual experience, and move humankind into a new tribalism. We would soon find ourselves living in "a global village."

In his second seminal work, *Understanding Media: The Extensions of Man* (1964), McLuhan elaborated. He argued that change in delivery systems, or media, notably from print to electronics, is more significant than any specific content those media deliver. It is not the message, he explained, but the "medium that shapes and controls the scale and form of human association and action." And so he coined that telling phrase "the medium is the message." By bringing us all into closer (instantaneous) proximity, McLuhan argued, the technological revolution would transform us as human beings. Like it or not, we would find ourselves dealing with contradictory reports and multiple perspectives. "All media work us over completely," McLuhan explained. "They are so pervasive in their personal, political, economic, aesthetic, psychological, moral, ethical and social consequences that they leave no part of us untouched, unaffected, unaltered." To cope, we would have to activate the right side of the brain. This would lead, McLuhan predicted, to the end of left-brain tyranny, and would terminate what media analyst Neil Postman later described as "the days of the print-oriented bastards."

From the late 1960s onwards, thanks to *The Gutenberg Galaxy* and *Understanding Media*, McLuhan became the most influential English professor of the age. He was a celebrity intellectual. Cultural critics cited his work—not just Woody Allen, but everyone from Postman to Camille Paglia and Timothy Leary, and from postmodern theorist Jean Baudrillard to pop-culture artist Andy Warhol. McLuhan remains the central figure in what is widely called the Toronto School of Communications, which includes Harold Adams Innis, Eric A. Havelock, and Derrick de Kerckhove.

Today, McLuhan is often identified as the Apostle of the Electronic Age. Speed, multi-directionality, interactivity: he predicted that electronic technology would transform communications, and so our world, and eventually ourselves. In his 1999 book *Digital McLuhan*, Paul Levinson argues that McLuhan's global village became a reality only when the World Wide Web allowed people to interact online. McLuhan became the first postmodernist, according to Glenn Willmott, by anticipating that transformative interactivity. He elaborates in *McLuhan, or Modernism in Reverse*, highlighting McLuhan's suggestion that the electronic media drove the evolution of modernity from one period to another.

As individuals, we have moved beyond modernist linearity. Single-mindedness has become a state of the past. In *The Future of the Self: Inventing the Postmodern Person*, Walter Truett Anderson builds on this idea. He argues that, for the first time in history, humans are developing changeable identities and multiple selves. This he attributes to the advent of the digital universe. The rapid-fire delivery of sometimes contradictory information and perspectives makes unprec-edented demands on the individual. The modern self, which is linear and single, cannot accommodate so many conflicting demands. To handle the overload, digital-age humans create multiple selves. These notions derive from Marshall McLuhan. When we moved into the global village, we became postmodern man . . . and woman.

11

JANE JACOBS

A matronly cyclist changes the way we inhabit The City

One evening in 1968, with the government of Metropolitan Toronto preparing to build a six-lane expressway through the centre of town, concerned citizens began meeting regularly at the urging of a woman named Bobbi Speck. Decades later, Speck would recall that the organizers didn't really know what they were doing. And none of them recognized the matronly newcomer who arrived late, a grey-haired woman wearing thick, black-framed glasses. But that woman, after listening awhile, rose to her feet and laid out a detailed plan of action to stop the Spadina Expressway. In *Jane Jacobs: Urban Visionary*, biographer Alice Sparberg Alexiou quotes Speck, reminiscing: "It was stunning. I was thinking as she was talking, this woman is incredible! She has everything down pat! Her thoughts came out in paragraph form, and put our instincts into a broader context." But not until after the meeting, when Speck checked the sign-up sheet, did she realize that this latest recruit was not just another neighbour. Jane Jacobs, already celebrated as the author of *The Death and Life of Great American Cities*, had recently led a battle to halt the construction of a New York City expressway. Apparently, she had moved to Toronto. And, clearly, she was ready to join the fight.

The newly arrived immigrant had been born Jane Butzner in Scranton, Pennsylvania, on May 4, 1916. She was the second daughter of a staunchly Presbyterian family. Her father was a doctor, her mother a school teacher, and both encouraged independent thinking. Jane was a feisty girl, free-spirited, and later remembered as clever, funny, and fearless. New York City lay 200 kilometres east and south of her industrial hometown, and Jane visited for the first time when she was twelve. Later, she would remember being "flabbergasted at all the people in the streets. The city was just jumping." Jane graduated from Scranton's Central High School in 1933. With the Great Depression at its worst, she worked for *The Scranton Tribune* as an unpaid gopher. After a few months, she joined her sister, six years older, in New York City. She hoped to become a reporter but found newspapers to be a male preserve. Instead, having trained as a stenographer, she took temporary jobs as a secretary at companies dealing variously in candy, clocks, hardware, and steel. At times, while sharing a sixth-floor Brooklyn walk-up, she and her sister subsisted on Pablum, milk, and bananas.

While job-hunting, Jane explored the neighbourhoods of New York. One afternoon, emerging from the subway on a whim, she discovered the lively bohemian area known as Greenwich Village, and soon convinced her sister to move there. In 1935, Jane began freelancing colour stories to magazines. She developed a clear, detailed writing style by conducting imaginary conversations with people from other eras. By "conversing" with Thomas Jefferson and Benjamin Franklin, and later with an imaginary ancient, an Anglo-Saxon, she taught herself precision. Jane sold an early article to *Cue* magazine, about manhole covers, and placed several pieces with the better-known *Vogue*. In 1940, she landed a staff position with *The Iron Age* magazine. Three years later, with most of the globe engulfed in the Second World War, Jane began working as a feature writer for the U.S. Office of War Information.

Meanwhile, she had been taking courses at Columbia University's School of General Studies, delving into law, economics, zoology, and geology. In 1944, she met and married Robert Jacobs, a budding architect. In Greenwich Village, the two bought an old three-storey building that housed a candy store. They renovated this while Jane wrote for the U.S. State Department and also gave birth to sons in 1948 and 1950. The couple remained in the Village to raise their children, adding a daughter and rejecting the post-war exodus to the suburbs. "Suburbs are perfectly valid places to want to live," she would later tell a magazine writer, "but they are inherently parasitic, economically and socially, too, because they live off the answers found in cities."

In 1952, when the State Department moved to Washington, Jane got a tryout with the upscale *Architectural Forum*. Because she was female and lacked a college degree, she looked like a long shot. But she wrote so vividly that she landed the job and began writing about schools and hospitals. She lugged home and studied great stacks of architectural blueprints, and, while turning herself into an amateur expert, also influenced her husband to begin specializing in designing hospitals. Now Jane rode her bicycle to work, and one editor would later describe her as "a wonderfully likeable, contentious, opinionated woman." Assigned to write about "urban renewal" and "slum clearance" projects, Jane went observing—first to Philadelphia, then to East Harlem in New York. Having started without an opinion, she concluded that razing a flawed but viable neighbourhood to build isolating high rises was a mistake. She stunned her editors by arguing that the expert urban planners were doing everything wrong. In April 1956, her bosses, expecting to jolt her back on track, sent her to Harvard University to speak at a conference on urban design. Jacobs gave a ten-minute speech drawing on her recent visit to East Harlem. She argued that urban planners were obsessed with order and control, and so were doing more harm than good: they were destroying a way of life.

To her own surprise, the audience of experts responded enthusiastically. Later, Jacobs surmised that probably "the speech was a big hit because nobody had heard anybody saying these things before." Crucially, the crowd included William Hollingsworth Whyte, a superb writer (*The Organization Man*) who doubled as a senior editor at *Fortune* magazine. Whyte invited Jacobs to write a story about downtowns. She declined, citing unpreparedness. But then, when his second choice of writer took ill, Jacobs accepted the assignment. She drafted an article, "Downtown Is for People." In it, she politely lambasted grandiose redevelopment plans for downtowns across the country, including one for New York's Lincoln Center. This draft drew the ire of *Fortune's* publisher. But Whyte stood firm and ran the article in April 1958. The response was overwhelmingly positive. Before long, Jacobs received a phone call from the Rockefeller Foundation, offering her a grant to expand her article into a book. She accepted and developed an outline. Meanwhile, Jason Epstein, a senior editor at Random House, had read her article and invited her to lunch. He offered her a publishing contract. She accepted. And in the autumn of 1958, Jane Jacobs took a leave from her job to write a book.

The end result, *The Death and Life of Great American Cities*, is arguably the most influential work in the history of urban planning. Eloquently written and fiercely critical of mainstream thinking, *Death and Life* changed the world, revolutionizing the way we see the urban landscape, and the way we have regarded cities ever since. Jacobs denounced top-down urban planning for destroying communities and replacing them with high-rise canyons empty of people. She championed mixed-use neighbourhoods, contended that they develop organically, and used New York's Greenwich Village as an example.

In a well-known passage that runs four pages, Jacobs wrote, "The stretch of Hudson Street where I live is each day the scene of an intricate sidewalk ballet. I make my own first entrance into it a little after eight when I put out the garbage can, surely a prosaic occupation, but

I enjoy my part, my little clang, as the droves of junior high school students walk by the center of the stage dropping candy wrappers. . . . When I get home after work, the ballet is reaching its crescendo. This is the time of roller skates and stilts and tricycles, and games in the lee of the stoop with bottletops and plastic cowboys; this is the time of bundles and packages, zigzagging from the drug store to the fruit stand and back over to the butcher's; this is the time when teenagers, all dressed up, are pausing to ask if their slips show or their collars look right . . . this is the time when anybody you know around Hudson Street will go by."

Jacobs argued that streets should serve several purposes; blocks should be short, buildings should vary in use and condition, and population density should be high. This proved incendiary. The scholar Lewis Mumford, for example, originally sympathetic, wrote a scathing rebuttal that appeared in *The New Yorker* under the headline, "Mother Jacobs' Home Remedy for Urban Cancer." Yet neither Mumford nor anybody else could turn the tide of popular opinion. While watching a parade from the sidewalk, Jacobs had cried out that the emperors of urban renewal had no clothes. When people took a second look, they saw that she was right.

Throughout North America, Jane Jacobs is rightly celebrated for what she did next. She led a triumphant, six-year battle to halt the construction of a ten-lane superhighway that would have destroyed several New York City neighbourhoods. Author Anthony Flint tells that story in his 2009 book *Wrestling with Moses: How Jane Jacobs Took On New York's Master Builder and Transformed the American City*. One prominent critic lauded the work as telling the story of how "Jane Jacobs, crownless queen of cities, defended New York against the assault that would have destroyed the pattern of its daily life."

As it happens, Jacobs did at least as much for Toronto as she did for New York City. Indeed, Canadian sociologist Barry Wellman has argued that in truth she did more. "Despite her well-deserved American fame," Wellman wrote in 2006, "Jane made an even more sustained, active and varied contribution to Toronto's urbanity. When she arrived, she plunged into the ongoing fight to stop the building of the Spadina Expressway. This was similar to her battle in New York City against Robert Moses' Lower Manhattan Expressway, except more important. The Spadina Expressway would have dumped a great deal of traffic into the heart of many Toronto residential neighbourhoods." Thanks largely to Jane Jacobs, he added, a mass movement developed that led Ontario premier William Davis to kill the project "with a Jacobsean pronouncement: 'If we are building a transportation system to serve the automobile, the Spadina Expressway would be a good place to start. But if we are building a transportation system to serve the people, the Spadina Expressway would be a good place to stop.'"

Jacobs had moved to Toronto with her family in 1968, when American involvement in the Vietnam War—which she fiercely opposed—meant her two sons could be drafted into the military at any time. In 1974, she became a Canadian, renouncing her American citizenship. During the next three decades, while based in Toronto, she produced more original and provocative works, among them *The Nature of Economies, The Question of Separatism, Systems of Survival, Cities and the Wealth of Nations,* and *Dark Age Ahead.*

American writers have been known to claim that Jacobs was "the quintessential American." But while the inveterate rabble-rouser could have returned to the United States at any time, she chose to reside in Canada for the last thirty-eight years of her life. In 1996, Jacobs was made an Officer of the Order of Canada. She was repeatedly honoured in this country, and remained politically engaged into her eighties. She inspired prizes, university courses, seminars, and symposiums all over the world. In the final analysis, however, given her long residence and her celebration of diversity, Jacobs proved to be "the quintessential Canadian"—one who transformed the way we conceive and inhabit The City.

12

DOUGLAS CARDINAL

A pioneering architect builds on his Aboriginal heritage

"There were claw marks all the way into the 21st century." Alberta-born Douglas Cardinal was recalling the late 1960s, when he started dragging architecture into the computer age. He makes this remark in *Radical Attitudes: The Architecture of Douglas Cardinal*, a documentary profile directed by Jim Hamm. Driven to computers by the demands of his organic, curvilinear approach to creating buildings, and the complexity of the attendant calculations, Cardinal pioneered computer-assisted design in architecture. His groundbreaking, holistic approach, according to Trevor Boddy, author of *The Architecture of Douglas Cardinal*, is rooted in his Aboriginal heritage. It reflects baroque and art nouveau influences from Europe, Mexico, and the American Southwest. But the Aboriginal dimension, the flowing shapes and curves, the insistence on a process of consultation and inclusion, have earned him global recognition.

Born March 7, 1934, in Calgary, Alberta, Douglas Joseph Cardinal was the oldest of eight children. His father, Joseph Cardinal, was of Blackfoot ancestry. A renowned outdoorsman, he worked as a guide and a game warden. Cardinal's mother, a nurse named Frances Marguerite Rach, had both German and Metis ancestors. Both parents were integrated into the mainstream communities of southern Alberta, and Cardinal was raised a Roman Catholic. When his mother fell ill, Cardinal and two of his brothers were sent to St. Joseph's

Convent residential school near Red Deer. During this period, according to Boddy, the boy became fiercely independent: a loner. He hiked
in the woods and studied literature, music, and art. After poring over
photo books celebrating the cathedrals of Europe, the boy vowed to
become an architect.

In his late teens, while on a hunting trip with his father, Cardinal
visited an old Blackfoot woman who lived on an Alberta reserve.
She was his own great-grandmother, though his father did not make
that explicit, and a decade would pass before, reconnecting with
his Aboriginal heritage, the young man would realize it. After high
school, Cardinal helped his father run a trapline, and built structures
for a mink ranching business. At eighteen, he began studying architecture at the University of British Columbia (UBC), the first member
of his family to undertake post-secondary education. Socially awk-
ward, given to long walks in the woods and along the water, Cardinal
existed in what Boddy describes as "a fine but inescapable web of sep-
arateness."

Under the influence of architect Bert Binning, Cardinal discovered the bold modernist paintings of Group of Seven founder Lawren
Harris. These sprang out of a setting and a sensibility he understood.
In his second year at UBC, Cardinal won a prize for his design work.
But then, enamored of curves, Cardinal came up against rectilinear
orthodoxy. He refused to conform, failed in design studio, and flunked
out of university. At an exit interview, the program director told him
he had "the wrong family background" to become an architect.

Back in Red Deer, Alberta, Cardinal began working as a draftsman
for a firm of architects. He progressed from junior to senior draftsman and, in the late 1940s and early 1950s, with Alberta enjoying an oil
boom, he designed numerous elementary schools. In 1957, Cardinal
completed his first circular building, a six-room primary school for
the town of Rocky Mountain House. His dismissal from UBC had

the effect of barring him from other Canadian universities. Cardinal looked southwards, and after an extended driving tour through the American Southwest and Mexico, which presented radically different architectural influences, Cardinal headed for Austin, Texas. He found work as a draftsman, impressed a leading designer, and got accepted to study architecture at the University of Texas. Here, in a more open environment, he developed superb technical skills, earning top marks and gaining entrance to honour societies.

Cardinal admired the work of Antoni Gaudí, the turn-of-the-century Catalan who designed curvilinear masterpieces, among them Barcelona's spectacular Sagrada Família. In that symbolic edifice, Cardinal found confirmation that architecture was an art: it could both criticize and articulate a culture. "I had a professor," he told a reporter in 2011, "who taught me about organic architecture and the importance of balance, harmony and connectedness." In Texas, he also became politicized. It happened after an incident at a beer garden, when he and some Arab friends were attacked by members of an athletic fraternity. Cardinal led the quest for justice and eventually got the attackers expelled.

After graduating from the University of Texas with honours, Cardinal returned to Red Deer, Alberta. He served the requisite year as an apprentice and, in 1964, hung out his shingle as an independent architect. He landed the contract to design a church for a Catholic parish. Taking an approach that would distinguish his career, and that reflected his as-yet-unproclaimed Aboriginal roots, Cardinal insisted on having the intense involvement of those who would use the building. The end result, his dramatic, curvilinear St. Mary's Church, was hailed almost immediately as a groundbreaking work.

As an artist speaking in stone, Douglas Cardinal had found his voice. He changed the world by introducing an Aboriginal sensibility into architecture, highlighting organic shape and forms and introducing a consultative, grassroots approach. While creating the complex church, Cardinal had begun using computer-aided drafting and design systems (CADD). In *Radical Attitudes,* he notes that the first computer he used, a Chicago mainframe with a memory of half a megabyte, was worth $250,000. And the 120-megabyte disk on which he stored his data cost $60,000. Today, tablet computers boasting more than 8,000 megabytes of internal memory, or 16,000 times that of the early mainframe, are selling for $200.

After St. Mary's Church, while struggling through marital difficulties, Cardinal produced a series of stunningly original buildings in Alberta. These helped to define "prairie expressionism." Key works included the Grande Prairie Regional College in Grande Prairie; the Alberta Government Services Building in Ponoka; and St. Albert Place, a civic and cultural centre in St. Albert, adjacent to Edmonton. Cardinal also began winning honours and awards. Here at home, these would eventually include the Order of Canada, the Canada Council's Molson Prize for the Arts, the National Aboriginal Achievement Award, the Gold Medal of the Royal Architectural Institute of Canada, and the Governor General's Award for Visual and Media Arts.

In 1981, the federal government of Pierre Elliott Trudeau recognized Cardinal as a pioneer in computer-assisted architectural design. Those in charge selected him to test and advance Canadian CADD technology. Out of this came his most celebrated building, the Canadian Museum of Civilization in Gatineau, Quebec, across the Ottawa river from Canada's Parliament Buildings, and recently renamed the Canadian Museum of History. Designing the complex structure, which involved 81,000 simultaneous equations, has been recognized internationally as a landmark technical achievement. That recognition has included the Gold Medal of the Union of Architects of Russia, the World Master of Contemporary Architecture prize of Bulgaria, the Outstanding Professional Achievement Award from the American Society of Landscape Architects, and the Juan Torres Higueras Award from the Federation of Pan American Associations of Architects.

The Canadian Museum proclaimed a shift in the public expression of First Nations history and culture. In 1993, the Smithsonian Institution hired Cardinal to design the National Museum of the American Indian. Situated on the National Mall in Washington, D.C., that building faces the United States Capitol. Contractual disputes led to Cardinal leaving the project in 1998, before it was completed, but he continued to provide input into the building's design. In a section-front story in the *Washington Post*, architecture critic Benjamin Forgey summarized this way: "Fortunately, back in 1999 the Commission of Fine Arts stepped in to block ruinous design changes proposed by the Smithsonian after Cardinal's dismissal, so it is possible to say with certainty that in the big, bold moves—the shape, the character, the basic floor plan—this building is a Cardinal."

Since the 1990s, when he got more in touch with his Aboriginal roots, Cardinal has repeatedly given architectural expression to Aboriginal culture. His projects have included the Saskatchewan Federated Indian College (now the First Nations University of Canada) in Regina; the Institute of American Indian Arts in Santa Fe, New Mexico; the Kainai Multi-Purpose Cultural Resource Centre in Alberta; and the Cree village of Oujé-Bougoumou in northern Quebec. This last earned a United Nations award of excellence for environmental design and was celebrated at Expo 2000 in Hanover, Germany.

In 2011, Cardinal was working on Cardinal House, a New York City housing complex for Aboriginal people; the Bo Hai Tidal Bridge in China, which will run 126 kilometres; and a Regina entertainment facility for the Independent First Nations of Saskatchewan, which will include a stadium that will hold 35,000.

Cardinal's buildings, immediately recognizable, proclaim the architect's disdain for the "meaningless boxes designed for obsolescence" that litter North America cityscapes. His buildings proclaim that, architecturally, we have options. As Cardinal puts it, "you should create places to elevate the human spirit."

13

FARLEY MOWAT

A feisty animal lover champions the natural world

The year he turned eighty-nine, Farley Mowat was still raging. That same year, he published his forty-fourth and final book, *Eastern Passage.* In it, the old battler made a compelling case that a dramatic drop in the beluga whale population in the St. Lawrence River was the result of an accident involving a nuclear bomb. He described how, in summer 1954, he was sailing down the St. Lawrence River, making an "Eastern Passage" from Montreal to Halifax. A deckhand "spotted a large, corpse-white something just beneath the surface directly in our path," he writes. Mowat swung the tiller hard and avoided a collision, but recognized the semi-submerged object as a twenty-foot beluga whale, clearly sick or injured.

Farther downriver, from an old sailor, he learned that a tremendous explosion had occurred in this vicinity four years before—the result, apparently, of an American plane having jettisoned several bombs. Half a century elapsed, Mowat tells us, before newspaper articles enabled him to piece together the whole story. An American bomber had run into engine trouble while transporting a version of "Fat Man," the nuclear bomb that in 1945 had obliterated the Japanese city of Nagasaki. The pilot, acting on standing orders, released the bomb into the St. Lawrence before attempting an emergency landing. The official version of what happened claimed an empty "Fat-Man casing" and three conventional bombs were released, while acknowledging that the blast

"was felt for 25 miles." Mowat quotes from a 1988 *New York Times* article. It notes that, since 1950, "a mysterious die-off of beluga whales" in
the St. Lawrence had shrunk the colony from 1,200 to 450. It added that
the area "has Canada's highest level of human birth defects, although
no direct cause-effect relationship has been shown."

Mowat makes his outrage palpable—as, down through the
decades, he has done so often. A pioneering champion of the natural world, he has always taken cutting-edge positions. While serving
as international chair of the Sea Shepherd Conservation Society, he
had a ship named after him. For six years, before it was seized by the
Canadian government, the *RV Farley Mowat* monitored violations of
international fisheries agreements.

Yet Mowat made his greatest impact as an author. Here in Canada,
few realize just how influential he has been internationally. Fewer
still are aware that, among Canadian writers of his generation (born
in the 1920s), this visionary conservationist proved a lonely giant in
having always commanded an international audience. Published in
twenty-five countries, he has sold twenty million copies of his forty-
four books in fifty-two languages. Mowat is almost certainly the most
influential Canadian author of all time. He changed the world by alter-
ing attitudes, insofar as they could be altered, towards the earth's environment, and towards the other life forms with whom we share it.

Farley Mowat is descended from fighting Scots on both sides.
His mother's family arrived in Canada in 1795. One of her ances-
tors, Alexander Grant, served as a Royal Navy officer in the Seven
Years' War and later became administrator of Upper Canada. On his
paternal side, the first Mowat to arrive in these parts fought in the
War of 1812 and settled in Kingston. He fathered Oliver Mowat, who
eventually became premier of Ontario and great-grand-uncle of
Farley. The author's father, Angus Mowat, fought in the First World
War, survived the Battle of Vimy Ridge, and subsequently became a

strong-minded librarian with an adventurous streak. He introduced young Farley—born May 12, 1921, in Belleville, Ontario—to sailing on Lake Ontario. Then, during the Great Depression, he moved the family to Saskatoon, Saskatchewan. There, young Farley fell in love with the natural world. A lonely boy who was small for his age, he discovered gophers, meadowlarks, and ponds alive with ducks and shorebirds.

The youth also had a way with words, and in his mid-teens he began writing a column about birds for the *Saskatoon Star-Phoenix.* Later, in *The Dog Who Wouldn't Be* (1957), Mowat would describe how he rambled around the prairies with his dog Mutt. At home, he kept a rattlesnake, a squirrel, two owls, an alligator, several cats, and hundreds if not thousands of pet insects. At school, he set up the Beaver Club of Amateur Naturalists. And by fifteen, when he travelled to the Arctic with a great-uncle who was an amateur birder, he had discovered his vocation as a naturalist.

In 1939, when the Second World War erupted, the eighteen-year-old Mowat was commissioned as a second lieutenant. He saw action during the Allied invasion of Sicily, where he served as a platoon commander. He then worked as an intelligence officer in Italy and the Netherlands, and in 1945, when the war ended, he emerged as a captain. Later, he would write about narrowly surviving these horrible years, most memorably in *And No Birds Sang* (1979).

After the war, while studying biology at the University of Toronto, Mowat took a field trip to the Canadian Arctic. He encountered a group of forty Inuit, the Ihalmiut, whose way of life was being destroyed by the arrival of the white man. An outraged Mowat, who had started publishing magazine articles, told their story in *People of the Deer*. When it appeared in 1952, that book shamed the Canadian government into shipping food to people whose existence it had previously denied, and also launched a spectacular literary career.

Over the next couple of decades, Mowat would publish bestselling works in a variety of genres. He produced children's books such as *Lost in the Barrens* and *The Curse of the Viking Grave*. He wrote memoirs—both serious (*The Regiment*) and light-hearted (*The Dog Who Wouldn't Be* and *Owls in the Family*). But it was as a champion of the natural world that Mowat would gain his international reputation, starting in 1963 with *Never Cry Wolf: The Amazing True Story of Life Among Arctic Wolves*. In that work, Mowat described how, having travelled to the Arctic to study declining caribou herds, he set up an observation camp. And he argued that, contrary to popular opinion, wolves were actually strengthening caribou herds by killing off the weakest animals. For the decreasing size of those herds, he blamed human trappers. This passionate book became an international sensation, and influenced the Soviet Union to ban the killing of wolves.

Mowat would produce more bestsellers in this conservationist mode. These books include *A Whale for the Killing*, which depicted the shooting of a trapped whale; *Sea of Slaughter*, a jeremiad attacking "the destruction of animal life in the north Atlantic"; and *Virunga: The Passion of Dian Fossey*, which tells the story of an anthropologist who studied and championed gorillas and was brutally murdered for her passionate commitment. Introducing his 1984 classic *Sea of Slaughter*, Mowat wrote that some early readers found the stories in the book "so appalling that they wondered why I had committed myself to five years in such a pit of horrors." He described the book as recording "what we have accomplished in one special region during 500 years of tenure as the most lethal animal ever to have appeared upon this wasting planet."

In April 1985, when he sought to enter the United States to promote *Sea of Slaughter*, Mowat was turned back at the American border. This kilt-swirling conservationist, whose twenty-seven books had already sold more than ten million copies around the world, was

judged a dangerous subversive. He wrote a book about the experience, *My Discovery of America*, demonstrating that his rejection was
farcically ill-founded. Ironically, the experience gave him a new faith
in the United States, if only because so many Americans backed him
in rejecting the "bullying, arrogant, astonishingly insensitive" postur-
ing of their leaders, and their "authoritarian, undemocratic, and frequently underhanded procedures." Mowat has never been one to pull
his punches. But what surprises most is that, at age sixty-three, he
could be judged so dangerous and subversive that America's security
experts would bar him from entering their country.

In 1996, when he was seventy-five years old, Farley Mowat weathered an assault on his reputation. A now defunct magazine, *Saturday
Night*, published a cover article slamming the author for stretching
the truth in books he had published more than three and four decades
before: *People of the Deer* (1952) and *Never Cry Wolf* (1963). The article
charged, for example, that the author had spent less time in the Arctic
than he claimed.

But Mowat had already written a cogent rebuttal. In 1974, twenty-
two years before the article appeared, Mowat wrote that he had realized early that his "métier lay somewhere in between what was then
a grey void between fact and fiction." Cataloguers could not decide
where to place his work, while "reviewers and critics, who were
enraged that I should dare to sail the middle ground between fact and
fiction, knew where my work belonged, or thought they did, and were
not hesitant about saying so." Mowat credited Truman Capote, author
of the groundbreaking "non-fiction novel" *In Cold Blood*, with having
brought respectability to what is now called creative non-fiction. As
early as 1952, Mowat had done what Capote later did. He fashioned a
real-life narrative using narrative techniques associated mainly with
fiction, incorporating scenes and dialogue.

Certainly, Mowat exaggerated the "truth" of his arctic experience beyond what today would be regarded as acceptable limits. But he was writing fifty and sixty years ago, before prevailing conventions had been established. To criticize him for transgressing borders that had yet to be drawn is patently unfair. As a writer, Farley Mowat was ahead of his time.

And as a conservationist, he was even more so. *Sea of Slaughter* remains emblematic. One reviewer described this denunciation of human destructiveness as "a hymn and a plea for life, yet also a symphony of death . . . a caring, compassionate, prophetic vision." Another called it a masterpiece in which "Canada's most beloved naturalist-author is as angry about the assault on the living sea as Rachel Carson was about the land in *Silent Spring*." Mowat himself hoped that "with luck, this record of our outrageous behaviour in and around the Sea of Slaughter . . . will help to change our attitudes and modify our future activities so that we do not become the ultimate destroyers of the living world . . . of which we are a part."

14

DON TAPSCOTT

A cyber-guru hails the arrival of digital collaboration

The developed world has reached a crisis point. Fifteen million young people (ages fifteen to twenty-four) are out of work in North America and Europe. Not long ago, youth unemployment reached 25 percent in France and 45 percent in Spain. "We are talking about structural unemployment for the whole generation," Don Tapscott warns in *Macrowikinomics: Rebooting Business and the World*. "Is there a way forward? Don't look to government or big corporations for the answers."

At a conference in São Paulo, Brazil, Tapscott elaborated, finding hope in digital technology, in young people themselves, and in the collaborative innovations made possible by the Internet. "We need to rebuild many of the institutions that have served us for decades or even centuries," Tapscott said. Addressing young people in an interview available online, he reiterated that existing institutions, including those created after the Second World War, "have taken us as far as they can on the old model . . . but now they are stalled."

Tapscott is a renowned cyber-guru and the Canadian author of fourteen books, among them a couple of blockbusters available in more than twenty-five languages. In 2011, he turned up at number nine in the Thinkers50 global ranking of outstanding business thinkers. Widely quoted in the international media, Tapscott is chairman of the think tank Moxie Insight (formerly New Paradigm, then nGenera

Insight) and an adjunct professor at the Joseph L. Rotman School of Management, University of Toronto. He is changing the world by clearing the way for, and hastening the arrival of, a digitally driven culture of collaboration.

In *Macrowikinomics*, which he co-authored with Anthony D. Williams, Tapscott says tinkering will not provide the answer to the present situation. He offers a road map to rebuild our cities, our models of government, and our institutions for wealth creation, as well as our transportation system, our energy grid, and our models of health care, science, and education. He finds hope in "lighthouse" innovators such as the start-up car company staffed by 4,500 competing designers; in a micro-lending community comprising 570,000 individuals making a difference around the world; and in an astronomer mapping the universe with the help of 250,000 citizens. "My objective," Tapscott said in Brazil, "is to be as influential as I possibly can be in bringing about these changes to our cities and to our models of government." In *Macrowikinomics*, he lays out a series of "ground rules for reinvention." Don't just create, but instead curate a context for people to self-organize. Find and strengthen the vanguard. Create a culture of collaboration. Empower the Net Generation.

Tapscott holds a bachelor's degree in psychology and statistics, a master's of education in research methodology, and several honorary doctor of laws degrees. But these did not come easily. Born in Toronto on June 1, 1947, Tapscott grew up in Niagara Falls and remembers his grade two teacher warning that he would never graduate from high school because he had "bad penmanship and bad spelling." In junior high, he ran into trouble for asking "dumb questions." In the middle of math class, he would demand to know why the tops of mountains were cold and covered in snow when they were closer to the sun than to ground level.

In 1966, Tapscott graduated from Trent University in Peterborough,

Ontario, and then became what he calls "a radical." He protested the Vietnam War and got involved in the civil rights and women's movements that arose in the United States. In the mid-1970s, he realized that the anticipated "revolution" might be slower in coming that he had hoped, and went looking for work in Toronto. In 1978, he joined the "Office of the Future" research group at Bell Northern Research. There, he studied the links between technology and human behaviour, gained a reputation for predicting trends, and quickly rose through the ranks.

Out of this work, in 1981, he produced a first book: *Office Automation: A User-Driven Method*. The following year, with several colleagues, Tapscott set up Trigon Systems Group, an independent consulting firm that rapidly grew from six to 140 employees. Trigon was acquired by DMR, an international corporation, and before long Tapscott left to found New Paradigm, a think tank specializing in how best to capitalize on the emerging information technology. In 1992, Tapscott published his breakthrough book, *Paradigm Shift: The New Promise of Information Technology*. Incorporating the results of a large-scale research project, the book detailed the impact of the new communications technologies on corporations and offered strategies and practical advice. An international bestseller, the book gave Tapscott a global platform. The ensuing kudos inspired more works. In 1995, Tapscott brought out *The Digital Economy: Promise and Peril in the Age of Networked Intelligence*, one of the first books to explore the impact of the Internet on the business world.

Three years later, in *Growing Up Digital: The Rise of the Net Generation*, Tapscott turned his attention to those born between 1977 and 1997—the first generation to arrive into and grow up in a digital world. In 2008, drawing on a study of more than 11,000 young people, he revisited this subject with *Grown Up Digital: How the Net Generation Is Changing Your World*. In that book, he argues that the "Net Geners" differ profoundly from their Baby Boomer parents. The digital world has taught them boundless freedom, customization, and interactivity, along with instant communication and a belief in collaboration.

Where Baby Boomers are "digital immigrants" who entered the new world in mid-life, the young are "digital natives." They will change the way we do business, Tapscott says, "because they are bringing a whole new mode of operation into the corporation." They are natural collaborators: "They work differently, they are very social, and of course they exist through social networks." Interviewed about that book in the *World Future Review*, Tapscott explained that Net Geners are different from their parents because they "have grown up spending their time differently, especially during adolescence." From the ages of eight to eighteen, he notes, a critical period of brain development, Baby Boomers "watched TV for 24 hours a week, and that creates a certain kind of brain. And these kids have spent that amount of time interacting, collaborating, composing their thoughts, scrutinizing, authenticating, organizing information . . . and this creates a different kind of brain." After surveying 11,000 young people in ten countries, and interviewing numerous neuroscientists, Tapscott concluded that the young are not simply better at multi-tasking but have "better active working memory and better switching abilities than their parents." And that has implications for the future.

Two years before he published *Grown Up Digital*, along with co-author Anthony D. Williams, Tapscott published *Wikinomics: How Mass Collaboration Changes Everything*. An international bestseller, it rocketed to number one on the management book charts, appeared in two dozen languages, and was a finalist for several prestigious business book awards. Based on a $9-million research project Tapscott had led, the book explored how people are collaborating to create TV news stories, sequence the human genome, design software, find cures for diseases, build motorcycles, you name it.

Again with Williams, Tapscott co-authored a hefty sequel, *Macrowikinomics: Rebooting Business and the World*, that appeared in 2010. This acclaimed work, a finalist for the Thinkers50 Book Award, argues that in the wake of the global financial crisis, the principles enunciated in *Wikinomics*—and particularly collaboration—have become more important than ever. The book shows that in virtually every field, from finance to health care to education and the environment, we face a choice: cling to the old industrial era models and institutions or use collaborative innovation to change the way we work, learn, govern, and care for each other.

Ours is a time of transformation, Tapscott writes, "not for tinkering with old models and structures." The old institutions are incapable, for example, of coping with massive youth unemployment. "We need to get beyond the tired debates," Tapscott insists, "and reach beyond the parameters of a failing framework." The process of transformation "is proving to be challenging, exhilarating, and sometimes agonizing. But given the stakes we have no choice but to forge this new future."

In December 2012, thanks to a new initiative by Thinkers50, Tapscott began creating a "compendium app" that will amalgamate essays, articles, interviews, and podcasts. The app will explore ten areas that Tapscott believes are undergoing radical change, among them education, banking, health, and science. While working on another book, called *Radical Openness*, Tapscott insisted in an article in the *Toronto Star* that he will never again rely exclusively on the written word. In future, every book he writes will "come with an app, or some kind of deep, interactive learning environment." For Don Tapscott, tomorrow has already arrived.

15

WADE DAVIS

A wayfinder explores the planet's "ethnosphere"

In recent decades, climate change has increased global awareness of the biosphere, the interconnected system that comprises the earth and all living organisms. People have realized that it needs protection. But according to Wade Davis, the planet's "ethnosphere"—the intellectual and spiritual web that makes up all the earth's cultures—is suffering far worse than the biosphere. In his 2009 Massey Lectures, published internationally as *The Wayfinders: Why Ancient Wisdom Matters in the Modern World*, Davis warned that human cultures are disappearing at an alarming rate. Where biologists say that 18 percent of mammals and 11 percent of birds are threatened with extinction, anthropologists predict that half the world's 7,000 languages will disappear within the next few decades. And when languages die, Davis explains, with them go knowledge, stories, songs, and ways of viewing the world.

The British Columbia–born Davis, known internationally as an explorer, an anthropologist, and an ethnobotanist, elaborated in January 2010 in San Francisco, where he addressed the Long Foundation. If alien anthropologists arrived from Mars, he said, and they measured success in terms of technological achievement, "we would come out shining." If those interplanetary visitors assessed social structure, however, they would judge western societies harshly. They would find ours to be a hubristic, extremist civilization that "rips down ancient rainforests, tears holes in the heavens, depopulates the oceans, and changes the biophysics of the atmosphere."

Davis is changing the world by shaking us awake to connectedness. In a video readily available online, Davis said he hoped climate change would "finally teach us that we're not the paragon of humanity's potential. Climate change is humanity's problem, but it wasn't humanity that created the problem." Rather, it was "a very small subset of humanity that had a particular world view. We think of that world view as being absolute, as the real world, and believe that everyone else is failing to keep up with us or something. But it's not like that." Other peoples, cultures, and societies "are not failed attempts," Davis added. "They are just alternatives. And you would think the fact that we have brought on this climate crisis would give us a little bit of humility about the impact we've had on the planet."

Davis, designated one of the Explorers for the Millennium by the U.S.-based National Geographic Society, has been publicly elaborating these views for more than three decades. He has been described as "a rare combination of scientist, scholar, poet and passionate defender of all of life's diversity." Born December 14, 1953, in British Columbia, and raised in Quebec, the multifaceted Davis earned degrees in anthropology, biology, and ethnobotany from Harvard University. He sprang to prominence at thirty-two when he published *The Serpent and the Rainbow*, an international bestseller that investigated psychoactive plants and Haitian zombies. Since then, he has produced fifteen books, more than 180 articles, and numerous documentary films. These last include his ethnographic series *Light at the Edge of the World*. Filmed in Rapa Nui, Tahiti, the Marquesas, Nunavut, Greenland, Nepal, and Peru, it has aired in 165 countries.

More than once, Davis has traced his interest in diverse cultures to having spent his childhood in a community on the outskirts of Montreal during the era of Two Solitudes. He realized at age five or six that neighbours who lived "on the other side of Jacques Cartier Boulevard" had "another language, another religion, another way of being." Intrigued, he crossed the divide and lived in both worlds, French and English—an experience that proved to be a catalyst.

When he was fourteen, his father told him that Spanish was the language of the future. He sent him with a teacher and six older boys on a student program to Colombia. By chance, while all the other students were billeted with wealthy families in the city of Cali, Davis spent eight weeks living with "a more modest family in the mountains," speaking nothing but Spanish. "Apparently a lot of the other lads were homesick, but I, by contrast, felt like I had found home." At nineteen, Davis returned to Colombia and lived there for a year and a half as a botanical explorer, "basically on the streets."

At twenty, travelling on foot, Davis crossed the infamous Darién Gap—an area of undeveloped swamp and forest separating Central America from South America—with the English author-explorer Sebastian Snow. He then spent more than three years in the Amazon and the Andes, living among fifteen indigenous groups in eight Latin American nations. Having collected 6,000 botanical specimens, he went to Haiti, where he investigated folk medicines known to turn people into zombies. This work culminated in his 1985 book *The Serpent and the Rainbow*, an international bestseller published in ten languages (it later became a feature film that Davis disavowed).

Since then, while rambling the world, Davis has produced more than a dozen books, among them *Penan: Voice for the Borneo Rainforest*; *The Clouded Leopard: A Book of Travels*; *The Lost Amazon: The Photographic Journey of Richard Evans Schultes*; *Grand Canyon: River at Risk*; *Book of Peoples of the World: A Guide to Cultures*; *One River: Explorations and Discoveries in the Amazon Rain Forest*; and *The Wayfinders*. These works have earned him honorary degrees and numerous awards, including the Lowell Thomas Medal (from the Explorers Club) and the Lannan Foundation's literary award for non-fiction. In recent years, his work has taken him to East Africa, Borneo, Nepal, Peru, Polynesia, Tibet, Mali, Benin, Togo, New Guinea, Vanuatu, Nunavut, and Greenland.

In 2011, Davis published two books. One was a short, fierce work entitled *The Sacred Headwaters: The Fight to Save the Stikine, Skeena, and Nass*, in which he battles to preserve an area where he has spent much of each summer for thirty years, and where mining companies have begun clear-cutting and digging while searching for gold and copper: "In a rugged knot of mountains in the remote reaches of Northern British Columbia," he writes, "lies a stunningly beautiful valley known to the First Nations as the Sacred Headwaters. There, on the southern edge of the Spatsizi Wilderness, the Serengeti of Canada, are born in remarkably close proximity three of Canada's most important salmon rivers: the Stikine, Skeena and the Nass. Against the wishes of all First Nations, the government of British Columbia has opened the Sacred Headwaters to industrial development." In a *Toronto Star* article published on January 13, 2013, Davis elaborated: "Not in my darkest imaginings did I ever think that a place so pristine and remote, of such overwhelming and breathless beauty, would one day fall prey to the same avaricious forces that have wreaked havoc over so much of the world. It's like drilling for oil in the Sistine Chapel."

In the second work he published in 2011, a 655-page tome called *Into the Silence: The Great War, Mallory, and the Conquest of Everest*, Davis produced his most ambitious book yet. Reviewing it in *The Globe and Mail*, I described the book as "a complex, subversive work— a post-colonial refashioning of an imperialist adventure." After noting that Davis "is rightly celebrated for introducing indigenous perspectives into the mainstream," I added that here he continues that work "while telling a terrific adventure story and affirming as sublime the hubristic madness of assaulting the highest mountain in the world 'because it's there.'"

That book, ten years in the making and clearly his most ambitious, was shortlisted in Canada for the Charles Taylor Prize and the Governor General's Award for Non-Fiction. In Britain, it won the leading non-fiction award, the Samuel Johnson Prize. *Into the Silence* illustrates what Davis meant when he told a magazine writer in 2007 that he was a storyteller—but that "storytelling can change the world." In a subsequent interview, Davis took this notion further, suggesting that storytellers shape vision and understanding and that "pessimism is an indulgence." In his lifetime, he noted, "women have gone from the kitchen to the boardroom, people of colour from the woodshed to the White House, gay people from the closet to the altar. Thirty years ago, when I was a kid, just getting people to stop throwing garbage out a car window was considered an environmental victory. Nobody spoke of the biosphere, and now that term is part of the language of school children."

History is like a river, Davis said, "that flows beneath the living. You never really know . . . where the current is going, and what the final direction of the river is going to be. But you have to be pretty inherently negative to look back at the last thirty years and not be optimistic." Recognizing that the world is also beset by darkness, and that humanity faces enormous challenges, Davis warned against negativity and pessimism: "Collectively, people can change history."

16

FRANK GEHRY

An ex-night-schooler takes architecture outside the box

Architects in their eighties don't typically make headlines. But Frank Gehry has never been typical. And in October 2012, when at eighty-three he unveiled a proposal that would revolutionize the Toronto skyline, he sparked a debate that started on front pages and overflowed into blogs, editorials, and commentaries. The tallest building in the city, aside from the CN Tower, is the seventy-two-storey First Canadian Place, which reaches 298 metres. Most of the city's tallest skyscrapers range between forty and sixty storeys. By 2015, however, Toronto will have forty-four high-rises exceeding forty-five stories— more than triple the number it had in 2005. Tallest among them will be the Trump International Tower (277 metres) and Canderel's condo project at Yonge and College (272 metres). Gehry, backed by Toronto businessman David Mirvish, is proposing to build three residential towers of eighty to eighty-six storeys, their heights exceeding any other city skyscrapers by 20 to 30 metres. The project would include a public museum, an art gallery, retail space, and classrooms devoted to art and design, but would involve tearing down the Princess of Wales Theatre, a Mirvish-owned playhouse just two decades old.

The *Toronto Star*, Canada's largest-circulation newspaper, described the initiative as making the kind of architectural statement that marks great world cities. It offered "a bold vision of what the city could be," and exemplified "the kind of dramatic thinking that

Toronto sees too rarely." One of the *Star*'s columnists, Rosie DiManno, took a contrary position. She portrayed the towers as "disproportionately humungous, ungracefully asymmetric, vertically overbearing," and declared this to be "a vanity project of gobsmacking arrogance."

Frank Gehry is no stranger to controversy. Unveiling this first architectural draft, he recalled that critics of his Walt Disney Concert Hall in Los Angeles denounced his design as "broken crockery." That hall is now widely viewed as a transformative masterwork. And in Bilbao, Spain, Gehry created the radical Guggenheim Museum, hailed by *The New York Times* as "the world's most celebrated new building." It has become a tourist attraction, and Gehry observed, "They wanted to shoot me when they saw the design, and now they get $500 million a year in revenue to the city." Did that change the world? Certainly in the view of most Spaniards it set a high-water mark. And Gehry is looking to repeat that accomplishment in Toronto, Canada's largest city, already recognized from one edge of town to the other as the Centre of the Universe.

In 2010, the World Architecture Survey cited Gehry's buildings as being among the most significant in contemporary architecture. At that point, not to be outdone, *Vanity Fair* called him "the most important architect of our age." By then, having become the only architect to win the world-famous Pritzker Architecture Prize and also to appear as himself in an episode of *The Simpsons*, Gehry could take it all in stride. He had become a world-beater.

Born Frank Owen Goldberg in Toronto on February 28, 1929, Gehry would change his name in the 1950s at the insistence of his first wife, who worried about the prevailing anti-Semitism. But that came later. His maternal grandparents had emigrated from Poland. They lived on Beverley Street in Toronto's Jewish ghetto, and owned a hardware store, Caplan's Hardware, around the corner. In the 1930s, young Frank spent many hours with his grandmother, building imaginary cities on the floor, complete with freeways. According to biographer Caroline Evensen Lazo, his grandmother "was my model of how an adult can play creatively. We made houses, we made cities, it was wonderful."

As he grew older, with the Great Depression dragging on, he worked in the store. That nurtured his talent, he later told writer Gillian MacKay, "learning to work with pipe, to cut pipe, put the threads on it, to cut glass, sell putty, sell nails, sell bolts. I used to love opening those boxes of bolts and looking at them, and making stuff with them." Later, he would become known for incorporating corrugated steel, chain-link fencing, and unpainted plywood into his creations.

When Gehry was eleven, his family moved 700 kilometres north to Timmins, Ontario. His father, originally from New York, made his living by leasing and servicing pinball machines and jukeboxes. As the only Jewish boy in his school, the young newcomer survived bullying. In an essay called "The Early Years," MacKay quoted Gehry, who remembered, "I used to go out at recess to play hockey and I'd get beat up. The French Canadians from the school next door shared the same rink, and they used to stand up for me."

In 1942, a government ban on pinball machines wiped out his father's business. The Goldbergs returned to Toronto, where Frank's father, something of a pop artist, tried to earn a living by "making things like wooden trays, smoking stands, lazy susans. Sometimes I worked with him. It makes me cry, with what I know now, to think how I could have helped him. We could have had fun together." That venture, too, went belly up, and the family crowded in with the grandparents.

The boy attended Bloor Collegiate, where he enjoyed art and shop. Having discovered atheism, he distinguished himself by seeking converts. He took an interest in architecture, attending lectures from the age of sixteen, and his mother encouraged him. But he analyzed the program at University of Toronto and judged it boring. Meanwhile, his father suffered a heart attack. A doctor suggested a change of climate, and suddenly, traumatically, the family moved to Los Angeles, where his father had two brothers.

His father found work driving a truck, and his mother worked in a department store. Frank Goldberg thought his life was over: "As the man in the family, it was my job to go to work. I thought I was never going to college. There was no future." He, too, found work driving a delivery truck, and then washing airplanes. He tried radio announcing but discovered he wasn't very good. He tried chemical engineering and didn't like that. While casting about, he remembered his early enthusiasm for drawing and building. He began taking night courses at the University of Southern California (USC). One of his teachers took him to a construction site, where an architect was guiding the building. Gehry was hooked. And he kept on studying.

At twenty-one, forced to choose, he became an American—though he would reclaim his Canadian citizenship decades later, in 2002, when Jean Chrétien welcomed him home. In 1952, he married. At the urging of his wife, he changed his name from Goldberg to Gehry. And in 1954, he received a bachelor of architecture degree from USC, graduating at the top of his class. Gehry served a year in the special services branch of the U.S. Army, and then, at twenty-seven, moved his wife and two children to Cambridge, Massachusetts, where he studied city planning at the Harvard Graduate School of Design. Interested in socially responsible architecture, he became disillusioned and dropped out after learning that one of the professors was secretly designing a palace for the Cuban dictator Fulgencio Batista (who would be overthrown by Fidel Castro a couple of years later, in 1959).

Back in Los Angeles, Gehry worked for a couple of architectural firms, and then, in 1962, opened his own office. Influenced by the pioneering French architect Le Corbusier, Gehry rejected the notion that every building must have straight angles and offer some variation on a box. Starting in 1966, when he used corrugated metal and telephone poles to build a California hay barn, he employed ordinary, inexpensive materials in sculptural ways. For four years beginning in 1969, Gehry produced a line of furniture he created out of corrugated cardboard. In 1977, having divorced, remarried, and fathered two more children, he bought a modest house in Santa Monica, a coastal suburb of Los Angeles. His remodelling of that house, using steel and chain-link fencing, prompted a *New York Times* critic to write about it, calling it "a major work of architecture—perhaps the most significant new house in Southern California in some years."

In 1981, after Gehry built a striking mini-campus for a law school, the California branch of the American Institute of Architects named him architect of the year—the first of many major honours that would come his way. He landed more work in southern California, and ever-larger commissions in France, Germany, and Japan, and invariably exceeded expectations. Gehry won the Arnold W. Brunner Memorial Prize for having "made a significant contribution to architecture as art." For the 1992 Olympics in Barcelona, Spain, Gehry used computer-aided design for the first time to create a monumental fish sculpture that turns up in many textbooks.

Through the 1980s, Gehry taught architecture at Harvard, Yale, and USC, and in 1989, he won the Pritzker Architecture Prize for lifetime achievement, the highest accolade in the field. The committee stated, "In an artistic climate that too often looks backward rather than toward the future [and where following older designs is safer than risking new ones], it is important to honor the architecture of Frank O. Gehry." The architect had discovered his voice as an artist. He was a contemporary cubist, a Picasso who worked in buildings and who sought ways to express his vision in three-dimensional objects.

Frank Gehry changed the world by producing revolutionary masterworks that go beyond the usual structural forms and definitions. These include the Frederick R. Weisman Art Museum in Minneapolis, the Guggenheim Museum in Bilbao, and the Walt Disney Concert Hall in Los Angeles. In 2007, Gehry completed an expansion of the Art Gallery of Ontario, located mere blocks from where he grew up. This building, filled with natural light, has become a favourite among Torontonians, and the redesign is not to be confused with that of the Royal Ontario Museum, which has attracted few champions.

As for the transformative, triple-tower project the architect proposes to build in downtown Toronto, Gehry is no stranger to tall buildings. In 2011, in Lower Manhattan, he completed a spectacular tower that soars seventy-six storeys and features an undulating exterior of titanium and glass. In Toronto, it is still early days. Will the three towers ever be built?

In 1883, in Barcelona, Spain, Antoni Gaudí launched an architectural project, the Sagrada Família, that has remained a work-in-progress through generations, though it is already a UNESCO World Heritage Site. Like Gaudí, Frank Gehry is an inspirational figure. He is not one to shrink from creating a revolutionary blueprint from which others can work.

17

GUY LALIBERTÉ

A fire-eating clown reinvents the circus

When people say that he recreated the circus, Guy Laliberté responds that he merely updated it. The circus has been around since Roman times, he says, or about 2,500 years: "It needs dusting off every twenty years or so." With Cirque du Soleil, he explains, "we repackaged it in a more modern way." Whether he repackaged, re-energized, or reinvented, this fire-eating ex-busker transformed the circus, turning it from an old-fashioned tiger-and-elephant show mixed with acrobatics into an imaginative theatrical experience.

Starting from scratch in small-town Quebec in the early 1980s, Laliberté changed the world by creating a global empire that mounts shows in more than 270 cities and on every continent except Antarctica. Early in 2013, the Cirque retrenched, laying off 400 of its 5,000 employees. But with almost 15 million people a year catching shows around the world, and annual revenues of nearly $1 billion, the empire remains a creative marvel. While he was reinventing the circus, incidentally vaulting a language barrier that has proven insurmountable to many another, Laliberté turned himself into Canada's youngest billionaire, with a net worth exceeding $2.5 billion. His is a rags-to-riches story that, if it weren't so contemporary, and so profoundly Québécois, might have come from the pen of Horatio Alger.

Guy Laliberté was born September 2, 1959, in Baie-Saint-Paul, a resort town on the St. Lawrence River, 100 kilometres northeast of

Quebec City. His father became a public relations executive with Alcan Aluminium in Montreal, and Laliberté grew up in Saint-Bruno, a suburb southeast of the city. He was a bright, adventurous child, and by age four he was selling lemonade outside the family home.

From his father, Laliberté learned to play the accordion. He loved to sing, dance, and entertain, and he developed a passion for folk music. After his parents took him to Montreal to see the Ringling Brothers and Barnum & Bailey Circus, he read a biography of P.T. Barnum and discovered a role model. At school, he gravitated to theatre arts and organized several events. Then he caught a concert in Montreal by Cajun artist Zachary Richard, who invited the audience to come to New Orleans for Mardi Gras. Laliberté organized a school trip to do just that, using garage sales, car washes, and concerts to raise the necessary funds.

As a teenager, Laliberté began hanging out with older musicians and performers. He played the accordion and the harmonica, and sometimes he sang. After high school, he joined a folk group called La Grande Gueule (The Big Mouth). In an authorized biography, Laliberté says the group played festivals around the province: "Some of the guys were working, so when they couldn't make it, I'd go alone, from festival to festival, from hostel to hostel."

As a street musician, an itinerant busker, the energetic youth specialized in Québécois accordion music and storytelling. After each performance, he collected money in a hat. At eighteen, having heard that buskers fared much better in Europe, he flew to London and spent his first night in town sleeping on a bench in Hyde Park. His English language skills were still shaky, so he headed to Paris. There, he fell in with other street performers and, while rambling around Europe, developed additional skills: juggling, magic, stilt-walking, and fire-breathing. This last would become his trademark.

Back home in Quebec, and hurting for money, Laliberté took what he calls a "straight job" at a hydroelectric dam in James Bay. But when, a few days after he started, the workers went on strike, he resumed his life as a busker. He joined a troupe called Les Échassiers de Baie-Saint-Paul (The Stilt-Walkers of Baie-Saint-Paul). In their leader, Gilles Ste-Croix, he found the first of several key allies who would help him change the world.

Laliberté worked with Ste-Croix and a few others to create La Fête Foraine, a street festival that sprang to life in 1982. He served both as general manager and as show-stopping fire-eater. The festival lost money the first year, but Laliberté expanded it and turned a profit. "I had a business goal, always," he says. "I think it's a quality I have. I'm capable of finding a balance between business and creativity, and see how creativity can grow out of that balance."

In 1983, Laliberté spotted an opportunity. The provincial government, led by Quebec nationalist premier René Lévesque, was funding projects to celebrate the 450th anniversary of the arrival in the New World of French explorer Jacques Cartier. While lying on a beach in Hawaii, watching the sun go down, Laliberté conceived of mounting a Cirque du Soleil (Circus of the Sun). "The sun stands for energy and youth," he says, "which is what I thought the circus should be about." That vision, inspired by a Hawaiian sunset, would not only gain provincial government support, but would give rise to a global empire that, even after retrenchment, today employs more than 4,500 people from forty countries.

Back home again, Laliberté applied for provincial government funding to mount a circus show under a big tent. But the government "wanted an activity that would tour the regions," he explained later. "They didn't want a show, per se. They wanted animation, an impact that would be larger than just a show. So the compromise was to have this gathering of street performers descend on eleven towns over thirteen weeks. Within that, we'd have an opening and closing show—the embryo of what would become Cirque du Soleil."

In rural Quebec, the first crowds were sparse. Laliberté refined his marketing techniques. He sent costumed performers into communities in advance and the crowds grew larger. The Cirque du Soleil became the runaway hit of the summer of 1984. After thirteen performances around the province, the Cirque went to Toronto and Vancouver. Laliberté had pitched and sold the circus as a one-year extravaganza, but he always had a long-term vision. He sought backing for expansion in 1985, under the auspices of the International Year of Youth.

This time, the federal government quickly agreed to provide funding, but certain powerful Quebec ministers provided resistance. Laliberté eventually triumphed, but only with the personal support of then-premier René Lévesque. From that time on, the Cirque would be not just a travelling show but a full-blown circus.

The original tent could seat no more than 800, so Laliberté went to Europe and bought a much larger tent. He also hired a first artistic director, Guy Caron, who had been running a circus school in Montreal. That same year, Belgian Franco Dragone came aboard to direct the show. These young men shared a common vision: they wanted to make of the Cirque a unique theatrical experience—an experience that, while rooted in traditional circus antics (minus the animals), also included music and a loose narrative.

The Cirque had finished 1984 with $60,000 in the bank, but had committed to spending $1.6 million the following year. "We ended up running after money," Laliberté says, "and chasing our tails all the time. We had some government funding, but never the amount we needed, or when we needed it." But here, too, Laliberté had installed a crucial ally, an administrative and logistical wizard named Daniel Gauthier. With him, Laliberté started expanding into Ottawa, Toronto, and Niagara, though most people there had never heard of the Cirque. "We had good critical reaction," Laliberté says, "but we weren't able to generate the word-of-mouth we needed to be successful." The result was a year-end deficit of $750,000. Technically bankrupt, Laliberté pushed ahead, and with the 1986 show, *La Magie Continue,* he turned things around.

That show was the first to include an original music score. It also gave rise to *Le Cirque Réinventé,* on which director and costume designer collaborated, taking a painterly approach to creating characters and, indeed, an entire show. *Le Cirque Réinventé* toured North America in 1987 and 1989 to great acclaim. Finances remained a challenge, but as an artist himself, Laliberté understood the creative process. He would choose his key people and give them room to work. With any given show, even today, he approves the creative team, the acrobatic skeleton, and the general direction. He then steps back and allows the specialists to work. As the show nears completion, he steps in again to hone the production, whether that involves simply changing the rhythm or introducing radical last-minute changes.

Artistically, 1990 brought *Nouvelle Expérience,* a breakthrough show based on a novel by Jules Verne in which a meteorite made of gold is about to hit the earth. Backed by Laliberté, director Franco Dragone put his performers through extensive workshopping sessions, encouraging them to experiment. This process became a model for future shows, all of which are mounted between 385 and 490 times a year. Each Cirque is distinctive and has a unique theme and storyline. In recent years, some shows have focused on iconic pop stars such as Elvis and the Beatles. *Michael Jackson: The Immortal World Tour* has been especially successful. All of these shows use live music to draw the audience into the experience, and sustain the magic by having performers rather than stagehands change the scenery.

As he became increasingly successful, Laliberté remembered his old friends and generously hosted extravagant parties. But never for a moment did he lose sight of his objectives. At one point, he undertook an intensive study of successful business people and applied every lesson that suited. An inveterate high-stakes gambler, he was always willing to spend money to make money. Step by step, he expanded into the United States. In each successive market, he identified key players and brought them aboard. He won over Los Angeles, New York, and then Las Vegas, where in 2012, *Mystère* was still going strong after nineteen years. In New York, the Cirque's *Zarkana* brings in $3.2 million per week while top-grossing shows on Broadway draw perhaps $1.8 million. According to one Canadian documentary, with revenues of around $1 billion a year, the Cirque takes in as much as all of Broadway combined. After conquering the United States, Laliberté turned to Europe, where he discovered that different markets have different tastes. He responded accordingly and kept expanding.

Over the years, Laliberté became interested in water conservation. In 2009, when he became the first Canadian to travel into space as a tourist, he dedicated his flight to raising awareness of water issues. He also founded a charity, One Drop Foundation, which works to help developing countries improve access to drinkable water. Along the way, *Time* magazine recognized him as one of the 100 most influential people in the world. He has been inducted into the Order of Canada and the Canadian Business Hall of Fame, and has received a star on the Hollywood Walk of Fame.

Meanwhile, with some two dozen shows running simultaneously, the Cirque entertains 350,000 people each week. In Las Vegas alone, where it plays five venues, it attracts 9,000 people per night. Around the world, its various shows, seen by roughly ninety million people, have continued to earn prizes and distinctions. At last count, these included a BAMBI Award, a Rose d'Or, two Drama Desk Awards, three Gemini Awards, and four Emmy Awards. From busker and fire-eating clown to billionaire jet-setter, Guy Laliberté has travelled no small distance. That alone would not qualify him for this book. Along the way, to the delight of millions around the world, he re-imagined and reinvented the circus. That did it.

Part III

Artists:
Painters, Writers, and
Filmmakers

They change the way we see the world

Speaking in Jerusalem while accepting the Dan David Prize, Margaret Atwood noted that writers are easy to attack because they don't have armies and can't retaliate. She and Indian novelist Amitav Ghosh, with whom she shared the $1 million award, had "both received a number of letters," she said, "urging and indeed ordering us not to attend, on the grounds that anything connected with Israel is tabu."

Those letters "have ranged from courteous and sad," she added, "to factual and practical, to accusatory, outrageous, and untrue in their claims and statements; some have been frankly libelous, and even threatening. Some [of the correspondents] have been willing to listen to us, others have not: they want our supposedly valuable 'names,' but not our actual voices." In other words, Atwood said, "the all-or-nothings want to bully us into being their wholly owned puppets. The result of such a decision on our part would be—among other things—to turn us into sticks with which to beat other artists into submission, and that we refuse to do."

The Dan David Prize for the Present, as distinct from those prizes awarded for the Past and the Future, was earmarked in 2010 for "an outstanding author whose work provides vivid, compelling, and groundbreaking depictions of twentieth-century life, rousing public discussion and inspiring fellow writers." Atwood was cited specifically for enabling "the emergence of a defined Canadian identity while exploring . . . issues such as colonialism, feminism, structures of political power and oppression, and the violation and exploitation of nature."

Atwood, co-founder of PEN Canada, added in Jerusalem that "we are familiar with what other artists of many countries have been put through in similar circumstances." And she quoted a recent speech made by Anthony Appiah, president of PEN American Center, noting that she and Ghosh had been subjected to an offensive "urging them to reject the award as part of a campaign of cultural isolation against Israel."

Appiah had observed that the American literary community does not speak with a single voice on Palestine, but said, "I want to be clear about where the PEN American Center stands on one aspect of this vexed issue. We have to stand, as we have stood from the very beginning, against the very idea of a cultural boycott. We have to continue to say: Only connect. We have to stick with our founding conviction that writers must reach out across nations. To stand anywhere else would be to betray our history and our mission."

As an artist, and more specifically a writer, Margaret Atwood is more politicized than most. Here in Canada, she long ago established herself as the Warrior Queen of Canadian Letters. Globally, as we see from her words and actions in Jerusalem, she remains fearless. She defends the diminishing space afforded to art in the broad sense—the psychological space an artist, writer, or filmmaker requires to effect change. The American artist Jeff Koons put it this way: "Art to me is a humanitarian act, and I believe that there is a responsibility that art should somehow be able to affect mankind, to make the world a better place."

Atwood is a generational leader, an extraordinary talent, and commands appropriate attention in this section. She is like other painters, writers, and filmmakers, however, in that she works transformative magic from within. Artists change the world one person at a time. They change the way we experience and perceive. Almost by definition, they resist categorization. But the world-changing artists who turn up here in Part III include an Inuit painter who enriched the world's cultural web, a Booker Prize–winning author who created a country, and a blockbuster king who ushered movies into the digital era.

18

KENOJUAK ASHEVAK

An Inuit artist enriches world culture

Despite her recent passing at age eighty-five, Kenojuak Ashevak remains an artist of international renown. She is celebrated around the globe for having woven a distinctive thread into the cultural web that comprises all the cultures of the world. In her native land, in 1967, she became one of the first people to receive the Order of Canada. Already, she had been the subject of a National Film Board documentary highlighting her art.

One of her prints, *The Enchanted Owl*, was featured on a postage stamp in 1970 to commemorate the 100th anniversary of the Northwest Territories. She was elected to the Royal Canadian Academy of Arts and celebrated in Toronto by the World Wildlife Fund. She received honorary doctorates from Queen's University and the Law Faculty of the University of Toronto. Her prints turned up on more stamps in 1980 and 1993, and on a coin in 1999 to mark the birth of Nunavut.

With her art, she changed the world, weaving a colourful new thread into what Wade Davis calls "the ethnosphere." Kenojuak, as she is called, was born in an igloo on October 3, 1927, on south Baffin Island. Her father, a spirited, impulsive man, died when she was three. She grew up among members of her extended family, living off the land—hunting, fishing, and trapping. She travelled by dogsled from camp to camp, just as the Inuit have done for centuries.

She witnessed and became part of the dramatic changes that

engulfed the Inuit in the twentieth century. She saw the buying and selling of capitalism lay waste to a traditional culture based on sharing, and Christianity supersede an ancient belief in spirits. She witnessed the arrival of electricity, which would bring television, computers, and access to the Internet. She saw fixed settlements and towns replace movable hunting camps, wooden houses replace sod houses (*qarmaqs*) and igloos, and snowmobiles replace dog teams.

As a child, though embarrassed by being left-handed, she learned traditional Inuit handicrafts from her grandmother, showing unusual skill at sewing sealskins or doing beadwork. An uncle used the odd piece of driftwood to carve impressive figurines, but she did not try carving: that was men's work.

She was late to marry, nineteen years old. The young man who won the approval of her family, Johnniebo, looked to her like a *qallunaaq*, or white man. "I found him repulsive," she said later, "and I was not looking forward in the slightest to being married to him." During the first weeks of their union, she said later, "I threw rocks at him whenever he approached me. He laughed good-naturedly, and continued his pursuit. Eventually I grew very fond of this kind, gentle man."

The marriage proved successful and enduring. Over the years, Kenojuak gave birth to several children. They lit up her life, and when some of them died early as a result of illness, she grieved deeply.

At age twenty-five, she was diagnosed with tuberculosis. She spent three years in a Quebec City treatment centre. During this period, several *qallunaaq* visitors—notably the sculptor Harold Pfeiffer—provided patients with arts-and-crafts materials to do beadwork, sewing, leatherwork, and wood carving. Of the dolls Kenojuak created from textile and leather remnants, Pfeiffer exclaimed, "They are some of the best and most beautiful I have ever seen."

Back on Baffin Island, the *qallunaaq* couple James and Alma Houston had settled into Cape Dorset. They had begun leading workshops and encouraging talented Inuit to produce (and then sell) carvings and crafts, including boots (*kamiks*), mittens, parkas, wall hangings, and dolls decorated with beadwork. In the summer of 1955, when Kenojuak returned to Kungia camp, near Cape Dorset, and showed her work, Alma Houston said she had a gift. Kenojuak made sealskin and bead works and the white woman sold them for her, eventually through an Inuit co-operative, generating money for the family.

At one point, when the supply of beads ran out, James Houston urged Kenojuak to try drawing, which, like carving, was considered a male preserve. In an annual catalogue of Inuit works, she would recall, "The first time *Saumik* [James Houston] gave me a piece of paper and asked me to start drawing, I asked him what kind of drawing am I going to make. And then he just told me to draw anything that come into my mind. It could be anything. A lot of times I didn't know what to draw."

But draw she did. Soon she was devoting every spare moment to artistic activity: drawing, etching, and occasionally carving in soapstone. In *Kenojuak: The Life Story of an Inuit Artist,* author Ansgar Walk notes that the artist's first print, *Rabbit Eating Seaweed,* was based not on a drawing but on a silhouette cut-out she had made for a sealskin bag. *Saumik* had noticed and asked to examine the bag, which she had decorated by sewing a dark sealskin cut-out onto a lighter-coloured background. He asked, "What's this?" And she said, "A rabbit thinking about eating seaweed."

Almost from the first, although several of her contemporaries produced excellent drawings and prints, Kenojuak's work stood out for its originality. From down south, museums and collectors clamoured for more. In those early days, "I usually only drew in daylight, sitting in our *qarmaq,*" she would later recall. "Though I was highly motivated, my role as mother and wife was even more important than this beautiful new work." Eventually, she would give birth to or raise a dozen children, including some she adopted.

By 1962, she had attracted enough attention that the National Film Board produced a documentary called *Eskimo Artist: Kenojuak*. Four years after that, mainly to access better schooling for her children, she and Johnniebo moved to Cape Dorset, where in January of 2013 she passed away. Always, through a career lasting more than fifty years, Kenojuak was fascinated by birds, especially owls. Yet she drew many other figures, including humans, spirits, transformed beings, a sea goddess, and countless mammals, as well as the sun and moon, sleds, harpoons, fishing rods, snow knives—all the paraphernalia of traditional life.

In the *Encyclopedia of Native American Artists*, Deborah Everett writes that Kenojuak gave precedence to imagination and the life of the mind rather than documentary realism or narrative. She suggests that the most important and distinctive feature of the prints is the vibrancy and intensity of the life forms: "They are assertive and self-assured. They stare out at the viewer with a wide-eyed and inquisitive gaze. They don't decorate the page—they take control of it, energizing every inch."

Everett notes that Kenojuak always experimented artistically, exploring composition, using different figures, and playing with overlapping forms and foreshortening. Her works range in mood from playful to menacing, and reveal a deep sensitivity to the lives of animals.

As her reputation grew, Kenojuak began to receive commissions and invitations to travel abroad. In 1970, to see the enormous mural she created for the World's Fair, she flew to Osaka, Japan, one of the largest cities in the world. Ten years later, she journeyed to Rotterdam, in the Netherlands, to attend the opening of an exhibition featuring her prints. Her works have found their way into the permanent collections of leading Canadian museums and art galleries, as well as the Tate Gallery in London, the Vatican in Rome, the Amon Carter Museum in Texas, and the World Wildlife Fund collection in Switzerland. To attend openings or receive honours, Kenojuak travelled to major centres around the world.

Yet she always returned to her home on Baffin Island, where it all began. In 1993, remembering, she put it this way: "I will never forget when a bearded man called *Saumik* approached me to draw on a piece of paper. My heart started to pound like a heavy rock." She took home several pieces of paper and started drawing as Johnniebo looked over her shoulder. "When I first started to make a few lines he smiled at me and said, '*Inumn*,' which means, 'I love you.' I just knew inside his heart that he almost cried knowing that I was trying my best to say something on a piece of paper that would bring food to the family. I guess I was thinking of the animals and beautiful flowers that covered our beautiful, untouched land."

Kenojuak's passing, art critic Sarah Milroy wrote, "marked the end of an era." Art dealer and collector John Houston, son of James and Alma, recalled her bold energy and unique sense of design. When he heard the news of her death, he said in *The Globe and Mail*, he had an image of a balloon slowly deflating: "Canada just shrank." The same might be said of the whole wide world. With her art, Kenojuak Ashevak made the earth bigger.

19

ALICE MUNRO

A Booker Prize winner creates her own country

One celebrated author, Jonathan Franzen, declared in *The New York Times* that Alice Munro "has a strong claim to being the best fiction writer now working in North America." Another, Cynthia Ozick, called her "our Chekhov," drawing parallels with the Russian Anton Chekhov, often considered the greatest short-story writer of all time. And when, in 2009, Munro won the Man Booker International Prize for her body of work, she inspired the three-person jury to write that she "brings as much depth, wisdom and precision to every story as most novelists bring to a lifetime of novels." The Man Booker, worth more than $100,000, was just the most spectacular addition to a list of honours that includes three Governor General's Awards, two Giller Prizes, and an American National Book Critics Circle Award.

Alice Munro dazzles the critics. Many have remarked on the density and emotional depth of her work, and Helen Hoy marvels at her "remarkable precision." Garan Holcombe highlights her sense of passing time and her use of epiphany—"the sudden enlightenment, the concise, subtle, revelatory detail." Robert Thacker hails the "verisimilitude" of Munro's writing and the allusive way it communicates the feeling "of just being a human being." Even so, given the work of Chekhov himself, and also of William Trevor and Flannery O'Connor, few would contend that Alice Munro has revolutionized the short story. On the other hand, when readers contemplate Jane Austen, Thomas Hardy, or William Faulkner, they think of the fictional countries those writers created—Jane Austen Country, Thomas Hardy Country, Yoknapatawpha County—and how sojourning in these various worlds has changed the way we experience our own lives. To suggest that Alice Munro has done the same by creating a distinct and recognizable "Munro Country" is not just plausible, but irrefutable.

In *The View from Castle Rock*, a quasi-autobiographical book of stories published in 2006, Munro writes of visiting Scotland's Ettrick Valley, about 80 kilometres south of Edinburgh. This is the home country of her paternal ancestors, the Laidlaws, and she describes how, in Ettrick Churchyard, she discovered the gravestones of several of them. They included William Laidlaw, her great-great-great-great-grandfather, and his sister, Margaret Laidlaw Hogg. Margaret became the mother of the rustic poet James Hogg, celebrated throughout Britain as "the Ettrick shepherd."

The author's daughter, Sheila, surmises that Alice Munro derives her near-photographic memory from her Laidlaw ancestry. "How else can her almost freakish memory, her ability, for instance, to look at her old high-school photos and remember the colours of all the dresses the girls are wearing, be explained?" In her memoir *Lives of Mothers & Daughters: Growing Up with Alice Munro*, Sheila suggests that her mother's storytelling ability, "which so often relates the everyday to the macabre, the nightmare, even the supernatural, the way ballads do, has some affinity with that whole minstrel tradition." If this seems far-fetched, the fact remains that, down through the generations, the Laidlaw family continued to produce writers. Late in life, for example, Munro's father, Robert Laidlaw, published a novel. Equally enduring, however, was a strain of self-effacing Presbyterianism. "They spoke of calling attention," Munro writes at one point. "Calling attention to yourself." This theme, the tension between eloquence and stoicism, gave rise to one of the author's best-known titles: *Who Do You Think You Are?*

In *The View from Castle Rock,* her most transparently autobiographical work, Munro relates how in 1818 her ancestors sailed from Scotland and settled in southern Ontario. She was born Alice Laidlaw in Wingham, a Presbyterian town 200 kilometres west of Toronto, in 1931. By that time, her father had a Canadian rather than a Scottish accent. He had settled on a small farm just outside town. Through her stories, famously honest, compassionate, and insightful, Munro has fictionalized the surrounding area into that unmistakable "Alice Munro Country." The late Carol Shields, after declaring herself an "enormous fan" of Munro, put it this way: "Her use of language is very sophisticated, but I can always hear, underlying the sentence and its rhythms, that rural Ontario sound."

In *Alice Munro: A Double Life,* biographer Catherine Sheldrick Ross quotes Munro describing her native Huron County as having "a rural culture with a strong Scots-Irish background." The area also has "a big sense of righteousness," Munro added, "but with big bustings-out and grotesque crime. And ferocious sexual humour and the habit of getting drunk and killing each other off on the roads." Later, she would describe how in Huron County, "the everyday is side by side with the macabre." This was a rural area, so inevitably it produced "bloody accidents." And young Alice grew up with "the extreme, the grotesque" as part of her daily life on the outskirts of a town hit hard by the Great Depression.

The girl realized early that she wanted to become a writer. But she hid her ambition because "drawing attention" constituted a reckless challenge to those "supernatural powers always on the lookout for greed." To excel as a student proved acceptable, and Munro did so all through high school. She gained a sense of vocation at fifteen, after reading *Emily of New Moon,* L.M. Montgomery's novel about a girl who chooses to become a writer. Later, Munro would declare it "the watershed book of my life." At seventeen, Alice Laidlaw won scholarships to attend the University of Western Ontario in London, 115 kilometres south of Wingham. In 1950, while still a student, she published her first story, "The Dimensions of a Shadow." The following year, with her money running out, she left the university to marry James Munro and move to Vancouver, British Columbia. During the 1950s and '60s, while based in that province, she gave birth to four daughters, one of whom died hours after being born.

With her husband, she opened a bookstore in Victoria: Munro's Books. She was still helping out there in 1968 when she published her first collection of stories, *Dance of the Happy Shades*. Hailed as presenting "a perceptive young narrator's dawning awareness of the powerful and legendary shapes lying behind ordinary life in Huron County," the book won the Governor General's Award for Fiction—a spectacular debut. In 1971, Munro followed up with *Lives of Girls and Women*, a collection of linked stories in which she again drew extensively on her girlhood in southern Ontario. A review in the *Los Angeles Times* typified the reception, declaring Munro "a writer of enormous gifts and perception." Fifteen years and several books later, Munro still spoke of that book as possibly her most enduring: "It's perennially appealing because it's about childhood and adolescence," she told one literary journalist. "It has a charm that my other books don't have. It doesn't challenge people in any way they don't want to be challenged."

Munro divorced her husband in 1972 and returned to the surroundings that fuelled her fiction. She served for a year as writer-in-residence at the University of Western Ontario, and then, in 1976, married a geographer, Gerald Fremlin, from the same area. Eventually, they settled in the small town of Clinton, Ontario, about 35 kilometres from where she grew up. From that home base, by intensifying her vivid regional focus, Munro forged a spectacular international career. Book by book, like Austen, Hardy, Faulkner, and a few other great fiction writers, she built her distinctive fictional world.

In 1978, Munro won her second Governor General's Award with her collection *Who Do You Think You Are?*, which was also runner-up for the Booker Prize. While publishing regularly in magazines like *The New Yorker*, *Atlantic Monthly*, and *The Paris Review*, she kept winning awards. After her 1986 collection, *The Progress of Love*, won her a third Governor General's Award, the American critic and short-story writer Cynthia Ozick summed up the emerging consensus by calling her "our Chekhov." Around that time, during a wide-ranging interview in Calgary, Munro spoke of her return to Ontario from the West Coast. "I didn't go back for any literary purpose," she said. "I thought I was through with small-town Ontario, and that I'd be writing about my years in Vancouver and Victoria—that background." Apparently, the fates could take the writer out of Huron County, but not for long.

Munro had grown accustomed to hearing her work characterized as "Southern Ontario Gothic." And in an interview that turned up in a critical anthology called *Here and Now*, she said, "If I'm a regional writer, the region I'm writing about has many things in common with the American South. . . . [I am writing out of] a closed rural society with a pretty homogenous Scotch-Irish racial strain going slowly to decay." Regional, yes. But Munro has also proven universal. Writing in *The Globe and Mail*, critic Claire Messud noted that while Ozick called Munro our Chekhov, "she is our Flaubert, too. We couldn't ask for more."

20

Joe Shuster, Dave Sim, and Chester Brown

Graphic novelists create new channels of communication

While working in a Toronto photocopy shop in the early 1980s, a would-be cartoonist in his early twenties, an ex-Montrealer, discovered underground comics. Having tried and failed to find work in New York drawing superheroes, Chester Brown realized now that those particular comics had become "a dead-end genre." Other graphic artists, having recently reached the same conclusion, had turned to producing science fiction, fantasy, or detective stories. Brown chose a different route. As historian John Bell tells us, "in one of the most daring acts in comic-art history, he plunged headlong into his subconscious, embarking on a strip that he drew panel by panel without a script."

That comic strip evolved into a graphic novel called *Yummy Fur*, which spawned further revolutionary works. Chester Brown had helped to create a new genre. Working in anarchic concert with other Canadian artists, he transformed the lowly comic strip into a work of art: the graphic novel. Brown represents a new generation of graphic-narrative artists who have changed the world by creating a new channel of communication that erases the boundaries between art and "pop culture."

But that new generation did not spring out of nothingness. The story begins with Toronto-born artist Joe Shuster. At age twenty-four, working with writer-friend Jerry Siegel, he invented Superman, the comic book character who first appeared in June 1938 in *Action Comics #1*. Shuster, a first cousin of comedian Frank Shuster, created Superman's appearance, complete with colourful, skin-tight outfit and, on his chest, a huge letter "S."

Shuster had moved to Cleveland while still a boy and teamed up with Siegel in high school. In the early 1930s, while working for the company that became DC comics, the two created a telepathic evildoer called The Superman. After turning him into a good guy rather than a bad one, and landing the cover of Action Comics, they launched the syndicated Superman comic strip, with Shuster drawing on his native Toronto for the fictional cityscape of Metropolis. In 1946, rightly feeling grossly underpaid, Shuster and Siegel sued their employer, National Allied Publications (NAP), to determine who owned the rights to Superman. Their superhero with a secret identity had become one of the best-known fictional characters of the twentieth century.

The courts ruled that the co-creators had signed away their rights. They invented another crime fighter, Funnyman, but he failed to catch on. Work dried up at NAP, and Joe Shuster disappeared from view. In 1975, with the first Superman movie looming, and needing now to obscure the disappearance of Superman's creators, DC's parent company granted both Siegel and Shuster a pension of $20,000 a year. The Canadian cartoonist collected for seventeen years before passing away in 1992.

Seventeen years after that, comics historian Craig Yoe made a chance discovery. In *Secret Identity: The Fetish Art of Superman's Co-Creator Joe Shuster*, he demonstrated that, during the lean years, when he vanished from sight, Shuster had worked as an anonymous illustrator for *Nights of Horror*. That underground graphic series specialized in erotic sensationalism. Shuster's pornographic cartoons, tame by today's standards, anticipated the work of subversive

American cartoonist Robert Crumb. Shuster gained some recognition during his final decade, and in 2005, a series of awards recognizing achievements in Canadian comic books were named the Joe Shuster Awards.

Meanwhile, back in the early 1940s, a brief Golden Age of Comics arose in Canada. Adrian Dingle created Nelvana of the Northern Lights, the first recognizably Canadian superhero. A female derived from Inuit mythology, she personified the North. Then came the fearless Freelance by Ed Furness, and also Johnny Canuck, who in this first incarnation was a Nazi-battler. Created by Leo Bachle, he was billed as "Canada's super hero."

In *Invaders from the North: How Canada Conquered the Comic Book Universe*, archivist-historian John Bell relates how, in 1948, church organizations and parent teacher associations led a North America–wide crackdown on "crime comics." Three years later, the Canadian government lifted restrictions on U.S. imports, and the country was flooded by American comics. The Canadian industry struggled through the next couple of decades.

In 1975, a Winnipeg duo, Ron Leishman and Richard Comely, created Captain Canuck, who thrived while working alongside a francophone sidekick called Kebec. And Bell tells us that, for five years ending in 1989, two Montreal artists, Mark Shainblum and Gabriel Morrissette, tracked the adventures of Northguard, probably "the most mature depiction ever of a Canadian national superhero."

By this time, a first wave of alternative comics had arisen, challenging the idea of the superhero. As early as 1951, a Newfoundland woodcut artist named Laurence Hyde had produced a word-free graphic narrative entitled *Southern Cross: A Novel of the South Seas*. And in 1967, as a special issue of the experimental magazine *grOnk*, the concrete poet bpNichol wrote and drew an underground narrative called "Scraptures."

But not until December 1977, when Dave Sim produced the first issue of *Cerebus the Aardvark*, did a graphic narrative move beyond experimentation into the realm of serious and sustained art. *Cerebus* began as a parody of *Conan the Barbarian* and other sword-and-sorcery comics, but as John Bell notes, it "evolved into a sophisticated work of art" that attracted international attention. Provocative and opinionated, *Cerebus* would explore everything from Sim's personal life to politics, philosophy, and, controversially, feminism and gender issues.

Born in Hamilton in 1956, and raised in Kitchener, Ontario, Sim started drawing comics as a boy. At seventeen, he dropped out of high school to forge a career in the field. In the early 1970s, he published a "fanzine," profiled professional comics artists, and created a comic strip for the mainstream *Kitchener-Waterloo Record*. Sim launched *Cerebus* as a bimonthly, black-and-white comic book series. He began running complex storylines through a few issues, and then produced a twenty-five-issue narrative called *High Society*, focusing on politics and religion.

In the 1980s, by putting a lot of energy into promotion, Sim drove circulation to 36,000 copies. He kept *Cerebus* running for 300 issues and twenty-seven years. By the time the series ended, in March 2004, it was easily the longest-running original comic in Canadian history. Sim considers the collected work a 6,000-page novel, an opinion shared by academic experts. His art and storytelling innovations, notably the use of complex, multi-issue stories, influenced the evolution of graphic narrative. As comics historian John Bell writes, "probably no other person has made a greater contribution to the development of Canadian comic art."

Sim's main competition would be Chester Brown. To Brown, alone among the scores of artists he treats in his history, Bell devotes an entire chapter. He writes that Brown's main body of work consists of six graphic narratives that, together, "represent a breadth unmatched by any other comic artist in Canada." Only Dave Sim, he adds, with whom Brown has collaborated, comes close. Brown has also worked with the notable Seth (Gregory Gallant), best known for *Palookaville* and *It's a Good Life, If You Don't Weaken*. In a foreword to *Invaders from the North*, Seth writes that Brown "is without doubt one of the most important writers (or artists) in any of Canada's art forms."

Born in Montreal in 1960, and raised in the anglophone suburb of Châteauguay, Chester Brown gravitated to Toronto at nineteen and began his serious work. Bell argues that the strong-minded artist spearheaded three developments in graphic narrative: "the rejection of the tired and juvenile superhero adventures, the fearless search for new narratives, and the determination to establish comics as an adult art form."

Brown broke through with *Yummy Fur*, which gave rise, in the mid-1980s, to a surrealistic black comedy called *Ed the Happy Clown*. In one episode of the latter, the title character finds the head of his penis replaced by the head of American president Ronald Reagan, from another dimension. Brown produced other controversial episodes and encountered resistance from printers and distributors. In the late 1980s, after discovering the highly personal comics of Montreal artist Julie Doucet, he shifted into an autobiographical mode. Pulitzer Prize winner Art Spiegelman, best known for the graphic novel *Maus*, says Doucet, "proved definitely that girls can be as dirty-minded as boys." Partly in response to the confessional nature of her work, Brown produced *The Playboy*, a painfully honest graphic novel about his teenage obsession with masturbation. Then came *I Never Liked You*, a more conventional reminiscence.

Ever restless, Brown now made several false starts, including one in which he began illustrating the gospels of the New Testament. And in 2000, he changed direction again. After reading a Maggie Siggins biography of Louis Riel, Brown began a graphic narrative about that still-controversial nineteenth-century figure. Published in 2004, his acclaimed *Louis Riel* became a Canadian bestseller and was widely hailed as a graphic tour de force.

Brown worked with Montreal publisher Drawn & Quarterly to reprint *Ed the Happy Clown* as a serial comic, and also got involved in federal politics, running in two elections for the Libertarian Party of Canada as a champion of property rights. In 2011, he released *Paying for It*, which finds his cartoon alter ego—a singular fellow, to say the least—merrily frequenting prostitutes. Some critics hailed the work for its honesty, while others lambasted it as encouraging the exploitation of women.

Brown does not work within existing forms or conventions—not stylistically, and not in theme or subject matter. The same can be said of Dave Sim, creator of *Cerebus the Aardvark*. And the so-called "fetish art" of Joe Shuster reveals that he, too, had much to express that did not flow easily through well-established media. All three of these cartoonists were driven to work outside the Canadian mainstream. They blasted open channels of communication. They transformed juvenile entertainment into a new artistic genre: the graphic narrative.

21

JOY KOGAWA

A Japanese Canadian clears the way for minorities

"There it was in black and white," the narrator declares in *Obasan*, "our short, harsh history. Beside each date were the ugly facts of the treatment given to Japanese Canadians. 'Seizure and government sale of fishing boats. Suspension of fishing licences. Relocation camps. Liquidation of property. . . . Deportation. Revocation of nationality.'" The fictional Naomi is reading a pamphlet handed to her by Aunt Emily. This aunt, back in Canada after attending a California conference entitled The Asian Experience in North America, tells the younger woman that, although she hates to admit it, "for all we hear about the States, Canada's capacity for racism seems even worse." The American Japanese were interned during the Second World War after the 1941 surprise attack on Pearl Harbor, she adds, "but their property wasn't liquidated as ours was." And after the war, thanks partly to the American Bill of Rights, the internees were able to re-establish themselves in Los Angeles and California: "We weren't allowed to return to the West Coast like that. We've never recovered from the dispersal policy."

This vividly imagined dialogue takes place in 1972. Canadians would wait until 1982 before prime minister Pierre Elliott Trudeau managed to enact a Charter of Rights and Freedoms comparable to the American Bill of Rights. *Obasan*, a first novel by Joy Kogawa, had appeared the previous year. It proved a resounding success, both critically and commercially, and won literary awards in both Canada and the United States.

More than that, *Obasan* proved pivotal to the redress movement which, in 1988, gained federal government recognition that injustices had been done to Japanese Canadians. That recognition brought financial compensation to those who had been stripped of their rights and forcibly relocated, and also ensured that no minority would ever again suffer such abuse. A major review in *The New York Times* hailed *Obasan* for revealing a hidden history common to Canada and the United States—a shared history that explains why, three decades after its publication, *Obasan* has altered educated opinion in both countries. Not only that, but the book has ensured that immigrants remain connected with those who remain in their native lands. Acting indirectly through her art, Joy Kogawa changed the world by changing the way we treat immigrants. While she was at it, she helped turn Canada into a beacon of pluralism.

Joy Nozomi Nakayama was born a Nisei, a second-generation Canadian of Japanese descent, in Vancouver on June 6, 1935. Her father was an Anglican minister and her mother a musician and teacher. She was six years old in December 1941, when the bombing of Pearl Harbor by the Japanese air force gave rise to demands for the removal from the West Coast of all Japanese Canadians. Both the RCMP and the Canadian Armed Forces told the federal government that these citizens, two-thirds of whom had been born in Canada, posed no security threat. Half of them were children and teenagers who spoke English as their first language. Yet the government designated all those of Japanese ancestry "enemy aliens." In 1942, between March and November, 21,000 Japanese Canadians were stripped of their rights and properties. Able-bodied men were sent to labour camps in the Alberta Rockies; women and children went to ghost towns in the interior of British

Columbia, and there, in Slocan, the author-to-be grew up with her mother and siblings.

When the war ended in 1945, the Canadian government prohibited Japanese Canadians from returning to the West Coast, a policy of dispersal that remained in force until 1949. In the United States, where citizen rights were constitutionally protected, the government launched resettlement programs that enabled Japanese Americans to return to Los Angeles and San Francisco. Japanese Canadians could choose to return to Japan or resettle east of the Rockies.

In *Obasan*, Naomi's worst experience begins after the war, when with her family she is driven to live in a one-room shack, "a chicken-coop house," in the fictional town of Granton. The reality behind this fiction was Coaldale, Alberta, 17 kilometres east of Lethbridge, where the author-to-be spent several years. Like her fictional alter ego, she left home to study at the University of Alberta in Edmonton. She earned a teaching degree, then returned to Coaldale and taught school. The fictional Naomi is still teaching in "Granton" in 1972, when *Obasan* takes place.

In reality, the author taught for one year. At twenty, she escaped to Toronto, where she studied music at the University of Toronto and attended the Anglican Women's Training College. In 1956, she returned to Vancouver, married David Kogawa, and gave birth to her first child. Two years later, in Grand Forks, British Columbia, she had her second child and began writing seriously, focusing on poetry. With her husband and young family, Kogawa lived in Moose Jaw, Saskatoon, and Ottawa. By 1968, when she and her husband divorced, Kogawa had become a prolific poet. The previous year, she had published a first collection, *The Splintered Moon*. Over the next few years, she continued to publish poetry: *A Choice of Dreams* (1974), *Jericho Road* (1977), and *Woman in the Woods* (1985).

From 1974 to 1976, Kogawa worked as a staff writer in the Office of the Prime Minister (Pierre Elliott Trudeau). According to a long essay by Mason Harris in *Canadian Writers and Their Works*, which quotes from a number of journalistic profiles and interviews, Kogawa still showed little interest in her ethnic past. "I just felt like a White member of the writing community for the longest time, and didn't have the guts or consciousness to stand up and say, 'Well, I'm not.'" The transformation began in 1977, when Kogawa flew to California to meet Japanese American writers. She was struck by their energy and self-confidence, and noted that writers from California and Hawaii were far more ready to communicate their experience than Japanese Canadians, who still embraced a culture of silence. The following year, while serving as writer-in-residence at the University of Ottawa, Kogawa went to the National Archives to research an essay on Japanese Canadians in Coaldale.

There, she discovered the essays and letters of Muriel Kitagawa, a Japanese Canadian writer who had died in 1974, but who had been living as an adult in Vancouver when the internment began. Kitagawa wrote detailed letters to her brother, who was based in Toronto, describing events as they happened in 1942. These letters galvanized Kogawa. She had written a short story entitled *Obasan*, about a child and her aunt (*Oba* means "aunt," and *san* is an honorific). Now she transported these characters into a complex novel, drawing on Kitagawa's work for the outlook of Naomi's activist Aunt Emily. Throughout the writing, she would say, "Aunt Emily's voice was always outside of me." As she progressed, however, she found herself identifying more and more with Aunt Emily.

Published in 1981, *Obasan* was hailed as a masterpiece and won numerous awards, among them the Books in Canada First Novel Award, the Canadian Authors Association Book of the Year Award, and the American Book Award. In 1982, it became an American Library Association's Notable Book. *Obasan* remains a staple of university courses throughout North America. It is often read alongside Sky Lee's *Disappearing Moon Cafe* and Amy Tan's *The Joy Luck Club*, which also focus on mothers and daughters, the process of adjusting to a new culture, and the need for a viable ethnic community.

Meanwhile, following the logic of her fictional Aunt Emily, Joy Kogawa became an activist in the redress movement. Her 1992 novel *Itsuka* dramatizes this struggle, tracing the path of Japanese Canadians as they sought to gain acknowledgment of their mistreatment and achieve recognition as full citizens. In the real word, the key change happened in September 1988, when the Canadian Parliament offered Japanese Canadians "a formal and sincere apology" for past injustices, and offered a "solemn commitment and undertaking to Canadians of every origin that such violations will never again in this country be countenanced or repeated."

As an author, Kogawa has received numerous awards. Since 2004, Vancouver has celebrated a Joy Kogawa Day. The house in which she spent her early childhood has been turned into a writers' retreat.

22

MARGARET ATWOOD

A literary superstar doubles as an activist

"The list of persecuted writers is long, ancient, and international," Margaret Atwood said in Jerusalem, at the award ceremony that figures in the preamble to this section. "We feel we must defend the diminishing open space in which dialogue, exchange, and relatively free expression are still possible." To refuse the Dan David Prize, she said, as some correspondents had urged her to do, "would be to destroy our part in the work we have been doing with PEN for decades—work that involves thousands of writers around the world—jailed, exiled, censored, and murdered."

Alluding to issues she had raised in her recent novels, Atwood said, "Perhaps this vocation of ours will soon be obsolete. For coming towards us is a frightening change in our planet. Floods and droughts, deserts and famines and epidemics—will they draw the world into ever more destructive conflicts?" She took a beat, and then adverted to Amitav Ghosh, co-winner of the million-dollar award: "We are both here as an act of good faith, because we believe that there are many people here and around the world who think as we do."

Here we see Atwood at work on the world stage, eliciting thunderous applause. As a novelist, poet, essayist, and, indeed, activist, Margaret Atwood is a global figure. She has published more than fifty books and won a still greater number of awards, including prizes from France, Germany, Ireland, and the United States, as well as the UK-based Booker Prize (she has been shortlisted five times), the Giller Prize, and two Governor General's Awards (she has been a finalist seven times). Like other writers, Atwood has changed the world by changing her readers—by making them more aware of the dangers of religious fundamentalism, for example, and more recently of climate change. But she has also worked a profound transformation by showing that a serious literary artist can be an influential activist, and can make things happen in a universe more usually dominated by mayors, prime ministers, and corporations.

Here in Canada, Atwood has been doing cutting-edge work for decades. Her influence is so far-reaching that, in the minds of many, she leads a generation of writers: the Atwood Generation. Early in her career, in the 1970s, Atwood took a leadership role in founding such institutions as the Writers' Union of Canada, the Writers' Development Trust, and PEN Canada. In 2011, still politically engaged, she used Twitter to reach her 290,000 followers, to derail a cretinous mayoral initiative that would have damaged the Toronto Public Library.

Where she finds time and energy, nobody has deduced. Born November 18, 1939, in Ottawa, Margaret Eleanor Atwood spent her early childhood in the woods of northern Quebec, where her entomologist father conducted research. She read voraciously, everything from Grimm's fairy tales to comic books and bodice rippers. She began attending school full-time in grade eight, and graduated from Toronto's Leaside High School in 1957. She had been writing stories since the age of six, and realized at sixteen that she wanted to write professionally.

At the University of Toronto, she studied under influential literary critic Northrop Frye, graduating in 1961 with a bachelor of arts degree in honours English. She won the E.J. Pratt Medal for her first book of poems, *Double Persephone*, and a Woodrow Wilson fellowship that took her to Harvard's Radcliffe College in Boston for graduate studies. She received her master's degree in 1962, and devoted two years to a doctoral thesis on the metaphysical romance, leaving it uncompleted.

Through the late 1960s and early 1970s, while writing fiction, poetry, and literary criticism, Atwood taught English at universities in Vancouver, Montreal, Edmonton, and Toronto. In 1973, after a five-year marriage to editor Jim Polk, Atwood formed a relationship with fellow novelist Graeme Gibson. They lived on a farm near Alliston until 1980, when with their four-year-old daughter they returned to Toronto.

By this time, Atwood had published half a dozen books of poetry, a collection of stories (*Dancing Girls*), four novels (*The Edible Woman, Surfacing, Lady Oracle,* and *Life Before Man*), and *Survival: A Thematic Guide to Canadian Literature,* a book that informs Canadian studies to this day. She was at the forefront of a wave of Canadian nationalism, and active in lobbying governments on behalf of writers and publishers. Still in her early forties, she had become the voice of a generation.

In 1981, she published her fifth novel, *Bodily Harm,* which focuses on a Toronto journalist who, after a partial mastectomy, travels to the West Indies, gets whirled into a political maelstrom, and ends up in a dank prison cell. Clearly, she was becoming more overtly political. Four years later came *The Handmaid's Tale,* the dystopian novel that vaulted her to international celebrity (and incidentally became a film starring Natasha Richardson).

The novel itself is a political form, Atwood said in a Calgary interview, noting that the genre "has gone through occasional periods of privatism, but has also been used throughout the ages for social comment." She added, "The world is getting more explicitly political. It's no longer possible for us to live only in our private lives. We can't exist in that exclusively personal world any more." Soon afterwards, when she addressed a standing-room-only audience of 600 in a Calgary theatre, Atwood said, "Nothing in my book is pure invention, or has been cooked up out of my fevered brain." She insisted that trends such as the declining birth rate, increasing pollution, and creeping censorship made her vision of a bleak, theocratic future all too plausible: "The seeds of my scenario are not lacking."

In 1989, when Atwood published *Cat's Eye*, about a painter who is haunted by memories of a girlhood friend, one review suggested that the novel was "smaller" than *Handmaid's Tale*. Atwood disposed of that idea: "That's like saying Faulkner is smaller than Tolstoy because he didn't write about epic battles." *Cat's Eye* raises questions about feminism. "What happens to a woman," Atwood said, "whose traumatic experiences have been with other persons of the female gender, when then she hits feminism? That's what happens to my heroine."

She said "the assumption that all women are supposed to feel sisterly is naive. But the fact that I'm able to say this without people calling me a gender traitor—that's new in the air." Publishing this novel required courage, she admitted, because the book reveals more than usual about the author, and also "there is that risky feeling that you're saying things that might be wrongly construed as anti-women."

Seven years later, the indefatigable Atwood published *Alias Grace*, her ninth novel and thirty-third book, which rocketed to the top of Canadian bestseller lists and showed signs of staying forever. Interviewed about the work, which focuses on a real-life nineteenth-century murderess, Atwood said that writing it was like going on a treasure hunt: "One clue led to another which led to another which led to another which led to a dead end. Then I'd have to backtrack." After getting "about 100 pages into it [the book], I threw it all out and began again." She had been trying to tell the story from four points of view—two murder victims, two convicted killers—"but it just didn't work." The finished novel, by comparison, has "two main narrators and several auxiliary voices—two narrators and a chorus."

Atwood said she spent two years writing the novel. It traverses several decades in the nineteenth century, but she bridled at calling it a historical novel because "that conjures up 'ye bodice ripper.'" Most novels are set in the past, she said, "so where do you draw the line? How far back do you go? Does 'historical' mean anything with petticoats?" After setting *The Handmaid's Tale* in the future, Atwood found writing about the past more painstaking: "In the future, you get to arrange things as you please. When you're treating the past, if you're writing about stoves and you don't know what they look like, you jolly well have to find out."

As for contemporary relevance, Atwood said, "Since we seem to be going back to the nineteenth century at a very rapid rate, it might not be a bad thing to know something about it. By that I mean that the nineteenth century had a small class of very wealthy people, a small middle class of moderately wealthy people, and a huge class of very unwealthy people. That's why servants were so cheap."

Atwood's latest acclaimed novels, *Oryx and Crake* and *The Year of the Flood*, might be called environmentalist dystopias. They are overtly political. And they prove conclusively that those who wrote to Margaret Atwood urging her to reject the Dan David Prize do not know her work. If they did, they would never have dreamed they could tell her what to do.

23

Deepa Mehta

A transnational filmmaker gives voice to marginalized women

While visiting Toronto on a North American book tour, Salman Rushdie—one of the world's most celebrated authors—went for dinner at the home of filmmaker Deepa Mehta and her husband. At one point, during a conversation about projects, Rushdie said something about working together, maybe bringing one of his novels to the silver screen. Without thinking, Mehta blurted, "The only book I'd like to do is *Midnight's Children*." Widely recognized as one of the great novels of the past century, *Midnight's Children* won the 1981 Booker Prize and the Best of the Booker in 1993 and 2008, both times it was awarded.

But the book also runs 560 pages, features scores of characters, and ranges across time from 1917 to 1974 while moving in space through a welter of locations in India and Pakistan. According to Stephanie Nolan, writing in *The Globe and Mail*, Mehta immediately realized the magnitude of the task she had proposed and tried to retract: "No, no, forget I said that." But Rushdie had already responded: "Done." Fortunately, the acclaimed author also agreed to write the script, and somehow did so, turning his original, multi-layered narrative into a 130-page film script.

Then came the question of where to shoot the movie. Logic suggested either India or Pakistan, but Rushdie had outraged one set of fundamentalists (Muslim) with his novel *The Satanic Verses*, and

Mehta had scandalized another set (Hindu) with *Fire*, her 1996 movie. They settled on Sri Lanka, that teardrop country to the south of India. But even there they had to fly beneath the radar, and called the project *Winds of Change*.

The finished film, *Midnight's Children*, made its 2012 debut at the Toronto International Film Festival, where it drew a standing ovation. The critics proved less enthusiastic, mainly because Rushdie tried to include everything in his novel. In the British *Telegraph*, for example, a reviewer wrote that this "earnest slog of a movie, biting off the book's whole span over an inevitably episodic two and a half hours, feels like sumptuously illustrated *Cliffs Notes* rather than fluid cinema."

For Mehta, the movie served mainly to solidify her international status and signal her transnational outlook: a Hindu-born filmmaker tackles a literary masterpiece with a Muslim-born fiction writer. She did not make any special mark with *Midnight's Children*. Mehta changed the world, rather, by giving voice to the dispossessed women of the Indian subcontinent, and to dispossessed women in general, wherever they may live. To this we shall return.

Deepa Mehta is either a Canadian filmmaker who immigrated from India or a transnational filmmaker based in Canada, depending on who's talking. She herself has said, "Moving away from India [to Canada] provided me with perspective and made me fearless." She has also criticized her adopted homeland as multicultural in name only, a situation she has worked hard to change. This much nobody would deny: with her groundbreaking trilogy *Fire*, *Earth*, and *Water*, Mehta transformed the public perception of India.

Born January 1, 1950, in Amritsar, in northwestern India, Mehta moved with her parents to New Delhi as a child. She then attended an upper-class boarding school in Dehradun, 240 kilometres north of Delhi. Her father, a film distributor, owned a couple of movie houses. Her family spoke English at home, and she grew up into a movie-based world revolving around "Friday-night openings and Monday-morning grosses."

At the University of Delhi, Mehta majored in Hindu philosophy. While making short documentaries for an Indian studio, she met Canadian documentary filmmaker Paul Saltzman, then working in India. At twenty-three she married him and moved to Toronto. While raising a daughter, Mehta wrote scripts for children's films. With Saltzman and her filmmaker brother, Dilip Mehta, she also formed Sunrise Films. She became a Canadian citizen and made several documentaries, among them *At 99: A Portrait of Louise Tandy Murch*, which focused on a wonderfully active woman approaching 100 years of age.

In 1983, after ten years of marriage, Mehta and Saltzman divorced. She continued making documentaries, and in the late 1980s, she directed episodes of two Canadian television series—*The Twin* and *Danger Bay*. Also in 1988, with two other women, she made a feature-length film called *Martha, Ruth & Edie*. That enabled her to secure financing for a solo work set in Toronto, a cross-cultural feature called *Sam & Me*, which explored the relationship between an elderly Jewish man and his young immigrant caretaker, an Indian Muslim.

Already, she had identified her major subject areas: the situational plight of women and what it means to change cultures. Moving from documentaries into the feature drama of *Sam & Me* felt like a natural progression, she says in *Calling the Shots: Profiles of Women Filmmakers*. She appreciated the power of the script: "You can actually control something. You can create it. You can shape it. You have nothing to lose. You can write whatever you want. You can make something that has the power to reflect what you think and what you feel."

In 1991, Mehta brought *Sam & Me* to the Cannes Film Festival, where it won the prestigious Caméra d'Or Prize as the best work by a first-time filmmaker. It was a breakthrough accomplishment that landed Mehta a host of professional admirers, among them George Lucas, the director of *Star Wars*. He hired Mehta to direct several episodes of a television series. And here in Canada, she served as executive producer for *Skin Deep*, a drama with a lesbian theme, and one to which she would return.

Does she think her films are Canadian? In *Calling the Shots*, Mehta offers an emphatic yes and adds, "They're idealistic. They're self-deprecating. I think they have a lot of suppressed anger." And she agrees, as well, that they reflect the point of view of an East Indian woman: "They must. I am what I am. I am a woman. I am an East Indian. So my films must reflect that." The concept towards which she was moving, in the early 1990s, was that of the transnational—the postmodern, pluralist concept of the individual who has more than one identity.

By the early 1990s, Mehta wanted to undertake a more ambitious film. More specifically, she wanted to create *Fire*, a feature set in India and focusing on a lesbian relationship. A couple of years after her divorce, Mehta had become involved with David Hamilton, an Ottawa-based businessman. After marrying him, according to a memoir by her daughter, Devyani Saltzman, Hamilton had begun focusing his attention on the world of film. Now he felt ready, and he put together the financing for *Fire*.

That 1996 movie, unprecedented in India for its depiction of lesbianism, caused a furor in her native land. Towards the end of the movie, the older male lead, an observant Hindu called Ashok, tells his wife that desire brings ruin. "Does it, Ashok?" she responds. "When I lived without desire, I was dead. Without desire, there is no point in living. Do you know what else? I desire to live. I desire Sita. I desire her warmth, her compassion, her body. I desire to live again." It was all too much for fundamentalist Hindus. Even before the film reached the screen, they attacked and looted theatres that had booked it. Indian legislators furiously debated whether the movie should be shown at all. Eventually, after *Fire* won awards at fourteen film festivals around the world—and elections cost fundamentalists some political clout—the controversy receded and censors allowed the film to be shown.

Two years later, when Mehta released *Earth*, a thematic sequel, Hindu extremists protested, but their calls for banning remained relatively muted. Based on a novel by Bapsi Sidhwa, *Earth* tells the story of the Indian partition of 1947, when British colonial rulers withdrew from the land and Hindu India and Muslim Pakistan became separate countries. Millions of people caught in the "wrong country" streamed towards the borders—Mehta's parents among them. Hundreds of thousands were killed—a tragedy Mehta dramatized largely through the eyes of an eight-year-old girl, and not shrinking even from presenting such horrendous scenes as the arrival of a train pulling cars filled with the bodies of massacre victims.

In January 2000, Mehta began filming *Water*, the final film in her transformative trilogy, in the Hindu holy city of Varanasi (formerly Benares). There, violent protestors sought to prevent her from shooting the movie. They objected not only to Mehta's storyline, which explores the unhappy plight of widows in India, but even to the film's title, which alludes to the sacred River Ganges as mere water. They burned Mehta in effigy and set fire to movie sets. When extremists threatened to rape the female stars, Mehta suspended production. As one critic put it, "An Indian will never look at the issue [of widows] the way Mehta has. If he does, there is something wrong with his Indianness." Her antagonists had laid hands on a script. Mehta agreed to cut certain lines. But when she tried to resume filming, she faced renewed violence. Protestors trapped the movie's actors and crew in a Varanasi hotel. Local police failed to respond, and finally Mehta halted production and returned to Canada. Four years later, in Sri Lanka, she secretly finished shooting *Water*. When it screened at the Toronto International Film Festival, American filmmaker Steven Spielberg hailed it as the best film he had seen in five years.

Afterwards, looking back at the challenges she faced during filming, Mehta told a writer for the *Atlanta Journal-Constitution*, "It was a horrific time." But it made her think about "the relationship between politics and art and freedom of expression and what that means and what drives extremists. I realized it really wasn't about me."

During an interview in India, Mehta acknowledged that *Water* became the highest-grossing Hindi film in North America. Why such mainstream success? "It struck a chord with people from all across the world," Mehta said, "because many people, especially women, felt they have been marginalized in different ways. Black people in Detroit told me they felt like the widows in the movie because their ancestors were excluded and segregated—in this case because of colour. A Jewish widow from Europe, who saw the film in an American city, told me she had often wondered why in the old days (and even now in many societies) women had to wear black following the husband's death, as if to signal that all light, all life had gone from them."

Deepa Mehta changed the world by clearing a space for marginalized women, be they Indian, Jewish, or African American. She has given voice to the excluded, to the segregated, to the dispossessed of the earth.

24

CHRIS HANEY

Which playful inventor built a universe of trivia?

Who invaded Spain in the eighth century? What was the first name of the television detective Columbo? Which of these two questions inspired a $300 million lawsuit? Welcome to the universe of Trivial Pursuit, an international phenomenon that changed the way the world treats trivia. Can you name a Canadian author who rejected an opportunity to invest in the board game? Early in 1980, two Montreal journalists were beating the bushes for forty people to invest $1,000 each in a game they had invented. Word of the search reached the *Calgary Herald*, where a dozen journalists had recently taken refuge following the demise of the *Montreal Star*. I was one of those journalists, and was duly invited to invest.

On December 15, 1979, Chris Haney, a photo editor at *The Gazette*, had got talking over beers with Scott Abbott, a *Canadian Press* sports editor, about inventing a trivia game. Players would answer questions in various categories, and then move pieces around a circular board with six spokes leading to a centre. Flash forward a few months. Did the *Herald*'s books columnist want to kick in $1,000 for five shares? Seize the moment while there was moment yet to seize? That clever fellow responded: What, put my hard-earned cash into an untested board game? Did I look like I had just fallen off a turnip truck?

Chris Haney was born in Welland, Ontario, in 1950. He dropped out of high school at seventeen. Later, he would say that he regretted this decision, quipping that he should have dropped out sooner. His father, who worked for Canadian Press (CP), landed him a job at the news agency as a copy boy. He graduated to the photo desk, worked with CP in Montreal and Ottawa, and in the early 1970s became a photo editor at *The Gazette*. In 1975, assigned to cover the looming Summer Olympics, he became friends with sports writer Scott Abbott. The two got into the habit of having a few beers while playing the board game Scrabble. They played too much Scrabble, Haney felt. He began thinking about creating a different game. On December 15, 1979, after yet another Scrabble session, he proposed a trivia game. Over the next hour, working with Abbott, Haney roughed out a game using trivia questions in multiple categories and a circular board with six spokes. Not long afterwards, the two attended a Montreal toy fair and, posing as reporters, gleaned valuable information about the business of board games.

They learned they needed development funds: roughly $40,000. Haney talked his mother out of joining the venture: too risky. But he brought aboard his brother and a close friend. And then he went looking further afield, starting with his journalistic network. In the end, they raised the requisite funds from thirty-two investors. Haney devoted a planned holiday in Spain to developing trivia questions. And on November 10, 1981, he and Abbott trademarked Trivial Pursuit. Later that month, their company, Horn Abbott, sold 1,100 copies to retailers. The game featured 6,000 trivia questions on 1,000 cards divided into six categories. Initially, sales were slow. Horn Abbott lost money. The two principals sought backers at trade shows in Canada and the United States. They found none. But then, even in that long-ago, pre-Internet era, informal networks began to work magic. In 1983, Horn Abbott licensed the game to Selchow and Righter, a major U.S. game-maker. That proved a turning point. Selchow and Righter brought thousands of gamers out of the woodwork—and then tens of thousands, who soon became hundreds of thousands. In 1984, consumers spent more than $800 million buying twenty million copies of Trivial Pursuit.

High-profile money attracts lawsuits. October 1984 brought the first of two big ones. Fred L. Worth, an American author of trivia encyclopedias, launched a $300 million suit claiming that more than one-quarter of the questions in the original "Genus" edition of Trivial Pursuit had been plagiarized from his books. Worth cited typos and, most notably, one bit of misinformation he had deliberately planted. The game copied one of his books in stating that Columbo's first name was Philip, when in truth, judging from a badge that appears in an episode called "Dead Weight," it was Frank. Haney and Abbott admitted to using Worth's books, among others. But as ex-journalists, they knew that simple facts are not protected by copyright, only the expression of those facts. They won the original case, won again in appeals court, and won conclusively in 1988 in the U.S. Supreme Court.

Meanwhile, during the two years ending in 1985, their Wisconsin manufacturers, Northern Plastics, had churned out thirty million copies of Trivial Pursuit. In 1988, Horn Abbott leased rights to the game to the giant Parker Brothers. By 1992, Trivial Pursuit had become a pop culture fixture available in various editions—Baby Boomer, Celebrity, *Lord of the Rings*, and so on. That year, the game fuelled an episode of *Seinfeld*, when George Costanza got into a fight with "Bubble Boy." Reading from a card, George asked who invaded Spain in the eighth century. Bubble Boy answered correctly, "The Moors." But George insisted on the correctness of a typo on the card—"The Moops"—and the two came to blows. In 1993, Trivial Pursuit entered the Games Hall of Fame and *Time* magazine declared it "the biggest phenomenon in game history." A version of the game turned up on the Family Channel in the United States. A syndicated version, *Trivial Pursuit: America Plays*, would air for a year starting in 2008, and more variations would later surface on television in Britain, Germany, and Spain.

In 1994, Haney and Abbott faced a second major lawsuit. David Wall of Cape Breton claimed that, in the fall of 1979, he and a friend were hitchhiking in Nova Scotia when Chris Haney picked them up. Wall said that he told Haney he had an idea for a board game—the game that later took shape as Trivial Pursuit. Wall's mother testified that she had seen designs that had since been destroyed. Haney denied ever meeting Wall. He produced four dozen witnesses, while the hitchhiker's friend never took the stand. In June 2007, after much legal wrangling, the Nova Scotia Supreme Court ruled against Wall.

The following year, Hasbro bought the rights to Trivial Pursuit for $80 million. By then, almost 100 million copies of the game had been sold in twenty-six countries and seventeen languages. And people could log in, as they can today, to play online. By that time, Haney was spending his summers in Spain, crossing the Atlantic in cruise ships because he feared flying. However, he also struggled with heart and kidney disease, and in June 2010, he passed away, leaving a wife, an ex-wife, and three grown children. Meanwhile, Scott Abbott, the former sports editor, built a hockey team, the Brampton Battalion, and a racing stable on the outskirts of Toronto. In 2010, one of his horses, Smart Sky, placed seventh in the Queen's Plate.

Total sales of Trivial Pursuit have exceeded $1 billion. Of the thirty-two people who invested small sums in 1980, no record has been kept. Almost certainly, the vast majority of them have retired to the Caribbean, the Mediterranean, or the South Sea Islands. Can you name a Canadian author who lies awake at night, imagining what might have been?

25

JAMES CAMERON

A blockbuster king ushers movies into the digital era

For more than a century, starting around 1890, moviemakers shot most of their works using 35mm film. Movies themselves changed dramatically during that time, going from silent black-and-white comedies to colour-drenched musicals and on to blockbusters featuring spectacular visual effects. Yet the vast majority of these diverse works were filmed and projected using strips of celluloid 35 millimetres wide and with four perforations per frame along each edge.

Today, digital technology is transforming the film world. Early in 2012, the movie industry reached a crossover point. That was when, according to IHS Screen Digest's Cinema Intelligence Service, more movies were shot using digital technology than 35mm film. By the end of 2012, 63 percent of films were expected to be digital, and within three years, 83 percent—relegating 35mm to a niche format.

This stunning transformation, according to a report by David Hancock, head of IHS film and cinema research, was driven by "the popularity of a single movie: the seminal film *Avatar*." The release of that 3D film in December 2009 was a pivotal moment, as digital technology became the bedrock of the modern cinema environment. "Before *Avatar*, digital represented only a small portion of the market," Hancock said, "accounting for 15 percent of global screens in 2009." Within two years, that share had skyrocketed to almost

50 percent. "This single film," Hancock said, "has driven up demand for digital 3-D technology at the expense of traditional 35mm celluloid." The man who changed the world by triggering this high-tech revolution is Ontario native James Cameron.

The writer, director, and co-producer of *Avatar*, Cameron has an extraordinary track record. All of his films except *The Terminator*, his low-budget 1984 breakthrough picture, have won Academy Awards for special effects. His 1997 blockbuster *Titanic* won eleven of the fourteen Academy Awards for which it was nominated. With *Titanic* and *Avatar*, which earned revenues of $1.84 and $2.78 billion respectively, Cameron created the two highest-grossing films of all time. In 2010 alone, according to *Vanity Fair*, he earned $257 million, making him the top money-maker of the year in Hollywood. That same year, *Time* magazine included him as one of the 100 most influential people in the world. The British *New Statesman* included him in a list of the world's fifty most influential figures, and he glided into top spot in *The Guardian* Film Power 100 list.

James Francis Cameron was born August 16, 1954, in the town of Kapuskasing, 830 kilometres north of Toronto. His artistic mother worked as a nurse, and his father, a disciplinarian of Scottish Presbyterian background, was an electrical engineer who sold hydroelectric equipment. Cameron was still a child when the family moved to Chippawa, on the outskirts of Niagara Falls, Ontario. His father inspired him to lead his playmates in building things, among them a catapult, a miniature diving bell, and a go-kart. His mother encouraged his painting and helped him mount an exhibition. With her he visited museums, where he would sketch whatever he saw. Early on, he became a voracious reader. He devoured comic books, especially those Marvel titles devoted to such superheroes as Superman and Spiderman.

In 1962, when he saw *King Kong vs. Godzilla*, he declared it so bad that he could do better. And at twelve, according to *James Cameron:*

An Unauthorized Biography of the Filmmaker by Marc Shapiro, the boy insisted that he wanted to be a comic book artist. Cameron read science fiction on the school bus, one hour each way, polishing off three or four novels a week. He was drawn to the work of Arthur C. Clarke, Robert Heinlein, and Ray Bradbury, and to stories involving genetic mutations, alien life forms, and space travel.

Cameron was fifteen when he first saw the groundbreaking movie *2001: A Space Odyssey*, directed by Stanley Kubrick. Dazzled, he went back to see it ten times. He decided that, instead of a comic book artist, he wanted to be a filmmaker. He worried that "kids from a small town in Canada didn't get to direct movies," but he borrowed his father's Super 8 camera and started shooting film. At seventeen, he caught a life-changing break: his father accepted a promotion and a transfer to Los Angeles, California. The family was moving to Orange County, and wasn't that near Hollywood?

The town of Brea is 65 kilometres southeast of that moviemaker's mecca. To young Cameron, it still seemed a world away. He finished high school in Brea and spent two years at a community college (Fullerton), studying physics and then English. He dropped out to write and took a series of odd jobs, from working in a machine shop to driving a truck. In his spare time, he studied film technology and how to create special effects. He would drive into Los Angeles to the library at the University of Southern California, and there peruse esoteric papers treating everything from optical printing to front screen projection.

At twenty-three, Cameron saw *Star Wars* for the first time. Like the Kubrick classic, it galvanized him. He ransacked a book about screenwriting (*Screenplay* by Syd Field), developed story ideas, and rousted a couple of friends. Eventually, they raised enough money from a group of Orange County dentists to rent a 35mm camera and a studio. Cameron built models from scratch, figured out how to run the camera, and produced a twelve-minute mini-feature, *Xenogenesis*, that was notable for its special effects. He screened the short locally and, after receiving positive feedback, carried it into Los Angeles. He went straight to Roger Corman Studios, a leading maker of low-budget action movies, and a training ground for the likes of Martin Scorsese, Francis Ford Coppola, and Ron Howard. By showing his mini-feature, Cameron got himself hired to create miniature models. Enthusiastic, creative, and always on the run, he rocketed through the ranks. Soon he was working as art director on the science fiction movie *Battle Beyond the Stars* (1980). Then he designed special effects for *Escape from New York* (1981).

While working as production designer on *Galaxy of Terror* (1981), Cameron used an electric current to jolt a bunch of worms into wriggling activity—a bit of creativity that caught the eye of visiting producers. He was hired to create special effects for *Piranha II: The Spawning*, and became director when another fellow quit. At the studio in Jamaica, he learned that the project was underfinanced and his Italian crew spoke no English. Working under pressure, Cameron had a nightmare about a "metallic death figure" sent from the future to kill him, and immediately sat up and scribbled notes. This idea would evolve into *The Terminator*, the movie that would catapult him onto the A-list of Hollywood moviemakers. While shopping the idea, he helped write two screenplays: *Rambo: First Blood Part II* (1985) and *Aliens* (1986).

Studios liked his Terminator idea but wanted a veteran director. Cameron cut a deal with a producer (Gale Anne Hurd), who agreed to let him direct. With a budget of just $6.5 million, he created *The Terminator*, which drew international acclaim, made *Time* magazine's list of the top ten best movies, and grossed over $80 million. It turned Arnold Schwarzenegger into a star and Cameron into a player as both screenwriter and director.

Cameron directed *Aliens* (1986), a sequel to *Alien*, starring Sigourney Weaver. A box office smash hailed for its feminist subtext, the movie won Oscars for best actress, best sound effects editing, and best visual effects. Cameron wrote and directed *The Abyss* (1989), a $41 million picture in which oil rig workers contend with alien underwater creatures. Because many scenes took place underwater and digital technology was not yet able to create a suitable environment, Cameron installed two gargantuan water tanks in an unfinished nuclear power plant and did the photography there.

Meanwhile, explorer Robert Ballard had discovered the wreck of the fabled *Titanic*, the supposedly unsinkable ship that sank in 1912 after hitting an iceberg. Cameron debated whether to create a movie around that disaster, the most famous shipwreck in history. He would want to include footage of the contemporary wreck, though this entailed inventing a camera that could function at 12,000 feet below sea level, and also making a dozen round-trip dives of sixteen hours each. Having focused mainly on the future in previous films, Cameron went ahead with this "period movie" because he found the disaster so compelling. In bonus footage packaged with the eventual DVD, Cameron said he scripted a love story "to provide an emotional doorway for the audience to appreciate the tragedy of what happened to *Titanic*." Cameron wove his fictional young lovers—played by Kate Winslet and Leonardo DiCaprio—"through the pylons of events that were known to have happened."

Cameron paid unprecedented attention to historical detail, explaining, "If you're not breaking new ground, what's the point?" The cost of the three-hour film soared to about $200 million, making *Titanic* the most expensive movie yet made. Released in December 1997, it leaped to the top of box office charts and stayed there for months. Eventually, it grossed over $600 million in Canada and the United States, and more than $1.8 billion worldwide, setting a mark that would last until Cameron broke it twelve years later with *Avatar*. *Titanic* also tied records with fourteen Academy Award nominations and eleven wins, including Oscars for best picture and best director.

After *Titanic*, Cameron spent several years creating underwater IMAX documentaries, contributing to remote vehicle technologies, and co-developing the digital 3D Fusion Camera System he would use in *Avatar*. That movie, released in December 2009, cost more than $300 million and relied almost entirely on computer-generated animation. Cameron wrote the script in 2005, but explained that he had to wait until the technology he needed was sufficiently advanced. He then delayed another few months to allow theatres to install the requisite 3D projectors. *Avatar*, which sparked another avalanche of awards, became the first movie to earn more than $2 billion.

According to James Cameron, filmmaking is not about technology: "It's about ideas, it's about images, it's about imagination, it's about storytelling." Even so, he says, "If I had had the cameras I'm using now when I was shooting *Titanic*, I would have shot it using them." Cameron sees digital 3D projection as launching a new age of cinema, one that is only now becoming technically possible. The digital cinema, he says, provides "a stunning visual experience which 'turbo-charges' the viewing of the biggest, must-see movies. The biggest action, visual effects, and fantasy movies will soon be shot in 3D." To anyone who has watched a lot of movies, Cameron sounds like a revolutionary. He sounds like a man who has changed the world and knows it.

Part IV

Humanitarians

They strive to alleviate suffering

S tephen Lewis could tolerate no more. For the past two years, he had been criss-crossing Africa at a ferocious pace. As the United Nations Special Envoy for HIV/AIDs in Africa, he had visited schools, hospitals, and villages throughout the continent. And, as someone who had fallen in love with Africa four decades before, he found the experience excruciating. "It's not just the ruinous economic and social decline," he would write in his 2005 book *Race Against Time.* "It's the ravaging of the pandemic; it's the way in which a communicable disease called AIDS has taken countries by the throat and reduced them to spectral caricatures of their former selves."

In his early twenties, Lewis had lived, worked, and travelled in Africa for a year. He remembered the warmth and friendliness, the vibrant life of the people. Yet forty-five years later, he would write, "death stalks every waking moment." Lewis found himself unprepared "for the pervasiveness of death. It has shaken me to my core." As he confronted the continent-wide devastation of the pandemic and the "appalling paucity of response" from the world outside, Lewis sometimes felt helpless and overwhelmed. He fought off these feelings "because futility leads nowhere."

Instead of despairing, Lewis got angry. In a CBC-TV documentary called *Stephen Lewis: The Man Who Couldn't Sleep,* we encounter Lewis in 2003, declaring, "I am in an absolute rage, and I don't apologize for it at all." What made him furious was that antiretroviral drugs existed that could prolong life, but they were not reaching the dying millions: "You look around at these lovely, lovely people, and you know there is no reason they have to die." In *Race Against Time*, he used slightly different words: "It's hard not to be in a near stupor of anger."

Stephen Lewis is an activist, certainly. But he is also, and I would argue primarily, a humanitarian. Motivated by what he had witnessed in Africa, Lewis enlisted his daughter, the human rights lawyer Ilana Landsberg-Lewis. Together, in 2003, they created the Stephen Lewis Foundation, which provides care and support to women, orphans, grandmothers, and people living with HIV and AIDS. That is how a humanitarian changes the world: by finding a way to alleviate the suffering of others.

Here in Part IV, we will return to Stephen Lewis. We will also encounter the humanitarian response to anguish and suffering from other Canadians—among them the young man who, stricken with cancer, embarked on an inspirational, cross-country Marathon of Hope; the globe-trotting doctor who works mainly in war zones; and the precocious teenager who created the world's largest children's crusade. Only the last of these figures has spoken frequently of meeting Mother Teresa. Yet all of them have demonstrated that they share the world view she voiced: "At the end of life we will not be judged by how many diplomas we have received, how much money we have made, how many great things we have done. We will be judged by, 'I was hungry, and you gave me something to eat. I was naked and you clothed me. I was homeless, and you took me in.'"

26

TERRY FOX AND RICK HANSEN

A Marathon of Hope encircles the globe

On April 12, 1980, in St. John's, Newfoundland, a young western Canadian man dipped his artificial leg in the Atlantic Ocean. Then he faced west and set out to run to Vancouver, 7,500 kilometres away. Bent on raising money for cancer research, Terry Fox began his Marathon of Hope, using a distinctive hopping motion that anyone who saw it would never forget. The hope, courage, and commitment Fox displayed would inspire hundreds of thousands around the world. One of those he galvanized, a fellow British Columbian named Rick Hansen, would embark on a wheelchair journey to raise funds for spinal cord research, a tour that would take him through more than thirty countries. Together, Fox and Hansen changed the world by raising more than $600 million to combat two of the most debilitating conditions known to humankind.

Terry Fox himself did not dream of making that much difference when he set out to run across Canada. Born in Winnipeg on July 28, 1958, Fox grew up mostly in Port Coquitlam, British Columbia, where dogged persistence enabled him to excel both as an athlete and a student. But in March 1977, soon after learning he had a cancerous tumour, he had his right leg amputated 18 centimetres above the knee. Just before undergoing the operation, he read a magazine article about an amputee runner, Dick Traum, who had participated in the

New York Marathon. "I was lying in bed looking at this magazine," he said later, "thinking if he can do it, I can do it, too."

In a biography entitled *Terry Fox: His Story*, Leslie Scrivener describes how, at the hospital, during treatment, Terry heard doctors telling children they had a 15 percent chance of living. He heard youngsters crying in pain, and saw lives cut short by the disease. And when, after sixteen months of rehabilitation he finally went home, he began training for what he called his "Marathon of Hope."

Using what today's experts would term a rudimentary prosthesis, the young man whipped himself into shape by running more than 5,000 kilometres. He pushed his wheelchair along the sea wall at Vancouver's Stanley Park, and tackled steep trails and rough logging roads, pushing himself until his hands bled. "I'm not a dreamer," he told the Canadian Cancer Society when he sought their backing. "And I'm not saying this will initiate any kind of definitive answer or cure to cancer, but I believe in miracles. I have to."

On April 12, 1980, accompanied by a few friends and family members, Terry Fox started running west out of St. John's, Newfoundland. Initially, media coverage was light. But as weeks passed and Terry put distance behind him along the Trans-Canada Highway, news of his quixotic undertaking began to spread. By the time he reached Ontario, Canadians were lining the road to see him pass, pounding forward with his fists clenched, eyes fixed on the road ahead, his gait distinctive, unforgettable. Often, they wept. Terry would set out each morning before dawn, running in shorts and a T-shirt printed with a map of Canada. "Some people can't figure out what I'm doing," he said at one point. "It's not a walk-hop, it's not a trot, it's running, or as close as I can get to running, and it's harder than doing it on two legs. It makes me mad when people call this a walk. If I was walking it wouldn't be anything."

Donations began pouring in. One day in southern Ontario, his friends and family collected $20,000 on the highway. In Gravenhurst, population 8,000, locals raised more than $14,000. Terry Fox kept running. He refused to pause even to go for a checkup. "If I ran to a doctor every time I got a little cyst or abrasion," he said, "I'd still be in Nova Scotia. Or else I'd never have started. I've seen people in so much pain. The little bit of pain I'm going through is nothing. They can't shut it off, and I can't shut down every time I feel a little sore."

But on September 1, outside Thunder Bay, Terry Fox collapsed. "The day before I'd run twenty-six miles," he said later. "Now I couldn't even walk across the street." Doctors confirmed that the cancer had spread to his lungs. At a press conference, he said that he had to go home and "have some more x-rays or maybe an operation that will involve opening up my chest or more drugs. I'll do everything I can. I'm going to do my very best. I'll fight. I promise I won't give up."

His father, Rolly Fox, sitting beside him at a table, said, "I think it's unfair. Very unfair."

"I don't feel this is unfair," Terry said. "That's the thing about cancer. I'm not the only one. It happens all the time, to other people. I'm not special. This just intensifies what I did. It gives it more meaning. It'll inspire more people. I could have sat on my rear end, I could have forgotten what I'd seen in the hospital, but I didn't."

Over 143 days, pausing only to give short, inspirational speeches, Terry Fox had run a distance of 5,373 kilometres, covering the equivalent of almost one marathon each day. On June 28, 1981, as he neared his twenty-third birthday, and with his family around him, Terry Fox succumbed to cancer.

By that time, he had become the youngest-ever Companion of the Order of Canada. He had also received the American Cancer Society's Sword of Hope. After his death, the honours multiplied, culminating perhaps in 1999, when he was voted Canada's Greatest Hero. Statues were erected in his honour across the country, and buildings, roads, and parks were named after him, as well as a 8,658-foot peak in the Rocky Mountains. In Ontario, an 84-kilometre stretch of the Trans-Canada Highway between Nipigon and Thunder Bay is called the Terry Fox Courage Highway.

The annual Terry Fox Run, first held in 1981, has become the world's largest one-day fundraiser for cancer. It flourishes in more than fifty countries. The Terry Fox Foundation, inspired by the young man's courage and dedicated to preserving his ideals, has raised more than $550 million for cancer research. It has changed the world by inspiring hope and bringing desperately needed funds for medical research into one of the greatest medical challenges confronting humankind.

The story might have ended there. But the Marathon of Hope would not let it.

During his long convalescence from his amputation, Terry Fox played wheelchair basketball at the invitation of another British Columbian, Rick Hansen. The two became friends. Hansen, born August 26, 1957, on Vancouver Island, was roughly one year older. He had been raised in the interior of British Columbia, at Williams Lake, where as a young athlete he won awards in five sports. At fifteen, however, he was thrown from the back of a pickup truck and suffered a spinal cord injury. He lost the use of his legs.

He finished high school, then took a degree in physical education at the University of British Columbia, becoming the first student with a physical disability to do so. He won national championships in wheelchair volleyball and basketball, and at the Summer Paralympics in 1980 and 1984, won three gold, two silver, and one bronze medal. Hansen also won nineteen international wheelchair marathons, including three world championships.

On March 21, 1985, inspired by his late friend's Marathon of Hope, as he would repeatedly declare, Rick Hansen embarked from Vancouver on a Man in Motion World Tour. Again, media attention took time to develop. But it grew exponentially over the next twenty-six months, as he rolled through more than 40,000 kilometres in thirty-four countries on four continents. By the time Hansen reached home, on May 22, 1987, he had been hailed internationally and had raised $26 million for spinal cord research. He was appointed to the Order of Canada, his citation declaring he had inspired people "around the world to realize their potential."

Hansen then founded the Rick Hansen Foundation, where he continues to serve as president. The foundation has generated more than $280 million from around the world for spinal cord injury programs. Hansen himself has been hailed as "the driving force" in the development of an information network, ICORD (International Collaboration on Repair Discovery), designed to track and record "best practices" in spinal cord treatment across the country and internationally.

Rick Hansen's many honours include the 1983 Athlete of the Year Award, which he shared with hockey player Wayne Gretzky. And one of his finest moments came in 2010, when, at the Vancouver Winter Olympics, he brought the flame into the stadium and lit one of the final torches. As a direct result of the 2010 Vancouver Olympics and Paralympics, and with the help of former B.C. premier Mike Harcourt, Hansen led his foundation in creating planat.com, a consumer-driven online ratings site that ranks the accessibility of buildings and public spaces around the world. Modelled on opinion-driven travel sites such as TripAdvisor, planat.com provides answers to travellers who have questions about automatic door openers, policies on service animals, and the availability of Braille on elevator buttons. When Hansen travelled the world as a man in motion, he gathered information by word of mouth. Today, with 17,000 venues covered and thousands more coming, planat.com has made that world ancient history.

27

MICHAËLLE JEAN

A Haitian immigrant proves that pluralism works

In September 2005, when Michaëlle Jean became the twenty-seventh Governor General of Canada, prime minister Paul Martin described her as a woman of talent and achievement: "Her personal story is nothing short of extraordinary, and extraordinary is precisely what we seek in a governor-generalship." Among Governors General, Jean was the first of Caribbean origin, the third female (after Jeanne Sauvé and Adrienne Clarkson), and the fourth youngest.

Jean was also the second, after Clarkson, to belong to a visible minority, to have been born outside Canada, and to be in an interracial marriage. The motto on the coat of arms she chose to mark her tenure was *Briser les solitudes*, or "to break down solitudes." At her investiture in Ottawa, Jean picked up this theme, declaring that "the time of the Two Solitudes that for too long described the character of this country is past."

In *The Globe and Mail*, columnist John Ibbitson captured the moment: "Here is this beautiful young Canadian of Haitian birth, with a smile that makes you catch your breath, with a bemused older husband by her side, and a daughter who literally personifies our future, and you look at them and you think: Yes, this is our great achievement, this is the Canada that Canada wants to be, this is the Canada that will ultimately make way for different cultural identities."

Michaëlle Jean changed the world by symbolizing all that is best about Canada. She shines as a beacon of pluralism, bringing hope to the impoverished and the marginalized, having demonstrated that, yes, you may come from difficult circumstances, but you can still overcome barriers and obstacles and achieve great things.

Born September 6, 1957, in Port-au-Prince, Haiti, Jean spent her early years there, where her father was principal and philosophy teacher at an elite preparatory school. Despite this, she was educated at home so that she wouldn't have to pledge allegiance to dictator François Duvalier, as all schoolchildren did. Duvalier's regime arrested, tortured, and released her father. In 1967 he escaped to Canada. With her mother and sister, Michaëlle joined him in Thetford Mines, 230 kilometres east of Montreal. He taught at a community college, but he did not make an easy transition.

Later, according to *The Canadian Encyclopedia*, Jean would describe her father as "a broken man" prone to violence. With her mother and sister, she decamped to a basement apartment in Montreal. To support the household, her mother worked first in a clothing factory and then as a night orderly in a psychiatric hospital.

Michaëlle Jean responded by excelling at school. She enrolled at the Université de Montréal, where she earned a bachelor's degree in Italian and Spanish languages and literature. She then completed a master's degree in comparative literature, winning scholarships that took her to Italian universities in Perugia, Florence, and Milan. By the time she was done, she spoke five languages fluently: French, English, Haitian Creole, Italian, and Spanish.

For two years starting in 1984, while completing her formal studies, she taught Italian at Université de Montréal. Meanwhile, all through her twenties, Jean worked full time at a shelter for battered women. She also co-ordinated a government study on spousal abuse and later established a network of shelters across Canada. As well, she worked for Employment and Immigration Canada, assisting immigrants, and began writing about immigrant women's experiences.

At twenty-nine, Jean returned to Haiti to research an article on Haitian women. She impressed a National Film Board producer, who invited her to conduct interviews for a film on the 1987 Haitian elections, made possible by the overthrow of the latest dictator. The CBC's French-language arm, Radio-Canada, broadcast the finished product on a newsmagazine called *Le Point*—and then hired her in 1988, making her the first person of colour on French television news in Canada.

Jean worked on camera for several shows, including *Actuel, Montréal ce soir, Virages,* and *Le Point,* and then moved in 1995 to Radio-Canada's all-news network, RDI (Le Réseau de l'information). There, she anchored several programs—among them *Le Monde ce soir, L'Édition québécoise, Horizons francophones,* and *Les Grands reportages*—and won a number of awards, including a Gemini. Before long, she had her own French-language current affairs show, *Michaëlle.* She added English-language television to her activities, and in 1999 began hosting the CBC Newsworld programs *Rough Cuts* and *The Passionate Eye.*

Nine years before, in 1990, Jean had married Jean-Daniel Lafond, a Canadian documentary filmmaker originally from France. As the decade unfolded, she participated in four films Lafond directed: *A State of Blackness: Aimé Césaire's Way; Tropic North,* about the Black experience in Québec; *Last Call for Cuba,* marking the fortieth anniversary of the Cuban Revolution; and *Haïti in All Our Dreams,* which won an award for best political film at the Toronto Hot Docs festival. In this film, Jean travels to France to meet her uncle, writer-in-exile René Depestre, who had fled the Duvalier dictatorship.

Soon after Prime Minister Paul Martin announced her appointment as Governor General, controversy arose. Critics argued that

Jean could not serve as the Queen's representative in Canada, and as head of state, because she and her husband had supported Quebec separatism. She refuted that allegation. Then, because she had acquired French citizenship by marrying Lafond, critics charged that she would suffer divided loyalties. Jean responded by renouncing her French citizenship before she took office.

Following in the footsteps of Clarkson, Michaëlle Jean sought to reach out to all Canadians, regardless of background, and focusing especially on the young and the disadvantaged. Embarking on the traditional viceregal tours of the provinces and territories, she paid special attention to the plight of female victims of violence, and met with representatives of various women's groups. Early in her tenure, Jean visited Italy and also Haiti and five African countries—Algeria, Mali, Ghana, South Africa, and Morocco—where she spoke in support of women's rights.

Late in 2008, when three opposition parties expressed a lack of confidence in the government led by Prime Minister Stephen Harper, Jean found herself at the centre of a constitutional maelstrom. After seeking expert advice, she granted Harper a prorogation, or adjournment, on condition that Parliament soon reconvene and produce a passable budget. The following year, when the European Parliament announced a ban on the import of Canadian seal meat, Jean made a political gesture on behalf of the Inuit. While touring Nunavut, she participated in a traditional seal feast, gutting a recently killed seal, and eating a piece of the raw heart. Asked her reasons, Jean said, "Take from that [gesture] what you will."

In January 2010, when her native Haiti was devastated by an earthquake (magnitude 7.0), Jean made a tearful speech, partly in Haitian Creole, that was instrumental in galvanizing Canadian support. With roughly 316,000 killed, 300,000 injured, and one million rendered homeless, Canada turned its embassy into a base camp for the 6,000

Canadians in the stricken country, while mobilizing warships and the Disaster Assistance Response Team.

The government agreed to match contributions from Canadians (up to $50 million), and eased immigration rules for Haitians. In March, after officially opening the 2010 Winter Olympics and Paralympics in Vancouver, Jean visited Haiti to draw attention to the continuing humanitarian crisis. Already, during the previous year, Jean had connected with UNESCO, addressing the executive on the importance of dialogue between cultures. Now, with UNESCO's Director-General, she chaired a round table in Port-au-Prince about education.

In 2009, as she approached the end of her traditional five-year tenure as Governor General, Jean acted with her husband to create the Michaëlle Jean Foundation. With Lafond as full-time chief executive officer, the foundation supports and encourages creative initiatives, as its website says, "to offer opportunities for underserved youth to mobilize, develop their leadership skills, and act for change." The following year, Jean accepted an invitation from the United Nations Educational, Scientific, and Cultural Organization to become UNESCO Special Envoy for Haiti. Irina Bokova, Director-General of UNESCO, made the appointment in recognition of Jean's "dedication to the reconstruction and rebirth of Haiti in the fields of education, social and human sciences, natural and exact sciences, culture and communication, and her contribution to the promotion of the Organization's ideals."

Jean became UNESCO Special Envoy for Haiti in November 2010, ten months after a massive earthquake devastated the island. Early the following year, she began calling for the overhaul of Haiti's educational system as "the cornerstone of the impoverished nation's future prosperity." In May, after the Caribbean nation installed a stable government, she began arguing that Haiti needed investment, not charity. "Aid is good in a crisis situation," she said. "But once the crisis is over, you have to build on what's sustainable." She urged investors to support the Haitian government in creating infrastructure and jobs: "How can you build an economy that is sustainable on charity? The government doesn't have the necessary means to implement its own plans." She continues to drive home this message: "If the reconstruction is not about creating infrastructure or jobs, what's the point?"

As UNESCO Special Envoy for Haiti, Michaëlle Jean is striving to ease suffering and improve living conditions in the land of her birth. By providing a symbol of hope for the impoverished and the marginalized, and for those who must overcome seemingly insurmountable odds, Michaëlle Jean has already changed the world.

28

STEPHEN LEWIS

An eloquent humanitarian leads the war against AIDS

In *Race Against Time*, quoted in the opening to this section, Stephen Lewis reveals that he lives not just in hope, but also in rage: "I cannot abide the willful inattention of so much of the international community. I cannot expunge from my mind the heartless indifference, the criminal neglect of the last decade, during which time countless people have gone to their graves—people who should still be walking the open savannah of Africa." Why has the world struggled to respond effectively? Lewis repudiates "the easy canard . . . that Africa is a basket-case of anti-democratic chaos." Instead, with typical directness, he blames international financial institutions, and notably the World Bank and the International Monetary Fund (IMF).

In the late 1980s and '90s, these agencies enforced "structural adjustment programs" that weakened and curtailed African social sectors, especially health and education. These cutbacks spawned unaffordable users' fees and devastating shortages of nurses, doctors, and teachers. What makes Lewis "nearly apoplectic" is that the World Bank and the IMF were fully informed but refused to consider the human consequences of their actions: "They were so smug, so all-knowing, so incredibly arrogant, so wrong."

In a July 2010 interview aired on *Democracy Now!*, Lewis returned to this theme. He argued that "thirty, forty or fifty years of structural adjustment programs, berserk and lunatic economic applications,

[have] stripped the social sectors of Africa at the behest of the World Bank and the International Monetary Fund." But that, he said, is the essence of capitalism: "You do as little as you can for human well-being in order to encourage the profits of the few. And the few have been making obscene profits."

If Stephen Lewis is an eloquent Jeremiah who declines to mince words, he is also a world-changer. Consider the foundation he established with his daughter in 2003, to provide care and support to women, orphans, grandmothers, and people living with HIV and AIDS. The Stephen Lewis Foundation provides counselling about HIV prevention, care, and treatment; distributes food, medication, and other necessities; supports home-based health care; and helps orphans and children access education. By June 2011, the foundation had distributed more than $54 million in fifteen African countries in support of 300 community-based organizations and 700 initiatives. That is what a humanitarian transformation looks like.

Who is the man behind all this? Born in Ottawa on November 11, 1937, and given to making speeches from the age of three, Stephen Henry Lewis is today the patriarch of Canada's leading family of social democrats. His Russian-born father, David Lewis (1909–1981), was a Jewish lawyer who served as national secretary of the Co-operative Commonwealth Foundation, helped establish the New Democratic Party, and led that party federally from 1971 to 1975. Stephen's wife, Michele Landsberg, is a feminist author who inspired the Canadian Women's Foundation to create an award in her name. And their off-spring include not just the human rights lawyer Ilana Landsberg-Lewis, but also journalist-broadcaster Avi Lewis, husband of activist Naomi Klein.

After moving with his family to Toronto in 1950, Stephen Lewis went to Oakwood Collegiate and Harbord Collegiate before entering the University of Toronto. In 1957, as a member of a university

(Hart House) debating team, he debated the forty-year-old American senator John F. Kennedy, future president of the United States, on the question, "Has the United States failed in its responsibilities as a world leader?" Lewis led the affirmative and lost narrowly (204 to 194), with many audience members judging his performance the more outstanding.

Lewis spent one year at the University of British Columbia, then returned to the University of Toronto but "couldn't muster the energy for exams" and dropped out. In *Race Against Time*, he writes, "if I may set your collective minds at ease, I don't wander around recommending similar conduct to the post-secondary youth of today." In 1960, at twenty-two, Lewis took a research job in London with Socialist International, a worldwide organization of social democratic, socialist, and labour parties.

A few weeks after he began working, he spotted a general invitation to a week-long conference of the World Assembly of Youth in the city of Accra in Ghana, West Africa. Lewis went to Africa for a week and stayed for a year. Ghana had recently become independent, and he loved the sense of hope and possibility, and "the music, the energy, the kindness, the generosity, the camaraderie, the purposefulness of everything." He taught English and history at Accra High School, and worked three nights a week for the University of Ghana at Legon, travelling to nearby villages to conduct adult education classes.

In 1961, Lewis accepted an offer to teach at a village boarding school in Nigeria. He did that for "several exhilarating months," and then, with a friend, spent five weeks driving across the continent to Kenya. That August, while working in Nairobi, finding university places in North America for African students, Lewis received a letter from Tommy Douglas, asking him to return to Canada to work for the newly formed New Democratic Party (NDP).

"You couldn't say no to Tommy," Lewis writes, "the same Tommy

Douglas who that very month in 1961 had become the first leader of the NDP." Stephen Lewis became the party's first full-time organizer. Two years later, at twenty-six, he moved to provincial politics and got himself elected to the Ontario legislature. In 1970, he became leader of the provincial NDP, and took the party through a major surge and then into a slight slide. In 1978, after the NDP lost its official opposition status, he left provincial politics.

For six years, Lewis worked as a labour mediator, newspaper columnist, and broadcaster, serving with Toronto's Citytv and on CBC Radio as part of a weekly political panel on *Morningside*. His incisive, well-informed commentary led to his 1984 appointment, on the advice of Prime Minister Brian Mulroney, as Canadian ambassador to the United Nations. During his four-year term, Lewis orchestrated the drafting of a five-year Programme of Action for African Economic Recovery and Development.

In 1988, he chaired an International Conference on Climate Change, which drew up the first comprehensive policy on global warming. Lewis coordinated an international report, the Graça Machel study, on the impact of armed conflict on children. Starting in 1995, he devoted four years to working as deputy executive director of the United Nations International Children's Emergency Fund (UNICEF) at its global headquarters in New York. During this period, at the request of the Organization of African Unity, he served on the International Panel of Eminent Personalities to Investigate the 1994 Genocide in Rwanda and the Surrounding Events, and helped to draft the *Rwanda Report*, issued in 2000.

Meanwhile, a global epidemic called HIV/AIDS—short for "human immunodeficiency virus/acquired immune deficiency syndrome"—had begun to kill people in large numbers, a large percentage of them in Africa. Since the 1980s, nearly 30 million people have died from AIDS-related causes. According to AVERT (an international

HIV and AIDS charity), the number of people living with HIV rose from around 8 million in 1990 to 33.3 million by the end of 2009. Of that total, 22.5 million were in sub-Saharan Africa. In 2009, 1.8 million people died of AIDS-related causes, 72 percent of them (1.3 million) in sub-Saharan Africa. AVERT also reports that in recent years, the overall growth of the pandemic has stabilized. Both the annual number of new HIV infections and the number of AIDS-related deaths have steadily declined, thanks to a significant increase in numbers of people receiving treatment with antiretroviral drugs. The pandemic is far from over. But the situational improvement owes much to Lewis, who spent five years, starting in 2001, as the UN Secretary-General's Special Envoy for HIV/AIDS in Africa. During this period, he not only drew attention to the HIV/AIDS crisis, but convinced world leaders—among them former American president Bill Clinton and philanthropist Bill Gates—that they have a responsibility to respond. Lewis is a member of the board of directors of the Clinton Health Access Initiative, serves as a commissioner on the United Nations' Global Commission on HIV and the Law, and co-founded and directs AIDS-Free World, an international advocacy organization based out of New York.

Along the way, both at home and on the world stage, Lewis has earned an eye-glazing cavalcade of awards and honours. In 2003, he was made a Companion of the Order of Canada, and *Maclean's* magazine named him the inaugural "Canadian of the Year." Two years later, *Time* included Lewis on a list of the 100 most influential people in the world, and in 2007, the Kingdom of Lesotho in southern Africa invested him with a knighthood.

Lewis has received a multitude of other international accolades, including thirty-five honorary degrees. He uses the recognition as a platform from which to champion the global struggle against the HIV/AIDs pandemic. In his book *Race Against Time,* adapted from his 2005 Massey Lectures, he offers his most extended analysis. On the first page, he writes of studying the Rwandan genocide, and how it "felt like a descent into depravity from which there was no escape." While eventually that genocide came to an end, he writes, "the pandemic of HIV/AIDS feels as though it will go on forever."

Against that backdrop, Lewis has nothing but praise for the women of Africa, who sustain the continent while living in a universe of pain. They should have a definitive role, he writes, "in every single aspect of social, economic, political, civil, and cultural life, from peacekeeping to agriculture to trade to AIDS." To that end, the Stephen Lewis Foundation pays special attention to women, and especially to grandmothers caring for orphaned grandchildren. According to Lewis, "the grandmothers are the heroes of Africa."

With the caregivers in mind, Lewis battles to reverse the effects of the "structural adjustment programs" instituted by the faceless institutions of global capitalism. He knows he cannot accomplish this alone. That is why he has inspired committed followers and enlisted powerful allies. Stephen Lewis has changed the world by demonstrating that his Race Against Time is both a marathon and a relay race. And it is one that humankind cannot afford to lose.

29

MICHAEL J. FOX

A Hollywood hero takes on Parkinson's

He woke in the morning to find his little finger trembling. His left pinkie. He couldn't make it stop, couldn't control the twitching. Maybe he'd slept on it? He made a fist with his hand, once, twice, five times, and then shook it vigorously. His pinkie kept twitching. Still lying on his back, he intertwined the fingers of his two hands behind his head and stretched them up high. When he released, his finger was still going. But also his head was hurting. Maybe he had drunk too much last night while watching Monday Night Football? Maybe he was suffering delirium tremens?

Okay, that didn't make sense. But neither did this. Movie star Michael J. Fox was in a hotel room in Gainesville, Florida, where he was shooting *Doc Hollywood*. Last night, he and fellow actor Woody Harrelson had been wrestling and roughhousing, same old, same old. Maybe he had caught one upside the head and this was the result. His pinkie kept twitching. He wandered from room to room, trying to distract himself. No change. He picked up the phone and called Brigitte, his assistant. A superwoman. Trying to sound unruffled, he described his slightly embarrassing condition: an out-of-control pinkie.

Strangely enough, that twitching finger would give Michael J. Fox a chance to make a difference—one he would seize with both hands. Ten years after that morning in Gainesville, the wild-and-crazy actor would create the Michael J. Fox Foundation. And with that he changed the world. The foundation is dedicated to finding a cure for Parkinson's disease and to improving therapies for those who live with it. The world's largest private funder of Parkinson's research, the foundation has raised almost $180 million to pursue its goals.

Not that any of it came easily. That morning in Gainesville, Brigitte listened calmly, then said that the uncontrollable pinkie might suggest a neurological problem. Did he want to speak to her brother, a brain surgeon in Boston? This scared the hell out of Fox. No, no. Instead, he called his actress wife, Tracy Pollan, a fitness buff. She listened, admitted to being baffled, then said, "You know, Brigitte's brother is a brain surgeon. Why don't you give him a call?"

A few minutes later, with Brigitte in the room, Fox called Boston. Her brother listened. He ran through a list of possibilities, none of which sounded enticing, and then suggested a visit to a neurosurgeon. At this point, November 1990, the worried actor was already well known. No, let's be honest. He was famous, a Hollywood figure. He was Michael J. Fox, star of the TV series *Family Ties*, for which he had won three Emmy Awards and a Golden Globe Award. He was Michael J. Fox, star of the blockbuster Hollywood movie trilogy *Back to the Future*, in which he played the teenager Marty McFly, who travelled back and forth in time in a magical, mystery car, a refurbished DeLorean.

But that afternoon, Michael J. Fox was ushered into the neurology department at the University of Florida. The doctors ran him through a few tests, asked him to touch the tip of each finger to the tip of his thumb, things like that. They remained unconcerned, and when the testing was done, the senior neurologist said that in his view, the spasms were probably the result of a minor injury to his ulna, his funny bone.

More than a decade later, Fox would reveal all this in his memoir,

Lucky Man. His pinkie stopped twitching and he returned to work. He finished shooting *Doc Hollywood.* But every so often, his pinkie acted up, and sometimes a couple more fingers would join the action. Also, his left hand felt weak, and he felt stiff and sore in his left shoulder and on the left side of his chest.

Michael J. Fox soldiered on. *Doc Hollywood* came out that summer and did far better than he expected. He felt pretty good and one afternoon, while taking a holiday on Martha's Vineyard, an island retreat off the south coast of Cape Cod, Massachusetts, he went for a longer run than usual. He felt himself falter in the stretch, nothing serious, but when he arrived home, his wife, looking shocked and frightened, said, "The left side of your body is barely moving. Your arm isn't swinging at all."

She insisted that he see a doctor as soon as he got home to New York. Fox tracked down a sports medicine specialist. The man examined him and prescribed an exercise regimen. Great, Michael was getting this under control. But then, after his second visit, the doctor took him aside, handed him a business card, and told him to visit his neurologist friend as soon as possible. What? Fox had already seen a neurologist. The man had given him a clean bill of health. It turned out the sports medicine doctor had already phoned his wife and told her, "Make sure he goes." So he went.

This time, the neurologist said two words Michael J. Fox did not want to hear: "Parkinson's disease." He added a few more words: "Early-onset. Early-onset Parkinson's. Quite rare." The disease usually hits those between fifty and sixty-five. It's a degenerative condition, at present incurable. But Fox was so young. Maybe someone would discover a cure. Fox was having trouble breathing, as if someone had sucked the air out of the room.

The month was September, the year 1991. Fox had recently turned thirty. The doctor wasn't much older. Why was he saying these horrible things? Fox was nodding, understanding. What was he going to tell Tracy? The neurologist handed him a pamphlet. Or maybe it was the nurse. The doctor looked so composed. Suddenly, Fox hated him with a passion. In a daze, he walked out of his office. He must have taken the elevator, because he emerged into a rainy afternoon. He flagged a cab. How could this be? He was thirty years old. He was Michael J. Fox. How could this be happening?

Fox had added the "J" to distinguish himself from another actor with the same name. In the beginning, he had been plain Michael Fox, or in fact Michael Andrew Fox, a Canadian born June 9, 1961, in Edmonton, Alberta. His father was a member of the Canadian Armed Forces, a career military man, and when Michael was four, still just "an army brat," he moved with the family to Burnaby, British Columbia, a suburb of Vancouver. There he went to school, eventually to Burnaby Central Secondary School, where, given a choice of options, he chose creative writing and acting.

Meanwhile, he played hockey. He dreamed of becoming the next Bobby Orr, knowing that his small size worked against him. He played guitar in a couple of garage bands, rock and roll. But mainly he was witty, a class clown, and he put that gift to work in acting class. He could memorize lines easily. He revelled in laughter and attention. A drama teacher, Ross Jones, spotted his affinity for acting, his talent, and when he learned that the Canadian Broadcasting Corporation was looking for an actor to play a twelve-year-old boy, he set up a meet and told Fox to go. The boy was fifteen, but he was small. He could pass. He was going to be the funniest twelve-year-old anybody had ever met. At the audition, with a few prepared jokes and one-liners, he got onto a roll. Fox could be really, really funny. He landed the job.

Suddenly, at fifteen, he was co-starring with Brent Carver in a CBC-TV sitcom called *Leo and Me*—a show that survived for three years. His school work suffered, of course. But Fox landed a few roles in American TV movies shooting in Canada, and at eighteen, with his parents' blessing, he did what aspiring actors tend to do: he dropped out of school and moved to Los Angeles. He landed bit parts in a couple of TV series—*Family* and *Lou Grant*—and a regular one in *Palmerstown, U.S.A.* And then came another milestone, the role of Alex P. Keaton in the hit series *Family Ties*. For seven years, Fox played a right-wing teenager with left-leaning parents.

He won awards, becoming one of Hollywood's most bankable young actors. Director Robert Zemeckis wanted him for *Back to the Future*, and after surmounting a number of complications, Fox began work on that movie. While still shooting *Family Ties*, he also worked as Marty McFly, a teenager who travels back in time, meets his parents when they are in high school, and gets in the way of his own birth. The film became a smash hit. For eight weeks, it remained the number one grossing movie. Eventually, it earned over $380 million. Not only that, it spawned two wildly successful sequels, *Back to the Future* parts II and III. Michael J. Fox was on top of the world. In 1988, he married the sensational Tracy Pollan, whom he had met while filming *Family Ties*, and with whom he would have four children. He was living the dream.

It showed no signs of ending. Through the late 1980s, Fox starred in *Teen Wolf*; *Light of Day*; *The Secret of My Success*; *Bright Lights, Big City*; and *Casualties of War*. Then came *Doc Hollywood* . . . and the diagnosis. Parkinson's disease? Was this some kind of joke? Forget that. The roles kept coming. Fox kept working. Besides playing supporting roles in *The American President* and *Mars Attacks!*, he starred in *For Love or Money*, *Life with Mikey*, *Greedy*, Woody Allen's *Don't Drink the Water*, and *The Frighteners*. Along the way, he landed the role of Mike Flaherty in *Spin City*, another hit TV series that ran for years. For that, he won an Emmy, three Golden Globes, and two awards from the Screen Actors' Guild.

But the Parkinson's proved relentless. The shaking, the tremors. Fox had more and more trouble hiding his condition. He had always been a party animal. In 1992, he quit drinking. He kept working. And in 1998, he went public. In a *People* magazine article, and also in a television interview with Barbara Walters, he told the world. Michael J. Fox had early-onset Parkinson's. The disease had no known cure.

The flood of sympathy almost swept him away. He realized he was not alone, that tens of thousands of people were suffering with the same disease. But one thing set him apart: he had money, and fame. Possibly, just possibly, he could do something—something that might help not just himself, but all those suffering from Parkinson's.

In 2000, Fox cut back on his acting. He continued doing voice-overs, but he also turned his attention to his affliction. He faced it. He tells the story in his memoir, *Lucky Man*, which appeared in 2002. He would follow that with two more books: *Always Looking Up: The Adventures of an Incurable Optimist* and *A Funny Thing Happened on the Way to the Future: Twists and Turns and Lessons Learned*. In these, he tried to spread optimism and hope.

Also in 2000, the actor created the Michael J. Fox Foundation. He began devoting serious attention to finding a cure and easing symptoms. As a result of his work in this cause, Fox received international accolades. But he didn't do this work for the recognition. He already had that in spades. He didn't do it for himself alone, though certainly he could have gone ahead privately. Fox did it for the sake of all those suffering from Parkinson's. He was Michael J. Fox. Eventually, like everyone else on earth, he will go down. But this much he has already demonstrated: a Canadian humanitarian, he won't go down without doing everything he can to alleviate the suffering of others.

30

SAMANTHA NUTT

A globe-trotting doctor does her work in war zones

The date: May 1995. The place: Baidoa, Somalia. A petite, twenty-five-year-old blond woman sat at a table in the heat. She was interviewing women, most of them swaddling babies, as they passed her in a slow-moving line at a volunteer-run feeding clinic. Samantha Nutt had recently earned a medical degree. She had come to Baidoa to do research for an advanced degree focusing on women's health issues in failed states. She hoped and believed that here, in the so-called "City of Death," she would be able to make a significant contribution.

In Nairobi, Kenya, before flying here in a six-seater plane, Nutt had left a series of post-dated postcards to be sent to her mother in sequence. *Having a wonderful time on safari. Seeing tons of lions, zebras, giraffes, and elephants. Wish you were here.* Nutt had arrived ready for the stultifying heat and humidity. But driving to the clinic from the airstrip with a surly armed escort high on drugs, she had registered not just the smell of the tropics—plantains, palm oil, salt sea air—but what she would later describe as "the stench of rancid, burning garbage, rotting animal corpses, putrid water, and suppurating wounds." She had also noticed rifle-toting young men roaring around in Jeeps armed with rocket launchers.

Three years before, 300,000 Somalis had died as a result of war, famine, and disease. The health system had crumbled, and where once 180 non-governmental organizations had offered aid and assistance, today there were fewer than forty. Now, having asked her list of questions of the young mother at the front of the line—hardly more than a girl, really—Nutt reached out and inserted a finger into the hand of the baby draped over the girl's shoulder. That hand was cold. The baby was dead.

Shocked and upset—had the child died while she ran through her questions?—Nutt approached the clinic's intake nurse. He sat at another table, recording names. "The first woman in line over there," Nutt said. "Her baby is dead." The man did not look up. "Doctor, if you go up to all the women standing in this line," he said, "you will find many more dead children." The man finished writing, then turned to the next waiting woman.

In 2011, in a public interview at the Toronto Public Library, Samantha Nutt described that moment as life-changing. She was talking about her new book, *Damned Nations: Greed, Guns, Armies, and Aid.* In Baidoa, she realized that, as a volunteer with the United Nations International Children's Emergency Fund (UNICEF), she would not be heroically saving lives. The agency, she writes, "was overwhelmed, underfunded, and barely operational." Later, as she digested that initial experience and others all too similar, Nutt realized still more: that she could not stand idly by while around the world, women and children suffered and died as a result of war.

Four years after Baidoa, with her husband Eric Hoskins, a fellow physician, Nutt founded War Child Canada, a charitable humanitarian organization that has changed the world by delivering aid and development money to war-ravaged nations. As executive director, Nutt has worked in the Democratic Republic of Congo, Liberia, Sierra Leone, Somalia, Burundi, northern Uganda, and Ethiopia, and also on the Thai-Burmese border.

In recognition of this work, *Time* magazine named her one of Canada's five leading activists, and the World Economic Forum recognized her as one of 200 young global leaders. *The Globe and Mail* named her one of "Canada's Top 40 under 40," and also one of twenty-five "transformational Canadians." Nutt speaks excellent French, and Montreal-based *La Presse* named her a *personnalité de la semaine.* The recipient of numerous honorary degrees, she has been welcomed into both the Order of Ontario and the Order of Canada.

In *Damned Nations,* Nutt presents harrowing anecdotes set in some of the world's most dangerous hellholes. She also offers a blast of passionate opinion. On the back cover, Stephen Lewis describes the book as "extraordinarily riveting," and adds, "The anecdotes are heart-wrenching; the analysis is trenchant, principled, uncompromising." Roméo Dallaire applauds Nutt's scrupulous consistency and her "hard-nosed, direct, in-your-face style," as well as "her defiant resolve in her approach to war and the massive abuses to humanity, especially women and children." And David Suzuki calls the book extraordinary: "From its opening scenes, my heart was in my throat. Samantha Nutt is a genuine hero. All of us living in the comfort and affluence of industrialized countries owe it to the rest of humanity to read this powerful book."

Born in Toronto in October 1969, Samantha Nutt lived as a child in Brazil and South Africa. But mainly she grew up in suburban Toronto, between Scarborough and North York. Strongly influenced by "a fiercely feminist mother," she came early to gender equity. At fifteen, she was much taken with Live Aid, the two-venue concert extravaganza in London and New York that raised more than $140 million for people suffering from famine in Ethiopia. She also marched against South African apartheid.

An outstanding student and a self-described "drama geek," Nutt enrolled at McMaster University in Hamilton, where she studied theatre and English literature and graduated summa cum laude. At that same institution, she took a medical degree. Along the way, she joined a peace vigil during the 1991 Gulf War. "For me, it's all part of a continuum," she said at the Toronto Public Library. "Humanities, humanism, human rights, women's issues. They're all about empathy and understanding what people go through."

After McMaster, Nutt went to the London School of Hygiene and Tropical Medicine, where she earned a master's degree with distinction, building her thesis around her research in Somalia. Then came Burundi and Congo and the creation of War Child Canada (WCC), which has evolved into an $8 million organization that helps 250,000 people a year with a staff of 200. Focusing mainly on war-affected children and their families in nine countries, WCC works with local partners, spending 90 cents of every dollar on programs designed to break the cycle of violence, poverty, and despair. The focus is not short-term charity but long-term economic development. More specifically, the agency provides education for children who have been exploited as soldiers and labourers. It brings legal aid to women and children, and helps young people move into jobs.

As a woman, Nutt has learned things in war zones that would have been denied most men. The greatest roadblock to world peace, she argues, is the marginalization of women and girls. The way to break the cycle of poverty and violence in the developing world is to foster women's education: "Even the most effective humanitarian interventions are stymied by high rates of female illiteracy in such countries as Afghanistan and Somalia, where girls' education is often seen as antithetical to religious and social norms."

As a mother now herself, and also an assistant professor at the University of Toronto—and with her husband active in provincial politics—Nutt spends less time in the field than she did. But she draws on her long and varied experience to argue that the vast majority of conflicts around the globe will not be solved militarily. The answer, she says, is to promote human rights. This means more than throwing conscience money at worthy causes and short-term programs, an activity that only propagates "the myth of humanitarian aid as a noble response to an ignoble act."

Canadians should work to ensure that our corporate social policies and labour practices jibe with "the values that we defend and uphold as Canadians," she says. She insists that we are "implicated in horrific acts of violence around the world, while our personal interventions rarely do more than maintain the status quo." Too often, Nutt writes, we ignore situations "that implicate us in the death, mutilation and extermination of other human beings, whose lives we degrade by casting ourselves in the role of saviours offering ever-shifting cures for their misery."

For Samantha Nutt, changing the world begins at home. We have to start by thinking critically about ourselves. If that sounds like a long-term commitment, that is exactly what she intends.

31

CRAIG KIELBURGER

A precocious teen leads a children's crusade

At age thirteen, Craig Kielburger asked Mother Teresa, "How do you it? How do you work every day side by side with people who are suffering, and who are dying, knowing that you cannot help every person?" Years later, Kielburger told a Toronto audience that the tiny woman smiled, took his hands in hers, and looked into his eyes. "And when Mother Teresa looked into your eyes, you felt that she was looking into your soul," he said. The now-beatified missionary told him, "You have to realize that in our lives we do no great things. But we can do small things with great love. That's how we change this world for the better, with those small acts, those small things, and doing them with great love every day."

Kielburger was speaking in June 2011 while receiving an honorary degree from the University of Toronto. And few in the audience at Convocation Hall, knowing what the young man had achieved in the sixteen years since he met the Blessed Teresa of Calcutta, doubted that he had taken her message not only to heart but into the world. Born December 17, 1982, Craig Kielburger grew up in Thornhill, Ontario, a suburb of Toronto, where he attended Bishop Scalabrini Catholic School. At twelve, while flipping through the *Toronto Star*, he noticed a headline: "Battled child labour, boy, 12, murdered." The story described how at age four, a Pakistani boy named Iqbal Masih had been forced into bonded labour in a carpet factory. At twelve, having become an outspoken leader in the fight against child labour, the boy had been gunned down in the street.

Kielburger was shocked. But what could he do? Then he recalled how he had helped his older brother, Marc, acquire signatures on various petitions for environmental causes. He decided that if Marc could do it, he could, too. Both his parents were teachers, and with the help of a school librarian, he researched child labour. Then, though he was not a natural public speaker, he addressed his classmates and led them in founding a group called Twelve Twelve-Year-Olds.

Working out of his parents' house, Kielburger and his friends sent letters and petitions to political leaders around the world, urging them to protect children's rights. Renamed Free the Children (FTC), the tiny group grew quickly to thirty, fifty, 100 members—and then kept wildly growing. Eventually, FTC would become the largest network of children helping children in the world. Through this organization, thousands of young people have raised funds to build hundreds of primary schools in developing nations. Those schools have educated tens of thousands of children, and also provided millions of dollars' worth of medical supplies to needy children and their families.

A crucial turning point came early. While still twelve years old and in grade seven, Kielburger felt the need to see child labour conditions for himself. He begged and pleaded and, after personally raising half the airfare, talked his parents into letting him travel through Asia with a Bangladeshi friend of the family, a twenty-five-year-old human rights worker. Here again, he used a precedent set by brother Marc, six years older, who had taken time off from university to do volunteer work in Thailand with mothers and babies suffering from HIV/AIDS. As he turned thirteen, Kielburger spent seven weeks exploring Bangladesh, India, Pakistan, Thailand, and Nepal. He talked with children living in the streets and slaving at mindless, dangerous jobs. Later, he would write, "The trip had a profound effect on me, one that changed me forever. I would spread the word about the suffering of all the children I had met. I would let the world know that we, too, are part of the problem. I would not fail them."

While abroad, Kielburger learned that Canadian Prime Minister Jean Chrétien was coming to India. Initially denied a meeting, he organized a press conference and declared that the prime minister had a moral responsibility to take action on child labour. Chrétien agreed to meet him, listened, and later raised the issue with both Pakistani and Indian leaders. The international media picked up the story, and Free the Children began receiving attention around the world. Kielburger appeared on *The Oprah Winfrey Show*—not once but several times—and never looked back.

Over the years, FTC's international projects, most of them introduced as part of its Adopt a Village program, have brought over 650 schools and school rooms to youth. They have provided clean water, health care, and sanitation to one million people in forty-five countries around the world. In North America and the United Kingdom, domestic programs have engaged and empowered hundreds of thousands of young people. And that is how this humanitarian changed the world.

Kielburger told the story of Free the Children in a book of that title, which he co-authored with professional writer Kevin Major. A review in *Publishers Weekly*, the bible of the American book trade, described it as "an absorbing account, in the form of a travelogue, of a young man's awakening not only to injustice and bone-crushing poverty but also to the beauty and diversity of the world and its cultures. Kielburger's story of moral outrage followed by extraordinary dedication and action is inspirational." That book won a prestigious Christopher Award and was translated into eight languages.

At age seventeen, together with his older brother, Kielburger founded Leaders Today, tailoring it to encourage young people to become active global citizens. This evolved into Me to We, a commercial enterprise that sells ethically made organic clothing and motivational books, and organizes youth leadership camps and volunteer trips to Kenya, India, Ecuador, the Arizona-Mexico border, and rural China. It donates half its profits to growth and the other half to Free the Children. As part of this initiative, the brothers wrote a book called *Me to We*, which has been published with two different subtitles: *Finding Meaning in a Material World* and *Turning Self-Help on Its Head*. Me to We has received contributions from such international celebrities as Oprah Winfrey, Richard Gere, Jane Goodall, and Desmond Tutu.

Amidst this whirlwind of activity, Kielburger graduated from high school and then from the University of Toronto, taking a degree in peace and conflict studies. In 2009, he became the youngest-ever graduate to earn an Executive MBA from the Schulich School of Business at York University. Meanwhile, in 2007, Kielburger appeared in a documentary episode of the TV series *Degrassi: The Next Generation*. It aired in the United States as "Doing What Matters" and in Canada as "Degrassi in Kenya." Aimed at a teenage audience, the episode took cast members to Africa to help build schools for children. Kielburger later appeared in a regular-season episode of *Degrassi*, in which a student mounts a project with Free the Children.

Over the years, Kielburger has become increasingly adept at using the media to deliver his message of caring and involvement. For the *Toronto Star*, he writes a regular column, "Global Voices," about social activism around the world. In June 2010, he began creating special reports for a Toronto television station, doing interviews about such events as the controversial G20 summit, which brought clashes between protesters and police. In October of that year, for CTV, he began doing a show called *Shameless Idealists*, on which he has interviewed such socially active figures as K'naan, Cherie Blair, Al Gore, Jesse Jackson, and Martin Sheen.

The previous January, immediately after an earthquake destroyed much of Haiti, Kielburger had travelled to that country with a Free the Children team, "anxious to check on the status of our schools, our students, and our friends." The newspaper and TV reports he sent back, focusing on the way people were struggling to cope with devastation, were among the most moving to emerge from that crisis. Towards the end of the year, Kielburger returned to Haiti with actress-activist Mia Farrow and a *W5* documentary film crew. The ensuing program, which aired one year after the calamity occurred, served to raise awareness of the continuing crisis.

Kielburger spoke and wrote of staying in the capital city of Port-au-Prince, where each morning he would pass "a two-storey home that sat on a 45-degree angle." One wall had been reduced to a jumble of concrete, though the tilted roof and water system "unfairly preserved a lasting memory of someone's former life." He did not arrive in the country looking for a politically volatile situation, Kielburger wrote: "But what we found was a country that resembled the house we passed each morning—frozen in a moment from a year earlier thanks to the inefficiency of a national government and the slow response of the international community."

Craig Kielburger recently turned thirty. He remains furiously active, shows no sign of forgetting the children who inspired him, and won't be abandoning the world-changing business any time soon.

Part V

Performers:
Actors, Musicians, and Athletes

They showcase pluralism on the world stage

The lanky Canadian emerged from the shadows, acknowledged the audience, and sat down at the grand piano. The Great Hall of the Moscow State Conservatory, which seated 1,800, was only half full. Glenn Gould, a twenty-five-year-old from Toronto, did not notice. Already, he was fixated on the music. At the insistence of his hosts, and uncharacteristically, he had donned a tuxedo. But even that ceased to bother him. Hunching over the keyboard in a posture that nobody else ever assumed while performing, he launched into the music of Johann Sebastian Bach.

The date was May 7, 1957. Into the rapt silence of the Great Hall, Gould played the first half of the program: four fugues and the Partita No. 6. When he was done, the audience exploded into applause. At intermission, music aficionados rushed outside to call their friends. *Hurry, hurry, you have to come and hear this. You have to hear this.*

By the time Gould regained his seat, after intermission, the Great Hall was packed. In *Glenn Gould: A Musical Force*, author Vladimir Konieczny describes how the pianist resumed playing with great energy, imbuing each piece with his "special magic." The Russians sat entranced, stunned by his interpretive virtuosity. Suddenly, Gould launched into a sonata by Austrian composer Alban Berg, a piece never before played in that country, which had banned modern music as a product of the decadent West. Before Gould had finished playing, people were shouting, "Bravo! Encore! Encore!"

Rising slowly to his feet, the young pianist emerged from the flow, a state of concentration that, in musicians, athletes, or performers of any kind, culminates in an accomplishment that exceeds normal expectations and crosses boundaries. To Glenn Gould himself, we shall devote further attention. Here we need remark only that, like every performer who appears in this section of *50 Canadians*, Gould was at home in the flow.

According to Mihaly Csikszentmihalyi, who originated the concept in *Flow: The Psychology of Optimal Experience*, that absorptive trance ensues only when an exceptional performer comes up against a difficult challenge. In the flow state, the author tells us, "The ego falls away. Time flies. Every action, movement, and thought follows inevitably from the previous one, like playing jazz. Your whole being is involved, and you're using your skills to the utmost."

In Part V, those we encounter include a peerless nightingale who voices the spirit of French Canada, a flag-waving rapper addressing the turmoil in northern Africa, and an idiosyncratic athlete who changed the face of his sport. We know that these performers are familiar with the flow because changing the world demands performance at near superhuman levels, and the requisite energy can be found nowhere else. We know, too, that in their diversity—ethnic, linguistic, racial, regional—they showcase what Canadian pluralism can accomplish. They serve as ambassadors for a vision of transformation, and demonstrate that pluralism can create excellence.

32

JAY SILVERHEELS

A talented Mohawk blazes a trail for Aboriginal actors

Many readers will remember Tonto from *The Lone Ranger*. As the title character's monosyllabic sidekick, Tonto co-starred in one of the biggest television series of the 1950s, an eight-year hit that went into reruns and attracted millions of viewers throughout North America. Some readers will know that the actor who played Tonto was called Jay Silverheels. But few will be aware that he was a Canadian, and that he was born Harold J. Smith on the Six Nations Reserve near Brantford, Ontario, on May 26, 1912. And fewer still will realize that, at considerable personal cost, Smith/Silverheels/Tonto kicked down Hollywood doors for Native North Americans, preparing the way for the careers of such actors as Chief Dan George, Graham Greene, Tom Jackson, and Tantoo Cardinal.

Harold J. Smith sprang from a Mohawk people that has produced many leaders. The most illustrious of them was Joseph Brant, who led First Nations warriors in fighting alongside the British during the American Revolution, and whose resulting, well-earned land grant gave rise to Brantford. Generations later, the father of "Tonto," George Alexander Smith, became the most decorated Native officer in the First World War. Harold J., the third of eleven children, grew up with his siblings in a rambling Victorian home. As a boy, he proved naturally athletic. But he also worked at developing himself physically. In a documentary film entitled *Jay Silverheels: The Man Beside the Mask,* viewers learn that as a slim youth, he was taken with the bodybuilding ads in such magazines as *Liberty* and *Popular Mechanics*—ads in which, for example, Charles Atlas undertook to transform ninety-seven-pound weaklings. His brother Steve Smith reports that when others would be out mowing hay or cutting wood, Jay would be in the barn pounding on a makeshift punching bag or pumping iron using weights he had built out of steel rods and cement blocks.

The boy excelled at lacrosse, that tough, stamina-testing sport invented by First Nations peoples. When he was sixteen and playing for the Mohawk Stars, the team manager bought all the boys white running shoes. According to a fellow player, when Jay Smith raced down the field, all you could see was white feet flying. Somebody called him "White Heels," but he objected: they couldn't call him that "because he was Indian." Somebody else suggested "Silverheels" and the nickname stuck. During the Great Depression, while working at odd jobs in Buffalo, 150 kilometres east of Brantford, Silverheels played semi-professional lacrosse with the New York Iroquois. He joined a local gym and began training as a boxer for the New York State Championships. In 1936, he placed second in the middleweight division of the Golden Gloves tournament.

Strikingly handsome, and working out now with real barbells, Silverheels earned extra money by modelling for local advertisers. A caption beneath a 1936 photo suggested that his slim, muscular frame and his "wavy, jet black hair and sharply chiselled features . . . qualify him for matinee idol honors should he ever take a whirl at that industry." While visiting Los Angeles to play exhibition lacrosse with Canada's national team, Silverheels met comedian Joe E. Brown, a Hollywood star so popular that his name appeared above the titles of his movies. The funny man got him an acting card to perform as an extra, and Silverheels began working in motion pictures as a stunt man, appearing in low-budget westerns and serials. Soon enough, having acquired a Screen Actors Guild "A" card, Silverheels was landing better roles. He worked with such "name actors" as Tyrone Power (*Captain from Castile*), Humphrey Bogart (*Key Largo*), and Glenn Ford (*Lust for Gold*).

In 1948, while performing in a B movie called *The Cowboy and the Indians*, Silverheels met Clayton Moore, an actor about to begin starring in an ABC television series called *The Lone Ranger*. The concept came from a radio show born on a single station in 1933. By this time, *The Lone Ranger* had spawned comic books and movies and was airing on more than 400 radio stations. Urged on by Moore, Silverheels auditioned for the role of Tonto and, in competition with three dozen other actors, won the part—a turning point in his career. As Patrick Watson writes in *The Canadians*, *The Lone Ranger* "was not just another radio serial; it was an extended morality play that worked out simplistic but powerfully presented issues of good and evil and was listened to by millions and millions of American and Canadian kids."

The TV series did typecast Silverheels, as can be seen in an online clip of Tonto's 1969 appearance on *The Tonight Show*. Host Johnny Carson assumes the role of a personnel director for a large corporation. While interviewing prospective employees, he summons "Mr. Tonto" from the wings. At this point, Silverheels has been working in motion pictures for three decades. He emerges in his buckskin outfit looking tall, trim, and fabulous. But instead of being treated like the articulate veteran actor that he is, Silverheels has to play along with a demeaning script. Carson asks, Who was his last employer? Tonto responds in his characteristic broken English. He calls the Lone Ranger *Kemo Sabe*, usually translated as "trusty scout" or "trusted friend": "I work thirty years as faithful sidekick for *Kemo Sabe*. Hunt, fish, make food, sew clothes, sweep up. Stay awake all night, listen for enemies for *Kemo Sabe*. Risk life for *Kemo Sabe*." He takes a beat: "Thirty lousy years." What's this? A glimmer of irony? Immediately, Silverheels is driven back into his stereotypical role. Carson inquires, "For this, what was your salary?" And the simple-minded Tonto responds, "Salary? What salary?" Ha, ha, ha.

Why does the actor play along? Consider the times. This was an explicitly racist era. With the benefit of hindsight, we can see that no Native American could dream of entering mainstream society in any but the stereotypical guise of the "big dumb Indian." Playing along is what Silverheels had to do to break into television and then Hollywood. He was the first Native North American to star in a television series. That series typecast him, but it also moved him onto the A-list of Hollywood actors, making him instantly recognizable to millions. It gave him what today we would call a platform.

Using that platform, Silverheels changed the world for First Nations actors. He voiced his opposition to the tradition of white actors portraying Aboriginal leaders in movies, arguing that Native Americans could do so more credibly. And in 1966, with a friend, he set up the American Indian Actors Workshop, an institution dedicated to enabling First Nations actors to hone their craft. That workshop helped many of them move beyond the roles that were available when Silverheels himself began to work.

In the 1970s, Jay Silverheels was preparing to play a couple of complex, challenging movie roles when he suffered a stroke that would lead to his death in 1980. Fortunately, he had already created Tonto, an iconic figure known to every child (and then adult) in North America. One especially memorable and revealing exchange arose out of the TV series. Silverheels himself created it, and delivered the punch line spontaneously, while fooling around on the set. The Lone Ranger and Tonto ride furiously over a hill, chased by a score of whooping bad guys. Suddenly, they find themselves surrounded by a hundred hostile Indians. The Lone Ranger says, "What do we do now, Tonto?" And at last the faithful sidekick abandons his pidgin English, "What do you mean *we*, white man?"

33

WAYNE, SHUSTER, AND PETERS

The Canadian comedian makes the world laugh with us

In an early routine known as "The Whole World's Mixing," Canadian comedian Russell Peters insists that racial integration is happening and there's nothing we can do about it. In 300 years, he tells us, there won't be any more white people. There won't be any more black people. "Everyone's going to be beige. And I don't care. I'm already beige." Peters takes a beat: he's into the flow. Then he insists that people will be hybrids. "It's inevitable," he says. "You can run from us now. But sooner or later, we're going to hump you."

In 2004, when someone uploaded a video of this routine onto the Internet, the thirty-four-year-old comedian could not believe it. He strode around in furious circles, punching his hand with his fist. How would he be able to make his living? His entire show was available for viewing at the click of a button. Russell Peters felt sick. But then came something unexpected. On the Internet, the video went viral. And Peters began receiving invitations from around the world. "That was my tipping point," he writes in his autobiography, *Call Me Russell*, "my shot heard round the world."

Russell Peters is a latecomer in a long parade of Canadian comedians. Starting with Wayne and Shuster, who became famous in the 1950s, the lineup includes Dan Aykroyd, John Candy, Jim Carrey, Rick Moranis, Catherine O'Hara, Eugene Levy, Martin Short, Dave Thomas, and Mike Myers. Sceptics will protest: *Wait, these people are mere entertainers. They don't change the world.* Well, yes they do. They work indirectly, changing individuals from the inside out, broadening our experience. By making fun of racism, Peters strikes a blow against it. And he does that performance after performance, all over the globe.

In the never-ending battle for freedom of expression, comedians work in the front lines. They extend the limits of language and subject matter. By challenging taboos, by venturing into the danger zones where people feel threatened, they increase tolerance. By making us laugh, they push back the boundaries of what we can talk about.

Most of the comedians named above, starting with Peters, have emerged from the Toronto area. Does humour spring naturally out of Scottish-Presbyterian southern Ontario? More likely, this geographical concentration arises out of critical mass and infrastructure. There are more people in the Greater Toronto Area (over five million) than in Vancouver, Calgary, Edmonton, and Ottawa combined.

In the 1970s, Toronto developed a network of nightclubs, improvisational comedy troupes, and even television shows where comedians could refine their humour and develop audience and career. The cornerstone was Second City, a sketch comedy outfit that, having been born in Chicago in 1959, created a second base in Toronto, which then developed a school, a touring company, and a television show that ran from 1976 to 1984. During that period, Mark Breslin launched a Toronto comedy club called Yuk Yuk's, which then evolved into a national chain. This infrastructure has grown increasingly complex.

But the international story of the Canadian comedian begins in 1958, when Wayne and Shuster first performed on *The Ed Sullivan Show.* Over the next dozen years, the comedy duo appeared on that show sixty-seven times, far more often than any other act. They reached a North American audience comprising tens of millions.

Louis Weingarten (1918–1990), also known as Johnny Wayne, and

Frank Shuster (1916–2002) were both born in Toronto. They met as high school students at Harbord Collegiate Institute, and began working together while studying theatre at the University of Toronto. In 1941, they launched a radio show, *The Wife Preservers*, which found them dispensing ludicrous household advice. This led to a national CBC Radio show, *Shuster and Wayne*. Starting in 1942, during the Second World War, they joined the Canadian army and entertained the troops. "Why shouldn't they cheer?" Shuster said as in one skit they sailed away. "*They're* not going!"

After the war, they became an overnight sensation on *The Ed Sullivan Show* with a skit that lampooned the murder of Julius Caesar in the style of a police procedural. In *50 Years of Comedy*, a retrospective video, Johnny Wayne observes, "We got so popular with Americans that even some Canadians started to watch us." Their wacky humour landed them a weekly television show, and then a series of long-running comedy specials on CBC-TV that ran into the 1980s. Occasionally, Wayne and Shuster made fun of ethnic accents, so laying a foundation for later arrivals.

In the late 1960s, as if to deliberately forge a transition, Frank Shuster's daughter, Rosie, married comedian Lorne Michaels and began writing comedy with him. In 1975, while working for NBC TV, Michaels launched *Saturday Night Live* (*SNL*), a mix of music and sketch comedy that drew heavily on Toronto's Second City comedy troupe. The original *SNL* cast included Dan Aykroyd, and away we go, hurtling towards the present.

Born and raised in Ottawa, Aykroyd got hooked on the blues at a nightclub called Le Hibou, where he heard such performers as Muddy Waters, Howlin' Wolf, Buddy Guy, Sonny Terry, and Brownie McGhee. He cut his teeth as a comedian in southern Ontario nightclubs, and ran a speakeasy (Club 505) in Toronto. Aykroyd spent four years as *SNL*'s youngest writer and cast member. He dazzled viewers and fellow professionals with his impersonations (Jimmy Carter, Richard Nixon, Vincent Price), and introduced fellow cast member John Belushi to the blues. Together, backed by professional musicians, they began performing as the Blues Brothers, which gave rise in 1980 to the blockbuster movie of that title.

A dozen years later, Aykroyd played a leading role in founding the House of Blues, which promoted African American cultural contributions. For three years ending in 2007, when it was sold to Live Nation, it was the second-largest live music promoter in the world, with seven venues and twenty-two amphitheaters around North America. Meanwhile, Aykroyd co-wrote and starred in *Ghostbusters* (1984), a comedic blockbuster whose evildoers included a lumbering Stay Puft Marshmallow Man. He was nominated for an Oscar as best supporting actor for *Driving Miss Daisy* (1989). He directed his first picture, *Nothing But Trouble*, in 1991, and has since appeared in dozens of movies and television shows.

In *Nothing But Trouble*, Aykroyd directed John Candy (1950–1994), a Canadian funny man who cut his comedic teeth in The Second City improvisational troupe (Toronto branch) and its *Second City Television* (*SCTV*) series. Highlights of his career include starring roles in *Uncle Buck* and *Planes, Trains and Automobiles*. Born just north of Toronto (Newmarket) and raised in the city, Candy began acting in low-budget films in his early twenties. In 1976, he began starring on *SCTV* (which was picked up by NBC) and in the early 1980s, he won Emmy Awards. Candy created numerous squirm-inducing characters, among them the Leutonian clarinetist Yosh Shmenge, star of the mockumentary *The Last Polka*. A superb mimic, Candy impersonated such diverse figures as Orson Welles, Julia Child, Luciano Pavarotti, Jimmy the Greek, Jackie Gleason, and Gertrude Stein.

Early on, he had a supporting role as a probation officer in *The Blues Brothers*. He appeared a couple of times on *Saturday Night Live*, starred in *Going Berserk*, and enjoyed a breakout role in the comedy *Splash*, playing opposite Tom Hanks. Then came *Planes, Trains and Automobiles* (1987) and *Uncle Buck* (1989), which made him an international figure. The last movie Candy finished was *Canadian Bacon*, a Michael Moore satire in which he played an American sheriff who led an invasion of Canada. It surfaced in 1995, the year after he died of a heart attack.

By then, Jim Carrey had arrived on the scene. In 1994, he had three hit movies: *Ace Ventura: Pet Detective*; *Dumb and Dumber*; and *The Mask*. Born in Newmarket thirteen years after Candy, Carrey grew up in Toronto and Burlington. The first time he tried stand-up, at the Toronto comedy club Yuk Yuk's, he bombed. He polished his act and returned to the stage, and this time he caught on. He moved quickly from open-mic nights to paid gigs, and then began opening for the comedian Rodney Dangerfield, who brought him to Las Vegas. From there, at nineteen, Carrey went to Hollywood, where he played at The Comedy Store and An Evening at the Improv. At twenty, he surfaced on *The Tonight Show*.

Now performing steadily, Carrey landed supporting roles in *Peggy Sue Got Married* and *Earth Girls Are Easy*. Then came *Dumb and Dumber*, which grossed over $270 million—the first of several pictures to make Carrey a comedic force. In 1997, he earned a Golden Globe best actor nomination for his performance in *Liar Liar*, and then he won Golden Globes with *The Truman Show* and *Man on the Moon*. In 2000, he played the title role in *How the Grinch Stole Christmas*, which became one of the highest grossing Christmas films of all time. His recent hits include *I Love You Phillip Morris* and *A Christmas Carol*, a 3D animated film in which he plays multiple characters.

Meanwhile, yet another alumnus of *Saturday Night Live*, Mike Myers, had joined the ranks of comedic royalty with *Wayne's World* (1992), in which he played a basement-dwelling slacker with a public-access television show. Born in Toronto in 1963, which makes him the same age as Carrey, Myers began acting in commercials at age eight. After high school, he spent three years with the Second City touring company, then moved to England and co-founded the improvisational Comedy Store Players. Back in Toronto, he rejoined Second City, moved to Chicago, and trained at the ImprovOlympic.

In the early 1980s, while working for Toronto's Citytv, he had created the slacker character Wayne Campbell. Working with another Second City comedian, Dana Carvey, he built a sketch that became a hit on *Saturday Night Live.* Out of this, he developed *Wayne's World*, one of the top movies of 1992. "Shyeah, and then monkeys might fly out my butt." Myers followed that with *So I Married an Axe Murderer* and *Wayne's World 2:* "We're not worthy! WE'RE NOT WORTHY!"

In 1997, he wrote and starred in the first of three hit films featuring Austin Powers, that "international man of mystery." He played the title character, but also the villain, Dr. Evil, and an incredibly gross Scottish giant called Fat Bastard. In the 2000s, Myers starred in *The Cat in the Hat,* and also in a series of animated blockbusters built around the ogre Shrek. In 2005, Myers became the second Canadian (after Jim Carrey) to win the MTV Generation Award for developing a unique style of comedy.

That same year, Canadian Russell Peters became the first South Asian to headline at the fabled Apollo Theatre in Harlem, New York. He had got his start in the Yuk Yuk Comedy clubs of Toronto. At one of these, he began playing an all-black comedy night called *Kenny Robinson's Nubian Disciples of Pryor.* Here, comedians faced a tough audience, and Peters saw dozens booed off the stage. But the crowd took to him. "That's where my first wave of support came from," he writes. "The black Caribbean community in Canada. I've never forgotten that." In Harlem, Peters made a splash, and soon he was fielding more offers than he could handle.

While growing up in Toronto and suburban Brampton, Peters had thought of himself as Indian. But he visited India at age twenty-eight and realized that the only Indian things about him were his parents and his skin tone: "Culturally, I'm not Indian at all, and that trip to India in 1998 brought that realization home. I'm Canadian." Before long, Peters was focusing his observational comedy on race and culture, using accents and doing impersonations while highlighting similarities rather than differences. Various fans have told him, he writes, "that even though they were Greek or Italian or Lebanese, they too had a father just like mine—they too had an 'Indian' father."

Based mainly in Los Angeles since 2006, Peters has performed all over the world, from mainland China and Hong Kong to Iran, Iraq, Afghanistan, and Sri Lanka. A single show in Sydney, Australia, drew almost 14,000 people, an event that some have described as the largest stand-up comedy show in that country's history. In 2009, he set a new United Kingdom attendance record for a one-off comedy show, attracting almost 16,000 people. For a Canadian comedian, and indeed for a stand-up comic of any nationality, this would once have been the stuff of dreams.

But remember the Stay Puft Marshmallow Man, the larger-than-life monster Dan Aykroyd created for *Ghostbusters*? Down through the decades, acting together, Canadian comedians created their own collective version. They started small with Wayne and Shuster, but then added not only Aykroyd but John Candy, Jim Carrey, Mike Myers, Russell Peters, and others too numerous to name, until today the collective Canadian comedian is a lumbering, beige-coloured Stay Puft Marshmallow Man. The Canadian comedic enterprise is a testament to diversity and tolerance. It changed the world by demonstrating that pluralism accommodates and fosters a sense of the ridiculous.

34

OSCAR PETERSON

First this Montreal jazzman took Manhattan

The year was 1949. New York impresario Norman Granz, creator of a concert series called Jazz at the Philharmonic, was in a Montreal taxicab driving to the airport in suburban Dorval. "The cabby had some music playing," he would say later, "and I assumed that it was a disc that some disc jockey was playing, and I asked him if he knew the station. I'd like to call them and find out who the pianist was with the trio." The cabby told him it wasn't a record, but a live performance. Montreal native Oscar Peterson was playing at a downtown club called the Alberta Lounge. According to biographer Gene Lees, Granz said, "Well, forget the airport. Turn around and let's go to the club."

This story has become the stuff of jazz legend. In *Oscar Peterson: The Will to Swing*, Lees notes that Peterson, at age twenty-four, had already been the subject of rave reviews in various American jazz magazines, and that Granz must have known him by reputation. The fact remains, Granz went to the Alberta Lounge, caught Peterson in performance, and invited him to play with a stellar bunch of jazz musicians at Carnegie Hall. Because Peterson was not a member of the New York musicians' union, as Alex Barris explains in another biography, Granz hit upon the idea of pretending to spot him in the audience and inviting him onstage as if spontaneously. According to Lees, Peterson himself had suggested that he surface first at a smaller venue, but Granz insisted. "Take your best shot, you'll know in one shot," he said. "You won't have to dilly-dally. If you make it, you'll know it. If you don't make it, you'll know that too."

Peterson proved a sensation. A headline in the *Canadian High News* of October 7, 1949, said it all: "Oscar Sets New York Back on Its Heels." But Lees is also correct to wonder how much Granz knew. Five years before, when Peterson was nineteen, *Down Beat* magazine carried a story titled, "Count Basie raves about young Canadian pianist." Then there was the occasion at a nightspot called the Chez Maurice, where the well-known Dizzy Gillespie band was headlining. Lees describes how Peterson arrived with a friend named Gerry Macdonald, and the Montreal crowd started clapping rhythmically: "We want Oscar. We want Oscar."

"Dizzy looked around," Macdonald later reported, "as if to say, 'Who the hell is Oscar?' It got so loud that finally Dizzy beckoned him to come up on the stage. Oscar sat at the piano. They decided to play 'What Is This Thing Called Love.' Oscar took about sixteen bars of introduction, and Dizzy's eyes were like saucers with disbelief. They got into the tune and then Oscar took a long solo. The guys in Dizzy's band just wigged out. The audience was screaming and yelling."

After the gig, the piano-man went on jamming with Gillespie until eight o'clock the next morning. So it does seem unlikely that the aficionado Granz had never heard of Peterson. Yet he was right about knowing "in one shot." After that first appearance at Carnegie Hall, the Canadian never looked back. According to Barris, in *Oscar Peterson: A Musical Biography*, the experts agree that Peterson's only possible peer as a jazz pianist was the legendary Art Tatum, who died in 1956. Saxophonist Charlie Parker once said of Peterson, "I wish I could play like his right hand." Duke Ellington called him the "Maharajah of the keyboard." But Canadian trombone player Murray Ginsberg summarized best, "Oscar Peterson is to jazz what Glenn Gould is to classical music."

Born August 25, 1925, in Montreal, Peterson came from a musical family. His father, Daniel, had been a sailor who taught himself to play "a kind of little organ," he told Lees. The older Peterson had immigrated from St. Kitts in the West Indies, and found work with the Canadian Pacific Railway as a sleeping car porter. "If you were black in Montreal," Peterson said later, "and you were lucky enough to have a job, then you were working for the railroad." The man savoured classical music, and insisted that all of his children have music lessons. Oscar's older sister, Daisy, would become a well-known music teacher.

From the age of five, Oscar took trumpet lessons. But at seven, having contracted tuberculosis, he spent thirteen months in hospital. Emerging with weakened lungs, he switched instruments to piano, working at first with sister Daisy. He would start in the morning doing scales and exercises, and practising classical pieces. "I practised time," he told a musicologist in 1959, "by playing against myself and letting the left hand take a loose, undulating shape while making the right hand stay completely in time. Then I'd reverse the process, keeping the left hand rigid and making the right hand stretch and contract." When he wasn't at school, the boy would practise at least six hours a day. He would play from nine until noon, pause for lunch, practise again from one until six, and then return to the piano after dinner: "I'd keep practising until my mother would come in and drag me away from the piano so the family could get some sleep."

In his teens, Peterson absorbed classical music, everything from the fugues of Johann Sebastian Bach to the concertos of Sergei Rachmaninoff. At fourteen, he began studying with Paul de Marky, a Hungarian immigrant with a beautiful touch. Oscar would go early to his lesson and wait outside the studio just to listen to "this beautiful sound that he'd get out of the instrument." Oscar heard an older brother "fooling around" with a couple of jazz classics and he, too, started experimenting with boogie-woogie. His father brought home a record of the Benny Goodman band, with pianist Teddy Wilson, and according to a video, *Oscar Peterson: The Life of a Legend*, the young man realized, "This was it! This was exactly the form and direction that I needed in order to continue on my own in the jazz world."

At fifteen, Oscar Peterson won a national CBC-Radio competition, the prize being a weekly fifteen-minute radio slot. He was "feeling very smug" about his prowess at the piano, he would say later, in what became another oft-told story. His father produced a recording of "Tiger Rag" by Art Tatum, a virtuoso jazz pianist, nearly blind since birth, noted for his speed and dexterity. At first, young Peterson swore that there were two people playing. His father insisted otherwise. "When I finally admitted to myself that it was one man," Peterson said later, "I gave up the piano for a month. I figured it was hopeless to practise."

Peterson resumed playing. The entertainment scene was booming because, with the Second World War in progress, Montreal served as an armed forces staging area. Peterson played with his school band, the Victory Serenaders, and landed a few paying gigs with the Jump Crew. A radio broadcast caught the ear of Johnny Holmes, one of Montreal's top bandleaders. Peterson told his father he wanted to quit school to become a jazz pianist. The older man, always a perfectionist, responded, "I'm not going to let you quit school to become a jazz pianist. If you want to be the *best*, then I'll let you go. But you have to be the best. There is no second-best."

In 1942, at age seventeen, Oscar Peterson began playing professionally with the well-established Johnny Holmes Orchestra. Peterson needed no instruction in keyboard technique, but Holmes coached him in performance. Later, the pianist said, "I was overdoing boogie-woogie and was completely lost for slow tunes. Holmes was responsible for changing this. He built up my technique and was responsible for the style I put on records." Peterson put out the first of those records at age nineteen. Urged on by his mother, he had telephoned RCA Victor, got through to someone in artist development, and secured an audition. In 1945, he recorded boogie-woogie versions of "The Sheik of Araby" and "I Got Rhythm." They sold well, and soon he was recording regularly. He performed in Winnipeg and Toronto and got profiled in *Liberty* magazine. In *Metronome*, a reporter declared, "For a county reputedly as unhip as Canada in the creation of musicians, a miracle has occurred. His name is Oscar Peterson."

The young musician also came up against racial prejudice. Even well-meaning interviewers would patronize him, referring to him as "a coloured boy." In the early days, Peterson just ignored these remarks: "I overlooked that because I wanted to get to where I had some clout. That was the sole reason." Later, he would be more inclined to confront racism, sometimes to the point of physical altercation. For years Peterson was the only black musician in the Johnny Holmes Orchestra. He became the feature attraction. At one point, Holmes had to take a stand against the Ritz-Carlton Hotel: no Peterson, no band. The hotel caved. In the video about his life, Peterson noted, "During this time we actually broke the racial barrier by appearing in several uptown clubs where black musicians had not gone previously." Peterson would be engaged in this struggle for the rest of his life.

But now came his 1949 breakthrough at Carnegie Hall, when he played with Ella Fitzgerald, Coleman Hawkins, and Buddy Rich, among others. According to biographer Lees, "If he went through the shock of meeting and working with his idols, he also, by all evidence, went through a cultural trauma on touring for the first time in the United States, where the racial discrimination was not tacit and non-violent, but entrenched, obvious, accepted, and brutal." At the urging of Norman Granz, Peterson not only became a regular with Jazz at the Philharmonic, but began leading first one trio and then another. When he brought aboard guitarist Herb Ellis, a Caucasian, he learned that racism cut both ways: "I would get hate letters in Chicago about Herbie Ellis being with the group—from both sides. . . . I'd get hate letters about, 'What is that white cat doing in the band? He can't play nothing—he's white.' Whatever that had to do with it, I don't know." Even so, Peterson would insist that "the jazz world became the most integrated community in American society . . . the overall picture in the jazz world was one of thorough, albeit unheralded, integration, long before people started swapping bus seats in the south."

As a musician, Peterson proved fiercely competitive. With guitarist Joe Pass, he would engage in musical dialogues: "He inspired me so intensely that I seemed to have reached a creative level that might have gone undiscovered without him. Joe helped make me a better player." In the biographical video, Peterson says, "I think we had the finest trio in jazz." Few would argue. The name of the game, he said, was to outplay the competition: "It was almost like the old gunfighter syndrome. Whenever we met up with any of our competitors, we would systematically set out to intimidate and destroy them musically." In the video, we see an example. While playing opposite jazz pianist Count Basie, the superlative Peterson goes so far over the top that he leaves Basie hollering and punching chords in protest. Peterson recorded two albums with the over-modest Basie, who said of the Canadian, "Oh, he's a lovely fellow, but you never know when he's going to sneak up on you and destroy you with his playing. He can be a monster." Basie described how the two would trade choruses, but then Peterson would get carried away: "He was wonderful but he was also terrible. Sometimes I'd just think about how I was going to be with that monster that evening, and my whole day was ruined."

With Ray Brown and Herb Ellis, Peterson is said to have redefined the jazz trio, as the three men pushed each other to their musical limits. Landmark recordings include *The Oscar Peterson Trio at the Stratford Shakespearean Festival* and a live album recorded at the Town Tavern in Toronto, entitled *On the Town with the Oscar Peterson Trio*. The Oscar Peterson Trio became legendary, not just in Canada and the United States, but throughout Europe and around the world. In the mid-1970s, for three years, Peterson hosted a television program for the BBC, and brought aboard such guests as Ella Fitzgerald, Count Basie, and Jorge Bolet.

During a musical career that spanned sixty years, Peterson played thousands of concerts and made more than 200 recordings. Along the way, he won eight Grammy Awards, including one for lifetime achievement, and a multitude of other honours. Peterson recorded several vocal numbers, and also composed pieces for piano, trio, quartet, and big band, among them *Canadiana Suite* and "Hymn to Freedom," his heartfelt contribution to the American civil rights movement. In the 1960s, having moved to Toronto, he co-founded and headed the Advanced School of Contemporary Music. Later, he taught in the jazz program at York University, and then served with distinction as chancellor of that institution.

Peterson, who overcame a stroke in the 1990s and died of kidney failure in 2007, is remembered as an ambassador of his chosen musical genre. "Jazz itself will remain a unique and noble art," he insisted. "In spite of racism, in spite of the desire of music magnates to establish tyrannical control and dismantle all that jazz means and has achieved, it retains a devoted following throughout the world, and its vast legacy of recordings will never be forgotten." Many aficionados consider Peterson the greatest jazz pianist who ever lived. Peterson himself, looking back in the aforementioned video, reflected that if he brought anything distinctive to jazz, "it was my Canadian background." Peterson changed the world by carrying Canadian attitudes and values, especially those regarding racial equality and tolerance, far beyond this country's borders.

In 1993, then prime minister Jean Chrétien wanted to make the jazzman Lieutenant-Governor of Ontario, but Peterson declined for health reasons. "He was the most famous Canadian in the world," Chrétien said at the time. He also revealed that Nelson Mandela became emotional when meeting Peterson: "They were both moved to meet each other. These were two men with humble beginnings who rose to very illustrious levels."

While critical of the tendency of Canadians to disparage their fellows—"How can he play any good? He comes from here! He's a Canadian!"—Peterson said that he always felt more at home in Canada than in the United States. American president Bill Clinton would hail the musician as "the greatest jazz pianist in our times," but Peterson remained attached to the country that shaped him: "This is my country and I've always been comfortable here. I've always loved it."

35

JACQUES PLANTE

A nomadic netminder changes the face of hockey

The turning point came during a regular-season hockey game. The date was November 1, 1959. At thirty years of age, Jacques Plante was the best goaltender in the National Hockey League. He played for the best team, the Montreal Canadiens, and the toughest coach, Toe Blake. Plante was famous for his daring nomadic style. Where other goalies would remain in the crease, he loved nothing more than to challenge incoming opponents for the puck, no matter where it might be. During this particular game against the fifth-place New York Rangers, Plante raced star forward Andy Bathgate into the corner and gave him a poke check. Years later, Bathgate would recall, "I went head first into the boards, cutting my ear and cheek."

In *Jacques Plante: The Man Who Changed the Face of Hockey*, author Todd Denault gives the most complete and credible account of what happened next. Bathgate got stitches and returned to the game, bent on exacting revenge. During the next rush, he came down the left wing and waited until players jammed the front of the net. "Plante used to sort of sit with his rear end in the net so he could get across quickly," he said, "and his head was sticking out there just like a chicken, so he could see what was going on." Bathgate fired a wrist shot: "It wasn't a blast, and I wasn't trying to score because the angle was really bad, but his head was sticking out and I decided if he wanted to play those games . . ."

Plante didn't know what hit him. He sprawled onto his stomach, his face surrounded by a growing pool of blood. Bathgate, who had intended to administer "a little love tap," raced over and lifted his head. The Montreal trainer charged onto the ice. The puck had hit Plante square in the face, opening a two-inch gash that ran from the corner of his mouth to his nose. Ironically, this accident offered the goalie the chance he had been awaiting. Before the night was done, he would revolutionize the game of hockey simply by donning a mask— an action that, until now, had been regarded as not only sissified, but subversive.

Jacques Plante was arguably the most innovative goaltender of all time—not just because of the mask, but because of his adventurous style of play. Born January 17, 1929 on a farm near Mont Carmel, Quebec, the eldest of eleven children, he grew up in Shawinigan, where his father worked in a factory. At age three, he began playing hockey, using a stick his father carved from a tree root. At first he played defence, but he suffered from asthma and found he could not skate hard for long periods. Plante switched to goalie and wore potato-sack pads stuffed with rags and wooden panels. At Christmas 1936, he received his first regulation goaltender's stick. Because he played outdoors through freezing Quebec winters, and as a goalie never left the ice to warm up, he got into the habit of wearing a tuque. He learned from his mother how to knit, and would fashion his own tuques even later, after he began playing professionally.

From age twelve, Plante played organized hockey. At fourteen, he was playing for teams in four different age groups, from midget to intermediate. He also played for his father's factory team, earning fifty cents a game. Professional teams tried to lure him away, but his parents insisted that he finish high school. In 1947, he graduated at the top of his class. A few weeks later, Plante joined the Quebec Citadelles. And now he made his first innovation. Instead of remaining in his net to block shots, he began coming out to play the puck. Ahead of him were four defencemen with various flaws, he explained later in a documentary called *Jacques Plante: The Man Behind the Mask*: "One couldn't skate backwards. One couldn't shoot the puck up to the blue line. One of the other two could only turn one way. Somebody had to clear loose pucks, and I began to do the job myself. It worked so well that I kept right on doing it. Right up to the NHL."

In 1952, Jacques Plante played three games for the Montreal Royals. Two years later, he became starting goalie for the Canadiens, a position he kept for nine years. In 1955, the strong-minded Toe Blake, himself an ex–hockey star, became head coach—and so began a clash of wills. At this point in hockey history, although goalies kept taking pucks in the face, none of them wore masks. In 1930, a netminder named Clint Benedict, whose nose had been broken, briefly wore a leather protector. But he abandoned that when his nose healed. Conventional wisdom insisted that masks were for sissies. Also, that they reduced visibility and made a goalie less effective.

Jacques Plante wasn't so sure. He had been a catcher in baseball and a goalie in lacrosse, and in both those sports he wore a mask. In 1954, during a hockey practice, he suffered a fractured right cheek-bone and ended up missing five weeks. One year later, he got his left cheek fractured and missed more playing time. Not long afterwards, he received an anonymous gift: a small plastic mask that extended from just above his chin to halfway up his forehead. He tried it in practice and found that it obscured his vision: "I was just thinking of taking it off," he said later, "when a puck hit the mask right in front of the eyeholes." He continued wearing it in practice and began experimenting with alternatives.

During the 1958 Stanley Cup Finals, Plante was knocked cold when a puck hit him in the forehead. After a twenty-minute delay, he finished playing the game. But the incident got one hockey fan thinking. Bill Burchmore, a marketing representative for Fibreglass Canada, began wondering about making a fibreglass mask that could be moulded to fit a player's face. He wrote to Plante. Initially sceptical, the goalie agreed to have a plaster cast made of his face. Burchmore then constructed the mask, which proved lightweight and incredibly strong. What's more, because it was so thin, Plante found that it did not obstruct his vision. In September 1959, the goalie went to see NHL president Clarence Campbell, who gave the mask a green light for league play, hoping that it would reduce injuries.

Coach Toe Blake reacted differently. With Plante talking about wearing the mask all the time, Blake told reporters, "He can practise with one if he wants. But no goalie of mine is going to wear one in a game. We're here to win." The coach's opposition would have silenced most hockey players. But in the October 1959 issue of *Hockey Pictorial*, Plante turned up insisting that goalie masks should be mandatory, and blaming the lack of young goalies on the lack of facial protection. He claimed that a mask had saved him from injury twenty or twenty-five times in workouts, and insisted that "the day is coming when goalies will wear them—they'll have to." Blake continued to insist that a mask hampered vision, adding that it invited ridicule and suggested that a goalie was puck-shy. That was why, on November 1, 1959, Plante began the game without a mask and, when hit, suffered that terrible gash. Holding a white towel to his face, obviously badly injured, Plante made his way to the rinkside medical clinic.

Different writers provide subtly different versions of events. But in those days, teams dressed only one goalie, and had the option, if their netminder was felled, of bringing in an in-house amateur. If Plante left the game, the Canadiens could kiss victory goodbye. Hockey writer Red Fisher hurried to the clinic and, according to Denault, arrived in time to see Plante "staring into the mirror and using his fingers to separate the ghastly cut." Plante said, "Pretty ugly." The doctor scraped away bits of loose flesh, and the goalie lay stoically, without anesthetic, as the man stitched up his face: seven stitches. When Toe Blake arrived and asked how he felt, Plante said, from the table, "I want to play with my mask on."

"We'll see, we'll see."

With his white sweater caked in blood, Plante returned to the ice and skated to the Canadiens dressing room, where the coach waited. Blake took one look at the shape his goalie was in and said, "Why don't you wear a mask for the rest of the game." Plante intended to do exactly that. He reached into his kitbag and pulled out his white fibreglass mask. Then he made his way back onto the ice. He remained almost unbeatable, and the Canadiens won three goals to one. After the game, Plante told a reporter, "I may look like Frankenstein but I'm not out there to stop pucks with my face." Later, he would observe that, in his career, he had suffered four broken noses and two broken cheekbones, and had taken 200 stitches to his head.

For a while, the mask continued to meet resistance, even from other goaltenders. But Plante quieted the naysayers with his sensational play. Seven times, he won the Vezina Trophy as outstanding goalie, and once he won the Hart Trophy as most valuable player. Sports writer Red Fisher put it this way: "He was different. He was a splendid goaltender. He's certainly the best goaltender that I ever saw, and I've seen a few over the years." Today, no serious goaltender in the world would dream of playing hockey without a mask. And that is down to Jacques Plante, the stubborn French Canadian goalie who changed the face of hockey.

36

LEONARD COHEN

A Zen troubadour encircles the world with Magic

In the world of Leonard Cohen, the concept of flow gains resonance. The idea of entering an absorptive trance in which the ego falls away owes much to Zen Buddhism; the very word "Zen" translates as "meditative state" or "absorption." In the late 1990s, after years of training at the Mt. Baldy Zen Center, near Los Angeles, Cohen was ordained as a Zen Buddhist monk. And the corollary notion that flow gives rise to magical moments, to synchronicities that intrude upon humdrum existence, is one that resonates with Cohen. This is the author who, in a celebrated passage from *Beautiful Losers*, famously insisted: "Magic never hid, Magic never faltered, though many poor men lied, and many hurt men wondered, Magic never weakened, Magic is Alive."

As unlikely as it sounds, this incantation speaks to a phenomenon that has marked Cohen's whole life. The story of his miraculous resurrection, when in his seventies he went back on the road to international acclaim after being robbed of his life savings, is familiar to most Canadians. Most also know the magic that swept up his song "Hallelujah" twenty-five years after he wrote it, and turned it into a global phenomenon. But few realize that less dazzling synchronicities have also punctuated the singer-songwriter's life.

Consider the events of 1984, when Cohen passed through Calgary, Alberta, while promoting his *Book of Mercy*. He had agreed to meet a journalist for dinner in the downtown hotel where he was staying. But on arriving at the restaurant, the place looked all wrong: white linen tablecloths, hovering waiters, two businessmen eating alone. Exchanging a glance, the new arrivals agreed wordlessly to go elsewhere, anywhere else. Cohen retrieved his portable cassette tape player and, with the journalist, drove across the Bow River to a restaurant called Flix. Decorated with old movie posters, it boasted Montreal smoked meat sandwiches. Cohen and the journalist ate two of these with fries, and also drank a bottle of dry red wine. They briefly discussed his book, but Cohen was more interested in sharing the songs destined for his album *Various Positions*. He provided earphones, and grinned happily as the journalist listened to "Dance Me to the End of Love," "The Law," and "Hallelujah." Before leaving the restaurant, Cohen visited the washroom. On his way back to the table, a waitress stopped him. She handed him a note that began "Dearest Leonard" and was signed "Lorraine."

Suddenly excited, Cohen questioned the waitress. But the author of the note had already departed. Out front on the sidewalk, Cohen said, "Why didn't she come over to the table?" He put his hand to his forehead. "She didn't want to intrude. What delicacy!"

Eighteen years before, in 1966, Cohen had resided briefly in Edmonton, 280 kilometres north. One wintry night during a blizzard, he had arrived back at his hotel and found two young women with backpacks sheltering in the doorway. While hitchhiking, they had run out of money. Cohen insisted that they stay in his room. He gave them the double bed, sat down in the armchair and, while gazing out at the storm, composed the song "Sisters of Mercy."

Now, almost two decades later, in a different city, Cohen had received a note from Lorraine, one of those original "sisters." It said that the other sister, Barbara, had moved to San Francisco. As to how Lorraine ended up at this obscure eatery at the same moment as

Cohen, who had arrived in so unlikely a manner, he grinned: "What did I tell you? Magic is alive."

Leonard Cohen, who would appear to live permanently in the flow, was born in Montreal on September 21, 1934, to a Jewish family that resided in Upper Westmount. His father died when he was nine. At high school and then university, he shone, becoming president of the debating society and also of a fraternity, and winning awards for public speaking. At fifteen he discovered the poetry of Federico García Lorca, and the following year he started singing folk songs while working as a camp counsellor.

At Montreal's McGill University, Cohen met literary figures, among them Louis Dudek, F.R. Scott, A.M. Klein, Hugh MacLennan, and, most crucially of all, Irving Layton. These poets and fiction writers spotted Cohen's talent. He thrived. And in 1956, as a strikingly handsome undergraduate, he published his first book of poetry, *Let Us Compare Mythologies*. He tried a term at law school, then spent a year hanging out in New York at Columbia University. Back in Canada, he visited publisher Jack McClelland, an emerging power in Canadian publishing, and convinced him to bring out his second book of poems, *The Spice-Box of Earth*. When it appeared, critic Robert Weaver declared Cohen "probably the best young poet in English Canada right now."

Cohen landed a grant from the Canada Council and used it to buy a small house on the Greek island of Hydra. There, he devoted himself to writing. In 1963, he published an autobiographical first novel, *The Favourite Game*, which revealed what would become a life-long obsession with women and sexuality. Three years later, he brought out *Beautiful Losers*, which contains an early version of "Magic Is Alive," and has been rightly described as "by turns historical and surreal, religious and obscene, comic and ecstatic." One writer called it "the most radical (and beautiful) experimental novel ever published in Canada."

Some years before, as a McGill undergraduate, Cohen had dabbled in music. With a trio called the Buckskin Boys, he had played mostly in church basements and high school gymnasiums. In New York, he had heard Jack Kerouac and other Beat writers perform poetry to music. By the early 1960s, in Montreal, he was experimenting with this. But because he was spending part of each year in Greece, Cohen did not discover Bob Dylan until 1966. Dylan's work, with its mix of vernacular poetry and music, proved a revelation. His own acclaimed books of poetry had sold a couple of hundred copies. His two novels, which had demanded massive investments of time and energy, had sold a few thousand. Cohen saw that he could not make a living in literature. But what about songwriting? He hurried south to New York, to the centre of a burgeoning folk music scene, and banged on doors until they opened.

Singer Judy Collins scored a hit with his song "Suzanne," and repeated with "Bird on the Wire." In December 1967, Cohen released his first album: *Songs of Leonard Cohen*. At two-year intervals, he brought out *Songs from a Room* and *Songs of Love and Hate*. Through the 1970s, he continued to publish books of poetry (*The Energy of Slaves*; *Selected Poetry of Leonard Cohen*; *Death of a Lady's Man*). But he devoted most of his energy to songwriting and performing.

And it is as a singer-songwriter that he has made a difference internationally. Leonard Cohen changed the world by smuggling poetry—complex, highbrow work—into pop music. He set a new standard for lyrics. This he might disavow, but Cohen has always revelled in obfuscation. As early as 1965, in the documentary *Ladies and Gentlemen . . . Mr. Leonard Cohen*, we see him explaining his flat-out refusal to "drop the con." Decades later, while working on his album *I'm Your Man*, he would declare himself a mere entertainer. "I never thought I *was* in showbiz," he would say. "Now I know what I am. I'm not a novelist. I'm not the light of my generation. I'm not the spokesman for a new sensibility. I'm a songwriter living in L.A. and this is my record."

Accolades and honours have come in both literature and music. They include inductions into halls of fame and awards from Ireland, the United States, Croatia, and Spain, as well as a Governor General's Performing Arts Award for Lifetime Artistic Achievement. This last is especially notable because in 1968, Cohen made headlines by declining a Governor General's Literary Award for Poetry. Clearly, he'd had a change of heart. But at one point he came close to explaining his self-transformations: "You've got to recreate your personality so that you can live a life appropriate to your predicament."

In 1970, Cohen toured throughout the United States, Canada, and Europe, and shone especially at the Isle of Wight Festival in the United Kingdom. The next year, film director Robert Altman used several of his songs in the movie *McCabe & Mrs. Miller*. By 1976, Cohen was again touring Europe, where he found his most receptive audiences. In four months, he gave fifty-five shows, including one at the Montreux Jazz Festival. In 1979 and '80, Cohen toured Australia, Israel, and Europe, an adventure that spawned a film called *The Song of Leonard Cohen*. His 1984 album, *Various Positions*, included "Dance Me to the End of Love," which became his first video clip. Cohen conducted his biggest tour yet around Europe and Australia, and his first tour in North America since 1975. At a festival in Poland, which was under martial law, Cohen performed "The Partisan," and it became a hymn of the Polish Solidarity movement.

Cohen had a quiet period. But in 1987, a tribute album by Jennifer Warnes, *Famous Blue Raincoat*, rejuvenated his career. The following year, he released *I'm Your Man*, one of his most acclaimed albums. Again, he toured around the world, playing to packed houses. In the 1990s, Cohen's songs turned up in such movies as *Exotica* and *Natural Born Killers*. Cohen had practised Zen Buddhism for years, and in 1994, he began what became a five-year retreat at the Mt. Baldy Zen Center. He then resumed writing and recording songs, though by 1999, when he turned sixty-five, he had ceased touring.

In 2005, however, Cohen discovered with a shock that he had been robbed of his life savings. He sued his former business manager, Kelley Lynch, for stealing more than $5 million. Eventually found guilty in a jury trial, Lynch was sentenced to eighteen months in prison, plus five years' probation. According to *The Guardian*, Cohen said, "It gives me no pleasure to see my one-time friend shackled to a chair in a court of law, her considerable gifts bent to the service of darkness, deceit, and revenge." After noting that Lynch had accomplished "a massive depletion of my retirement savings and year earnings," Cohen added that he hoped a spirit of understanding would "convert her heart from hatred to remorse, from anger to kindness, from the deadly intoxication of revenge to the lowly practices of self-reform."

Cohen was awarded $9 million, but collecting would prove impossible. At age seventy-four, with no pension plan established, the singer-songwriter went back on the road. And here, again, we see magic: people turned out in droves, and critics exhausted their superlatives. In Ireland, Cohen won the Meteor Music Award for best international performance of the year. In New Zealand, a notoriously tough-minded reviewer wrote, "This was the best show I have ever seen." In Sydney, Australia, an audience of 12,000 gave Cohen five standing ovations. While he was there, on learning that the Yarra Valley had been devastated by fire, Cohen donated $200,000 to an emergency appeal.

Not long afterwards, in 2008, Cohen's song "Hallelujah" became a phenomenon in the United Kingdom. An emerging singer named Alexandra Burke won a national competition on a hit television show by singing a gospel version. Her sensational rendition rocketed to number one on the charts and became the fastest-selling single by a female artist in UK history. An older version by Jeff Buckley then shot to number two, and Cohen's original rendition, released on *Various*

Positions more than two decades before, climbed to number thirty-four. Driven by this British mania, "Hallelujah" sold more than five million digital copies by year's end, so becoming the fastest-selling single in European history. At last count, according to a 2012 biography entitled *I'm Your Man: The Life of Leonard Cohen*, the song has been covered by more than 300 artists. A writer in *Maclean's* called it "the closest thing pop music has to a sacred text," and biographer Sylvie Simmons echoed that sentiment, declaring the song "a kind of all-purpose, ecumenical/secular hymn for the new millennium."

Leonard Cohen was in the flow—indeed, rolling in the deep. He kept touring. In July 2010, when he played in Croatia, sixteen of his albums entered the Croatian top forty. In August, he played to sellout houses in Ireland, Austria, Belgium, Germany, and Scandinavia. Then came Italy, Germany, Portugal, Spain, Switzerland, and Austria. Cohen kept going: France, Poland, Slovenia, Slovakia. Then he returned to New Zealand and Australia before playing the west coast of North America. As this is written, late in 2012, Cohen remains on the road, forever young, forever a stranger. He shows no signs of stepping out of Magic, or of giving up the Holy Game of Poker. Some claim to see a highway, curling up like smoke above his shoulder.

37

GLENN GOULD

An eccentric pianist changes the way we hear music

In Moscow in 1957, before Glenn Gould had finished the inaugural performance introduced on page 203, audience members were on their feet shouting, "Bravo! Encore! Encore!" And when at last the twenty-five-year-old Canadian was spent and emerged from the flow to take a bow, the Great Hall of the Moscow State Conservatory swelled with applause. Slowly, slowly, the applause turned into a rhythmic clapping that reached to the rafters. This was the highest possible compliment. A giant basket of blue chrysanthemums appeared onstage, and still the audience was hollering, "Encore! Encore!"

So it began, the pianist's groundbreaking tour of Cold War Russia. Gould played the next night at Tchaikovsky Concert Hall with the Moscow Philharmonic Orchestra. A few nights later, he was back at the Great Hall, where he gave a recital and a talk. He focused now on "forbidden music," bent on introducing Russians not only to Berg, but to Arnold Schoenberg, Ernst Krenek, Anton Webern. Professors pleaded with Gould to play Bach and Beethoven, those far safer figures, because what if the authorities found out? At last he performed some Bach, offering up the Goldberg Variations—the work with which, two years before, he had originally stunned the music world. Again he elicited gasps of admiration, the experts floored by his virtuoso technique, his idiosyncratic stylings, and what they recognized as virtually a reinterpretation of one of the greatest composers in the history of music.

Gould travelled to Leningrad, but his reputation arrived first. The hall was overflowing, with extra chairs onstage, and people showered the stage with flowers and endless applause. In the street, Russian strangers cheered Gould or embraced him. He was almost pathologically averse to such physical contact, but in Russia, he tolerated it. He wrote a letter to his dog, Banquo, telling him that, as a result of the Second World War, few dogs lived in Russia: "You would have the field all to yourself." Onward to Berlin he went, there to play with the legendary conductor Herbert von Karajan and the Berlin Philharmonic Orchestra. The Germans, too, recognized and hailed Gould as a stupendous talent, comparing him with the greatest they had known. Onward to Frankfurt, then to Austria and the Vienna Festival. More applause, more flowers, more encores.

If Gould had never returned to Europe, already he had made such an impression that he would never be forgotten. But the following summer, and the summer after that, he went back. He performed at the Salzburg Festival and the Brussels World's Fair. He performed in Sweden, Germany, Italy, and Israel, giving eleven performances in eighteen days. In London, he made his debut with the London Symphony Orchestra and gave two recitals for the BBC. He received the Harriet Cohen Bach Medal, the first of numerous prestigious awards.

By now the year was 1959, and Gould had been a prodigy for longer than he could remember. Born in Toronto on September 25, 1932, to Presbyterian parents of Scottish and English ancestry, he had been listening to classical music since before he emerged into the world, kicking and screaming. Both his parents came from musical families, and his mother, in particular, had been bent on seeing him become a musician. As a baby, he did more humming than crying, and he wiggled his fingers so much that a doctor predicted he would become either a physician or a pianist. At age three, he demonstrated perfect pitch. He learned to read music before he read words and, unusually, he struck not chords but single notes on a piano and listened to them fade. At five, he told his father, "I'm going to be a concert pianist." Soon he was playing for family and friends, and at six, he performed one of his own pieces at the Emmanuel Presbyterian Church, near the family home in the Toronto Beaches district.

That year, his parents took him to hear a performance by the virtuoso pianist Josef Hofmann, who made what Gould would later describe as a staggering impression. He would remember how, driving home in the car, "I was in that wonderful state of half-awakeness in which you hear all sorts of incredible sounds going through your mind. They were all *orchestral* sounds, but *I* was playing them all, and suddenly I was Hofmann. I was enchanted." At age ten, having covered the basics with his mother, Gould entered the Royal Conservatory of Music. He studied piano with composer and pianist Alberto Guerrero, who taught him a singular technique: how to pull down on the piano keys rather than strike them from above.

At the family cottage on Lake Simcoe, Gould fell from a boat ramp and hurt his back. His father built him an adjustable-height chair, which enabled him to sit very low, and he used this chair, battered and unsightly as it became, for the rest of his performing life—one of his eccentricities.

Gould showed stunning dexterity in performing a vast repertoire and, at age twelve, passed the final Conservatory exam in piano at the top of his class. Through his teenage years, he continued to dazzle, showing extraordinary clarity and control despite such idiosyncrasies as vocalizing or humming to himself and swaying his body in a clockwise motion. At thirteen he gave a first public performance on the organ, and the following year, with the Toronto Symphony Orchestra, he played the first movement of Beethoven's 4th Piano Concerto. At fifteen he gave his first solo recital, and in 1950, his first recital on radio with the CBC.

In 1952, Gould became the first pianist to play on CBC-TV. Two years later, he performed with the Montreal Symphony Orchestra. And the year after that, he made American debuts in Washington, D.C., and at the Town Hall in New York. His childhood vision became a reality: he was the piano virtuoso, the Hofmann, and he gave concerts around the world. After his 1957 tour of the Soviet Union, when he became the first North American to play there since the end of the Second World War, Gould astonished one expert audience after another. But in the early 1960s, he began to wonder: Was this all there was? At first merely disillusioned with constantly performing, Gould began to see the public concert as "a force of evil," one that turned musicians into competitors before an audience watching only for errors. An eloquent writer, though sometimes florid, he elaborated on these views. "The justification of art," he wrote in 1962, "is the internal combustion it ignites in the hearts of men and not its shallow, externalized, public manifestations. The purpose of art is not the release of a momentary ejection of adrenaline but is, rather, the gradual, life-long construction of a state of wonder and serenity."

Despite such declarations, Gould stunned the music world when, after a concert in Los Angeles in 1964, at age thirty-two, he retired from performing. Where other pianists performed 100 concerts a year, Gould had given fewer than 200 in total, including only forty in Europe. And yet, he had changed the way the world listened to classical music, most notably that of Johann Sebastian Bach. Nor did he cease working. He had long enjoyed what he called a "love affair with the microphone," and for him that entailed recording music.

For Gould, the creation of a musical composition did not end with a musical score. A performer made creative choices. Not only that, but in the studio, where he could mix and match, he gained more options and greater control, and could develop the music more completely. Gould saw no point in re-recording old pieces unless he brought new perspective to the material. Later, pianist Robert Silverman would declare Gould much more than a talent: "He studied. He thought. He was a profound musicologist. He had more understanding of what he was playing than 99 per cent of pianists when they play on the concert stage."

So began a new phase: recording, writing, broadcasting. The new Gould likened music to film, and saw himself as playing the role of director. A two-hour film takes many hours to achieve, and undergoes countless revisions; given contemporary technology, why should music be any different? Gould explored these and other ideas in lectures, convocation speeches, articles, and radio and television documentaries. His outstanding productions—examples of his contrapuntal radio technique, using simultaneous voices— included the Solitude Trilogy, which comprised *The Idea of North*, *The Latecomers* (about Newfoundland), and *The Quiet in the Land* (about Mennonites in Manitoba). *The Idea of North*, created on request for the Canadian centennial year of 1967, would be hailed as one of his greatest creations—"the realization of his desire to move from the world of performance to that of 'composition.'" So said one music scholar: "It was with *The Idea of North* that Gould seriously launched his new genre, and began his creative adventure."

Gould won Juno Awards and Grammy Awards and, after his death, he inspired biographies, plays, works of critical analysis, and even a Genie-winning film entitled *Thirty Two Short Films About Glenn Gould*. Almost twenty hours of his broadcast work, drawn from the years 1954 to 1977, would become available in the twenty-first century as a package set: *Glenn Gould on Television/The Complete CBC Broadcasts*. Music lovers would create the Glenn Gould Foundation to preserve his memory and extend his legacy, awarding a $50,000 prize every three years for an original work by a Canadian artist. The foundation would rightly proclaim him "an individual who has earned international recognition as the result of a highly exceptional contribution to music and its communication, through the use of any communications technologies."

But Gould, always a hypochondriac and given to ingesting various prescription medications, would appear to have undermined his own health. On September 27, 1982, after complaining of a severe headache, he suffered a stroke. He was rushed to Toronto General Hospital, but his condition deteriorated. On October 4, having suffered brain damage, he was taken off life support.

Decades later, American composer Leonard Bernstein would write, "I worshipped the way he played. I admired his intellectual approach . . . his complete dedication to whatever he was doing, his constant inquiry into a new angle or a new possibility of the truth of the score." And virtuoso cellist Yo-Yo Ma would explain that Gould "transformed and reduced concepts of vast complexity into forms of profound beauty and simplicity. Gould's mind was a brilliant and shimmering prism through which sounds, senses and ideas were magically transformed." On hearing Gould's recording of Bach's Goldberg Variations for the first time, the cellist added, articulating the experience of many, "I experienced a musical epiphany that would fuel my musical thinking for years to come."

In February 2013, more than thirty years after his death, Glenn Gould was honoured posthumously with a special lifetime achievement award at the Grammy Awards in Los Angeles. Peter Simon, president of the Royal Conservatory of Music, observed that Gould was outstanding in many fields—not just as a pianist, but in broadcasting, writing, and producing television documentaries. Likening him to the visionary Marshall McLuhan, Simon said, "He was a complete creative artist. He foresaw the digital age."

38

JONI MITCHELL

A Picasso of song refines self-expression

For decades, Joni Mitchell has been evoking comparison with Bob Dylan. A 1972 *Melody Maker* article suggested that "few other rock musicians, male or female, have so refined personal expression that it succeeds as genuine art. She should be sitting at Dylan's right hand. The cards are face up, the king and queen." Thirty-nine years later, in 2011, *New Yorker* writer Adam Gopnik would raise the stakes, declaring that "Joni Mitchell is a poet and artist of a rare quality—better than Dylan." When she received a Grammy Award in 2002 for lifetime achievement, the citation moved beyond comparisons and described her as "one of the most important female recording artists of the rock era." That same year, a *Rolling Stone* article declared, "Let's face the facts: Joni Mitchell is one of the greatest songwriters ever—no gender required."

Her story begins on November 7, 1943, when Roberta Joan Anderson was born in Fort Macleod, Alberta, a dusty town near Lethbridge in the foothills of the Rocky Mountains. The child's father, an instructor at a Canadian air force academy, was of Scandinavian heritage, her mother Scottish and Irish. After the Second World War ended in 1945, the family moved to Saskatchewan, first to the small town of Maidstone, then to North Battleford, and finally to Saskatoon. Bill Anderson managed grocery stores for a chain, and her mother taught school. From ages seven through nine, the girl took piano lessons.

She quit in frustration, and focused mainly on drawing and painting, after the music teacher rapped her knuckles for composing her own melodies instead of sticking to the program. In 1952, stricken with polio and forced to spend Christmas in hospital, she took to singing Christmas carols and, according to biographer Mark Bego, discovered she was a ham: "That was the first time I started to sing to people."

As she moved into her teens, Mitchell painted, wrote poetry, and revelled in music of all kinds, from Russian pianist Sergei Rachmaninoff to obscure jazz trios and the emerging rock 'n' roll of Elvis Presley, Ray Charles, and Chuck Berry. At thirteen, she began calling herself Joni. She became a fanatical rock 'n' roller, a self-described "goodtime Charlie" who organized a Wednesday night dance so she could do the Lindy Hop more than one night a week. In her late teens, she wrote a column called "Fads and Fashions" for her high school newspaper. Using money she earned modelling dresses in a department store, Ricki's Ladies Wear, she bought a ukulele and began leading singalongs around campfires.

At eighteen, having perused Pete Seeger's *How to Play Folk-Style Guitar* and made adjustments for a left hand weakened by childhood polio, she began singing and playing on a local TV show. Distracted, popular, always on the go, she had to repeat a few courses to get her high school diploma. She made her professional debut on Halloween night at the Louis Riel café in Saskatoon. Then, in 1963, bent on becoming a painter, she moved to Calgary to train at the Alberta College of Art. She lasted a year, explaining later that the professors were obsessed with abstract expressionism while she wanted to paint portraits and landscapes. During that year, she became a popular performer in local folk-music clubs. In 1964, she caught a train east to Ontario to attend the Mariposa Folk Festival, held that summer in Orillia.

In Toronto, she gravitated to the Yorkville neighbourhood, where folk music was thriving in a variety of clubs. And, having recently lost her virginity to a fellow artist, she discovered that she was pregnant. Later, she would declare that, in 1964, to be pregnant and unmarried "was like you had killed somebody." She stayed in Toronto to hide her pregnancy from her parents and to protect them from scandal. She worked in a department store, played folk music at night and, in February 1965, gave birth to a girl. Unable to care for the infant, she relinquished the baby to foster care, an action she found so difficult that, in the file, the foster-care worker remarked on it.

Meanwhile, at the Penny Farthing folk club, she met an American musician, Chuck Mitchell. She married him in Michigan in June 1965, and then—after he refused to raise another man's child—reluctantly put her baby up for adoption. Having become Joni Mitchell, and based now in Detroit, she performed as a duo with Chuck and got to know many of the folk musicians of the era. She had already composed songs—"Urge for Going," "The Circle Game"—recorded by such performers as Tom Rush, Buffy Sainte-Marie, and Judy Collins. In 1967, her marriage broke down and Joni bailed, heading alone to New York City to check out the music scene in Greenwich Village.

When she wrote "Both Sides Now" and played it for Tom Rush, he insisted on phoning Judy Collins so Joni could play it to her over the phone. Collins put the song on her next record and saw it rocket to number eight on the *Billboard* charts. By now an accomplished guitar player, Joni Mitchell began touring the eastern seaboard, honing her chops. Late in 1967, with the help of David Crosby of the supergroup Crosby, Stills & Nash, the twenty-four-year-old Mitchell went to California and recorded her first album, *Joni Mitchell*, or *Song to a Seagull*.

Through 1968, she toured promoting that album, performing to enthusiastic audiences in places as varied as Los Angeles, Philadelphia, New York, Ontario (Mariposa), Florida, and London, England. In 1969, based now in Laurel Canyon, Los Angeles, where music flourished amidst the experimentalism of the era, Joni Mitchell toured the United States and worked on her second album. It would include her own versions of songs recorded by others, among them "Chelsea Morning," "Tin Angel," and "Both Sides Now." As with the first album, and virtually all those that would follow, she would design and paint the cover art.

That second album, *Clouds*, appeared in October 1969. Again the critics responded with enthusiasm, applauding "the craft, subtlety, and evocative power of her lyrics and harmonic style," as well as the sophisticated chord progressions. After still more touring, early in 1970, and still just twenty-six years old, Joni Mitchell took a break from recording and went travelling around Europe. She won her first Grammy Award for *Clouds* and continued to write songs as, also in 1970, she released *Ladies of the Canyon*, which included "Big Yellow Taxi" and her own version of "The Circle Game."

Early in 1971, back in California, Joni Mitchell went into the studio and recorded *Blue*, an album that included such songs as "California," "Carey," "River," and "A Case of You" (this last tune one of several that drew on an indelible, months-long love affair with Leonard Cohen). Released in June, *Blue* reached number fifteen in the United States and number three in the United Kingdom, and before long had sold over one million copies. Critically, the album made a still greater impact, music experts hailing it as inspired: a pop music masterpiece. One critic wrote of how *Blue* explored "territory previously untouched in such determined detail by any other performer, either male or female." In her ability to reach into herself and sculpt her perceptions with tempered irony, "Joni Mitchell absolutely demands to be set apart." Another wrote that, despite *Blue*'s intimacy, Mitchell proved "so perfect in her lyric, so vivid in her universal portrayal of desperate love . . . that she never once detached the listener. If anything, the feeling was almost sinful, intrusive, the sensation one would get from reading someone's personal diary."

Yet another writer would call *Blue* "the quintessential confessional singer/songwriter album," one in which tales of love and loss are "etched with stunning complexity." Mitchell herself would protest: "I don't think of myself as confessional. That's a name that was put on me." With *Blue*, she added, "People were kind of shocked at the intimacy. It was peculiar in the pop arena at the time, because you were supposed to portray yourself as bigger than life. I remember thinking, well if they're going to worship me, they should know who they're worshipping."

In 2008, at a sixty-fifth-anniversary tribute to Mitchell, fellow pop star David Crosby spoke for most singer-songwriters when he declared that, "by the time she did *Blue*, she was past me and rushing toward the horizon." If Mitchell had never produced another album, most rock critics agree, she would be remembered for *Blue*. But after releasing another outstanding pop music album (*Court and Spark*), the relentlessly experimental Mitchell would pioneer the incorporation of African rhythms, or what later became known as world music (*Hejira*). She would move from rock to jazz (*Mingus*) and albums of social commentary (*Dog Eat Dog*). Along the way, too adventurous for top-forty radio stations, she would struggle to retain access to the airwaves.

Even so, committed to songwriting as an art, Mitchell refused to confine herself to working within conventions she had exhausted, explaining rhetorically, "Would you ask Picasso to repaint his 'Blue Period?'" At one point, Mitchell said that, while some find the notion of creating "art songs" pretentious, for her, the word "art" never lost its vitality: "Love lost its meaning to me. God lost its meaning to me. But art never lost its meaning. I always knew what I meant by art." To put it simply, Joni Mitchell changed the world by making art out of popular music.

Of course, she earned acclaim not just with her lyrics, but with her original guitar stylings, which landed her on lists of the 100 best guitarists of all time. Musicians as diverse as Charles Mingus, Prince, and Madonna have hailed her work, and one of her songs, "Chelsea Morning," proved so important to Hillary Clinton, who became American Secretary of State, that she insisted on naming her daughter Chelsea. Speaking of mothers and daughters, Joni Mitchell regained contact with the daughter she had so sorrowfully relinquished into foster care, an ongoing reunion that has brought her joy.

But here we are concerned with global significance. "When the dust settles," one critic writes on a website called AllMusic, "Joni Mitchell may stand as the most important and influential female recording artist of the late 20th century." Hailing her as uncompromising, iconoclastic, and innovative, the writer notes that her music "evolved from deeply personal folk stylings into pop, jazz, avant-garde, and even world music, presaging the multicultural experimentation of the 1980s and 1990s by over a decade." Even so: that mitigating allusion to gender? The citation for her 2002 Grammy Lifetime Achievement Award set things straight by recognizing Mitchell as "a powerful influence on all artists who embrace diversity, imagination, and integrity." But music critic Carl Wilson, writing in the January/February 2013 issue of the *Literary Review of Canada*, offered what is probably the best one-sentence testimonial: "She opened doors that it is now hard to realize were ever closed, becoming the kind of innovator whose influence is so pervasive that it is paradoxically invisible, a figure lost in the background she herself had painted."

39

WAYNE GRETZKY

A gentleman superstar makes hockey a contender

On December 30, 1981, while driving to the arena with a teammate, twenty-year-old hockey player Wayne Gretzky had a premonition. "I suddenly got the strangest feeling," he wrote later. He turned to his fellow player and said, "Geez, I feel weird. I might get a couple tonight." Gretzky, in his second year with the Edmonton Oilers of the National Hockey League, was speaking of goals. He was chasing a record set in 1945 by Maurice "The Rocket" Richard: fifty goals in fifty games. The previous season, Mike Bossy had tied that record by scoring twice in the last four minutes of his fiftieth game. But the Rocket's mark had never been surpassed.

Yet this season had seen Gretzky accomplish miracles. During a recent four-game stretch, he had scored ten goals. Now, after thirty-eight games, he had forty-five—and twelve games in which to score five more. Turned out, he would not need that many. In *Gretzky: An Autobiography*, he would write, "It was almost eerie the way things happened." In the first period, he got a rebound off the boards and shot wide, but the puck bounced off the goalie's leg into the net. He would forget the details of his second goal. But he scored a third with a slap shot, and a fourth in the third period "on a slapper from the right on a power play."

That made forty-nine. If he scored again, Gretzky would have fifty goals in thirty-nine games—an almost inconceivable record.

"But then the magic suddenly left me," he writes. In the last ten minutes of the game, he proved unable to score, though he had "three absolutely point-blank chances." With ten seconds remaining in the game, and the Oilers leading six to five, the Flyers pulled their goalie in favour of an extra attacker. The puck bounced off the side of the Oilers' net, and Gretzky "took off like I was late for a bus." With seven seconds to go, the goalie got the puck to a winger and Gretzky called for a pass. At the three-second mark, he fired the puck past a sprawling Flyer "into the world's most beautiful net." Wayne Gretzky had scored fifty goals in thirty-nine games.

The performer, the challenge, the performance, the flow. After the game, recognizing the magic of that moment, the captain of the opposing team, Bobby Clarke, came to the Oilers' dressing room to shake the Great One's hand. "When I saw him," Gretzky wrote later, "I realized I had set a record that was going to be real tough to break."

Wayne Gretzky had been a child prodigy. Born in Brantford, Ontario, on January 26, 1961, he was skating at two, attracting national attention at six, and signing autographs at ten. At eleven, he inspired a national magazine article, and at fifteen, he was profiled on a television show that aired across Canada. For this early success, he has always credited his father, Walter Gretzky, who turned their backyard into a hockey rink every winter, set up flood lights, and conducted hockey drills until ten o'clock at night.

Fortunately, Wayne Gretzky loved the game. He excelled at other sports—baseball, lacrosse, cross-country running—but became passionate about hockey. At six, he started playing against ten-year-olds. At the end of the year, driving home from a banquet with his father, he started crying. He hadn't won a trophy: "Everybody won a trophy but me." His father said something he never forgot: "Wayne, keep practising and one day you're gonna have so many trophies, we're not gonna have room for them all."

That year, Gretzky had scored one goal. But in the next three years, the boy scored 27, 104, and 196. Then, at ten, he scored 378 goals in sixty-nine games—an age-group record that still stands. When at thirteen he had scored 1,000 goals, a newspaper article hailed him as "The Great Gretzky," a nickname that later evolved into "The Great One." Predictably, his stardom provoked jealousy and "Gretzky-bashing" among the parents of other boys. He was learning "that excellence has its price."

When, at fourteen, he was invited to Toronto to play hockey while living with a teammate's parents, he jumped at the chance. His own parents hesitated, but finally agreed to let him go, though it meant he was living 100 kilometres away. He was supposed to play Bantam League hockey but went straight to Junior B, where again he held his own against much older players. He was slight, roughly 135 pounds, but from lacrosse he had learned how to dodge checks. He also showed uncanny anticipation.

Later, Gretzky would allude to his father, Walter, when explaining: "It's not God-given, it's Wally-given. He used to stand at the blue line and say to me, 'Watch, this is how everybody does it.' Then he'd shoot a puck along the boards and into the corner and then go chasing after it. Then he'd come back and say, 'Now, this is how the smart player does it.' He'd shoot it into the corner again, only this time he cut across to the other side and picked it up over there. Who says anticipation can't be taught? It was something he taught me every day."

While living with his teammate, the boy went home on weekends, but he felt the difference. Decades later, Gretzky would remember his loneliness with some feeling: "I didn't leave Brantford to go play better hockey. I left because the people drove me out."

In 1978, after two years in Toronto, seventeen-year-old Gretzky went professional. He joined the World Hockey Association and played briefly with the Indianapolis Racers before being traded to the

Edmonton Oilers. The following year, the Oilers were one of the lucky WHA teams that, as part of a business shakeout, got absorbed into the National Hockey League. In his rookie year in the NHL, Gretzky tied Marcel Dionne for the scoring title and, to his own surprise, won the Hart Trophy as most valuable player.

Over the next few years, Gretzky would become the greatest goal scorer in hockey history. His single-season records include most goals (92), most assists (163), and most points (215). No other NHL player has ever tallied more than 200 points in a season, and Gretzky did that four times. He also racked up over 100 points in sixteen seasons, including fourteen seasons in a row.

In 1982, Gretzky won the Sportsman of the Year Award from *Sports Illustrated* magazine: "I think to this day that's the award I cherish most because I had to beat out great athletes from all sports." Through the mid-1980s, he played a crucial role in turning the Edmonton Oilers into an unstoppable force, leading them to one Stanley Cup after another. On May 26, 1988, delivering what hockey writer Stephen Brunt called "one of the finest playoff performances in the history of the sport," the Great One led the Oilers to their fourth Stanley Cup victory. After the game, during celebrations at a local restaurant, his father took him aside and gave Gretzky some shattering news he had kept secret all through the playoffs. The owner of the Oilers was going to trade him. Probably, the deal was already done.

At this point, Wayne Gretzky had raised the performance bar and changed hockey from within. No single player in the history of team sports had so dominated any game. Never heavier than 170 pounds, always opposed to the macho ethos of brawling, he had demonstrated that at its best, hockey is a game of speed and finesse. What happened next enabled Gretzky to elevate hockey in the great wide world, and to transform the profile of the sport in North America.

In an action that stirs emotions among hockey fans to this day, the Edmonton Oilers traded Wayne Gretzky to the Los Angeles Kings. Hockey aficionado Stephen Brunt tells the story in his book *Gretzky's Tears: Hockey, Canada, and the Day Everything Changed*. The controversial details need not detain us here. Some hockey fans jumped to the conclusion that the trade happened because Gretzky had recently married Janet Jones, a Californian. This is a red herring: Jones had been preparing to move to Edmonton.

In truth, the owner of the Oilers, Peter Pocklington, needed $15 million to cover business losses and the only major asset he had was Gretzky's contract. Pocklington's opposite number, Bruce McNall, had been trying to bring hockey into the American mainstream alongside baseball, basketball, and football. Adopting a Hollywood-specific strategy, McNall had been trying to turn excellent hockey players into celebrities. It hadn't worked. But what if he had the greatest hockey player of all time? In a celebrity culture, McNall believed, a marketing strategy built around The Great One might work magic.

Crucially, Gretzky himself bought into the idea. First, he learned that Pocklington had begun bad-mouthing him, calling him a whiner and too big for his britches. That stung his pride. Yes, he would have to leave a city he had grown to love. He would have to leave his teammates, among them most of his best friends. And he would have to abandon his dream of establishing a Stanley Cup–winning dynasty. But Pocklington wanted him gone. And maybe, just maybe, by joining the Los Angeles Kings, he could advance the development of the sport he loved.

Nobody's motives are ever unmixed. Gretzky's critics pointed out that, in Los Angeles, The Great One would earn more money and live a flashier lifestyle. That was true—but where was the crime? Critics argued that Gretzky betrayed the game of hockey by leaving a Stanley Cup contender, and the nation itself by moving to the United States. Yet surely the opposite is true: he advanced the game and did Canada proud. Of course, Gretzky had doubts and misgivings. He was twenty-seven years old. In his autobiography, he writes, "The Kings were a team that had been running brutal for twenty years. They were eighteenth in the league that year. What if I went down there and couldn't help them a bit?"

Fortunately, the McNall strategy worked. Hollywood royalty responded excitedly to the arrival of The Great One, turning out in force at receptions and soirees. Los Angeles sports fans followed their celebrities and movie stars. Overnight, hockey became chic. Before Gretzky laced on his skates, season's ticket sales jumped from 4,000 to 13,000, even though average prices doubled. And then, on the ice, Gretzky delivered. The Kings won forty-two games—twelve more than the previous year. They finished second in their division, and went from eighteenth to fourth in the league—one of the biggest turnarounds in hockey history. Gretzky received his ninth Hart Trophy.

Then, in the quarter-finals, he led the Kings to victory over the Oilers. "The sweetest part," he wrote later, "might have been proving it to [Pocklington]. He sent me to the worst team in the division because he figured that at best I'd help them from awful to sort-of-awful. I guess he underestimated us all." The following year, Gretzky became the NHL's all-time points leader. In 1993, he led the Kings to the Stanley Cup Finals. And the year after that, he became the NHL's all-time leading goal scorer. By the time he retired, in 1999, Gretzky held or shared sixty-one National Hockey League records, many of which remain unbroken.

Twelve years after he retired, and thirty after he scored fifty goals in thirty-nine games, Wayne Gretzky celebrated his fiftieth birthday with a long interview that can be found online. Citing the work of fellow hockey players in New York (Mark Messier), St. Louis (Brett Hull), and Pittsburgh (Mario Lemieux), Gretzky noted that the National Hockey League had expanded from six to twenty to thirty teams, and enjoyed a much higher profile around the world than ever before. Pushed to answer a hypothetical question, he admitted that, if he had stayed in Edmonton, he might have led the Oilers not just to the four Stanley Cups, but to "six, seven, or eight." He shrugged: "It wasn't meant to be."

What Gretzky didn't say was that, if he had stayed in Edmonton, hockey would be far less popular than it is. By accepting unavoidable change with grace, and then making good on his reputation, Gretzky did more than anyone else to turn hockey into a mainstream sport in the great wide world. Decades after he made the move south, a *Toronto Star* story about the American team winning the gold medal at the 2013 World Junior Hockey Championship carried the head-line, "U.S. rise part of Gretzky legacy." In that story, published on January 6, 2013, reporter Kevin McGran observed that the ascent of Team USA to the top of the hockey world "can be traced to the trade of Gretzky to the Los Angeles Kings in 1988 and the NHL's ensuing expansion into non-traditional markets." By moving to Los Angeles, The Great One changed the world of sport: he made hockey a global contender.

40

CÉLINE DION

A nightingale sings French Canada to the world

When she was in Spain to perform before an international audience, singer Céline Dion told a Montreal journalist that she was against political boundaries. The year was 1992. She was twenty-four. The man asked her what she thought of the separatist movement in Quebec. In her autobiography, Dion writes that the Canadian media sought to turn this exchange into a huge story, claiming that she "considered the possible secession of Quebec from the rest of Canada to be a horrible nightmare for Quebec."

Looking back, she wrote that she should have said politics was not her field, period. Her husband and manager, René Angélil, insisted that the journalist was out of line: "Did that writer ever think of asking the prime minister to sing in front of twenty million people, like you do?" The journalist was just doing his job, just trying to get a story. But Angélil had a point. A singer does not change the world by fomenting a revolution or achieving a scientific breakthrough. She works from within, she connects emotionally, she makes us feel more deeply.

Numbers tell the story in a different way. According to her distributor, Sony Music Entertainment, Dion has sold over 200 million albums. In 2004, when she passed the 175 million mark, she was honoured at the World Music Awards as the bestselling female artist of all time. Her 1995 album *D'eux* is the bestselling French-language album ever. She is the only female artist to have two singles sell more than a million copies in the United Kingdom. The list goes on and on.

Inevitably, given human nature, her fantastic success has engendered a small army of skeptics and naysayers. One of them, music critic Carl Wilson, wrote a book—*Let's Talk About Love: A Journey to the End of Taste*—in which he elaborated on virtually every criticism ever levelled at the singer. But even Wilson had to write, "If you have never heard Céline Dion in French, it's hard to believe it's the same singer. Her cadences are much more supple and controlled, her interpretations more detailed. Gone is the blank persona that reduces many of her English songs to vocal stunt work, replaced by what can only be called soul."

Millions would quarrel with "blank persona." Anybody who thinks there might be something to this criticism should go online and watch Dion perform "I'm Alive."

For some, Dion is the quintessential pop music translator: French to English, English to French. Others find inspiration in her rags-to-riches story, because here we have a musical Cinderella for whom a childhood dream became a fairy tale reality. In my view, Céline Dion changed the world not only by demonstrating the range of the human voice in the context of pop music, but above all by introducing the spirit of French Canada to those who have never known it.

Dion was born March 30, 1968 in Charlemagne, Quebec, just north of Montreal. She was the last of fourteen children in what she describes as an artistic working-class family. Her father played the accordion, her mother the fiddle, and often after supper, parents and adults would gather and sing rounds, everything from traditional folk songs, complete with clacking spoons, to hit tunes by Creedence Clearwater Revival.

She sang publicly for the first time when she was five, at the wedding of her brother, Michel. That day, she wrote later, she experienced "that unforgettable sensation felt by a singer when she realizes that she's captivated a listener, that she's being heard, applauded." That was the moment Dion knew she wanted to make music her life, the moment her dream was born. Her parents opened a piano bar, Le Vieux Baril (The Old Barrel) and, while still a child, Dion became a major attraction, standing on tabletops to belt out tunes by Quebec star Ginette Reno. By age twelve, she had attracted the attention of a Montreal agent who did not know what to do with her. Her brother Michel, frustrated, sent her demo tape to the promoter who handled Ginette Reno's career, René Angélil. A few weeks later, Michel followed up with a phone call, telling Angélil he knew the promoter hadn't listened to the tape because if he had, he would have called back immediately.

A few minutes later, having listened to the tape, Angélil did call back to set up an appointment. When the girl sang in his office, she did what she has done to so many others, both before and since: she brought tears to his eyes. Angélil heard Céline's stupendous voice. He heard the potential, he heard the desire and drive, and, as a skilled professional, he knew what to do with them.

Many have likened Angélil to Svengali, a fictional character who uses hypnosis to transform a young woman into a great singer. Dion herself has declared that, without Angélil, the superstar singer we know today would not exist. Unlike Svengali, Angélil has proven to be benign and essential, more protector and guide than creator. Although he is twenty-six years older, he is the love of Dion's life: her husband since 1994, and the father of her three children.

All that came later. In 1981, when she was thirteen, Angélil believed so strongly in Céline Dion that he mortgaged his house to finance her first record, *La voix du bon Dieu*. Today, online, an early performance of that tune looks schmaltzy. But the song became a hit in Quebec, and Dion was on her way. Still in the early 1980s, Céline became the first Canadian to have a gold record in France. She also won a gold medal at the Yamaha World Popular Song Festival. She quickly became known as the hardest-working singer in Quebec.

With the release of several French-language albums in quick succession, Dion became a star in her home province and well known in France. "One evening I'd sing with the Montreal Symphony Orchestra," she would write, "and the next, by suppertime, I'd be doing a TV broadcast with country music performers. I'd give a concert on a raft on a lake in the Laurentides in central Quebec. At night I'd record a Christmas song with a chorus of forty people, all from my family. Then Maman, René, and I would leave for a distant region of Quebec where I was performing in a festival."

At eighteen, after seeing Michael Jackson on television, Dion told Angélil she wanted superstardom. He said she would have to take time off and polish her appearance: cut her hair, pluck her eyebrows, cap her teeth. Oh, and she would also have to learn English. Dion said fine, whatever it took. She wore braces that made her feel as if she had "a giant orthodontic scaffold" in her mouth. For two months, she took English classes: nine hours a day, five days a week: "At times, it was a nightmare. I stopped understanding words in any human language at all. I started talking nonsense and all my ideas got mixed up. And then, all at once, everything became clear and intelligible. I watched a talk show in English on TV and understood all the conversation for long stretches. Or almost all. I discovered a new meaning in the songs that I'd known since childhood."

In 1990, the new-look Dion, no more a teenager, suddenly a woman, put out her first album in English: *Unison.* "When you change from one language to another," she would write, "the very texture of your voice changes, even its register." Later, she would realize that "for some reason, in English, I almost always sing spontaneously in a higher key, and I load the singing with my own inventions, a lot of ornamentation and volume." Americans enjoy these arabesques, she said, while in France, "singing is much more constrained, restrained, and personal. The words take on a much greater importance."

Dion's first English album included the soft rock ballad "Where Does My Heart Beat Now," her first single to reach the top ten on the American *Billboard* chart (it made number four). The following year, with Peabo Bryson, Dion sang the title track to Disney's *Beauty and the Beast*. It became her second American top-ten hit and won an Academy Award and a Grammy Award.

In 1992, her rising popularity in the English-speaking world made her Québécois fans restive. She regained their affection when she won a Félix Award for anglophone artist of the year and openly refused to accept it on the grounds that she was and always would be a French artist. Meanwhile, she maintained a killing pace in both of Canada's official languages. Between 1992 and 1996, Dion recorded six albums. The sixth, *Falling into You*, broke new ground, adding complex orchestration, chanting, and such little-heard instruments as the trombone and the cavaquinho. It won two Grammy awards, topped the charts in several countries, and became one of the bestselling albums of all time. It also earned Dion an invitation to perform at the opening ceremonies of the Atlanta Olympic Games.

And then came "My Heart Will Go On," the theme song to *Titanic*, James Cameron's blockbuster movie. She put it on her album *Let's Talk About Love*, which went platinum in twenty-four countries and became the fastest-selling album of her career. In Canada, it sold over 230,000 copies in its first week, setting a record that has yet to be broken. By now, anyone who listened to music had realized that, while most pop singers have a vocal range of three octaves, Céline Dion could soar through five.

Even so, she did experience setbacks. In 1989, during a concert tour, her voice fell apart. She consulted a specialist, who gave her a choice. She could have surgery on her vocal cords, or she could try to save them by remaining silent for three weeks and then undergoing a vocal formation, a challenging program to change the way she used her voice to create sound. She chose the latter and made it work. A few years later, she endured a devastating confrontation with the abusive music producer Phil Spector, an infamous bully who more than once reduced her to tears, and who has since become a convicted murderer.

In 1999, her husband was diagnosed with throat cancer. Dion took a break and helped him survive it. She gave birth to their first child, then returned to music in 2002 with an album, *A New Day Has Come*, that debuted at number one in seventeen countries. That same year, she announced yet another departure: a three-year contract to perform five nights a week and do 600 shows at Caesar's Palace in Las Vegas. She became the centrepiece of a multimedia program orchestrated by people involved in Quebec's Cirque du Soleil.

In 2008, ever mindful of her roots, Dion presented a free show in Quebec City, performing exclusively in French on the Plains of Abraham to celebrate the city's 400th anniversary. That year, too, she garnered France's highest award, the Legion of Honour. The next December, American pollsters announced that Dion was the bestselling solo act of the decade. She had grossed more than $520 million since 2000 and, according to a Harris Poll published a few months later, had become the most popular female musician in the United States.

In March 2011, Céline Dion began a second residency at Caesar's Palace, this one for seventy shows a year. Four years before, she had been ranked by *Forbes* as the fifth richest woman in entertainment, with an estimated net worth of more than $250 million. Why, then, does she keep on working? The answer is the same as it has always been: she lives to move people with her voice. Don't take anybody's word for it. Go online and check out "Where Does My Heart Beat Now." Show me another singer who can hit those notes with so little effort, and while investing them with such emotion, and I will show you another global superstar.

41

K'NAAN WARSAME

A flag-waving rapper tackles trouble in Somalia

"When I get older I will be stronger. They'll call me freedom, just like a wavin' flag." So it begins, the song that made K'naan world-famous as a champion of war-torn Somalia. That song, "Wavin' Flag," is familiar to tens of millions around the globe as the official anthem of the 2010 World Cup, which was held in South Africa. The Canadian rap musician, sometimes called "the dusty foot philosopher," offered up a celebration mix of the hit song for that occasion, complete with allusions to the Beautiful Game, with champions taking to the field and making everybody feel proud.

But the original, which subsequently went over the top as a result of the anthem exposure, carrying K'naan's *Troubadour* album with it, told the story of growing up in a "poor people zone" where life could be bleak. It evokes a picture of young people struggling to eat, wondering when they would become free, yearning for the day when, older and stronger, they would be free as a waving flag. K'naan Warsame changed the world by reaching young people with the message that they can make a difference.

In 2011, two decades after he emigrated from Somalia, K'naan returned to his native country to focus international attention on what the United Nations has called the worst famine in a generation. Tens of thousands have died, and aid workers were struggling to get food to the 3.2 million Somalis who needed it. K'naan visited malnourished children at Mogadishu's Banadir Hospital, where refugees reached out to touch him or shake his hand. According to a story in *The Globe and Mail*, he spoke in Somali, explaining his presence and promising, "I will do all I can to help my people in Somalia."

The following year, when K'naan put out a catchy follow-up album to *Troubadour*, called *Country, God or the Girl*, he also released a mini-documentary in which he speaks of injustice, inequality, and poverty, but also seeks to broaden his subject matter. "I'm so known for my focus on Somalia for very good reasons," he says. "But people in Somalia feel one plague similar to people in America and everyone else in the world, which is alienation, loneliness, desire to find commonality."

K'naan was born Keinan Abdi Warsame on February 1, 1978, in Mogadishu. His grandfather, Haji Mohammad, was a poet whose nickname was Ahyaa Wadani, which K'naan translates as "the passion" or "the soul of the country." His aunt Magool was one of East Africa's best-known singers. K'naan, a Muslim, grew up listening to hip-hop records sent from the United States by his estranged father. When he was ten, warlords began a series of feuds that would escalate into full-blown civil war. In "Wavin' Flag," he sings about how these warlords would make promises, talking about how love is the answer while luring the innocent and the naive into fighting their battles.

When he was eleven years old, K'naan had to run for his life from gunmen, dodging bullets that killed his three best friends. Two years later, with the United States embassy closing, K'naan, his mother, and three siblings managed to get on the last American plane out of Somalia. They stayed briefly in Harlem, New York City, before moving to the Toronto neighbourhood of Rexdale, which is home to a large Somali community. There, even before he learned English, K'naan started rapping along phonetically with the songs of established artists.

Still, the transition proved difficult. "Going to Toronto was great in all the textbook things," he said during a global tour that followed the World Cup. "Here was a place where you weren't in war. Great quality of life, good culture, good schools, but you have to understand that . . . those checked boxes and dreams don't apply to people equally in Canada. When you are an immigrant and a black immigrant where your parents don't come with a certain education and you are running from war and you have nothing, you are at the mercy of society." He lost friends in Toronto as he did in Somalia, he said, because "if I didn't lose them to death, I lost them to prison and deportation."

As a teenager he experienced anxiety attacks, hearing voices in his head that "were getting more opinionated than my own voice." He was already experimenting musically. He told an *Eye Weekly* reporter that he would "sit on those big garbage boxes and bang on them with the rhythm, and start rhyming off the top to kids. They thought it was fascinating. They were like, 'Man, you're going to be the first Somali rapper ever.' It turned out true." On good days, he might go to the mall with friends: "I would spend all my time inside Radio Shack playing their little keyboards until they kicked me out for not buying."

K'naan wrote his first songs while in a troubled state. One of them, called "Voices in My Head," he wrote "during a particularly torturous anxiety attack. I had gotten the news of a Somali boy who was a friend in Toronto, leaping to his death from the twenty-something floor of an old high-rise we once lived in."

After dropping out of high school in grade ten, K'naan spent two years rambling around North America, rapping when he got the chance, developing his act. Eventually, he signed up with Toronto promoter Sol Guy, who in 1999 got him a gig at a Geneva concert marking the fiftieth anniversary of the United Nations. While performing, K'naan suddenly felt the need to speak out. In mid-song, he stopped the band: "I needed that moment to go and justify the rest of my life. . . . It was this abrupt and tense feeling; some of the organizers in the UN knew my politics and had trouble with them. Someone had to bring the house down, let 'em know that they're still sitting on fire."

Unaccompanied, K'naan rapped out a poem blasting the United Nations for failed operations in Mogadishu in the mid-1990s. When he finished, he said later, "there was a gap of two seconds—the most uncomfortable time of my life. And then a standing ovation—a sea of people got up." One of the enthusiasts was Youssou N'Dour, the Senegalese superstar who took K'naan under his wing, bringing him on a world tour.

The albums followed. *The Dusty Foot Philosopher* won the 2006 Juno Award for rap recording of the year and the BBC Radio 3 Award for World Music in the newcomer category. *Troubadour*, released in 2010, brought more awards, more world tours, and collaborations with such artists as Nelly Furtado, Damian Marley, and Bryan Adams. It also featured the song "Wavin' Flag," and enabled K'naan to bring what he calls his "urgent music with a message" to a global audience. His next full-scale album, *Country, God or the Girl*, built on that success. Here we find collaborations with Furtado, Bono, Keith Richards, and the rapper Nas, and K'naan declaring that life's been difficult but he's not typical: "They never gonna cut me down."

In December 2012, in a first-person piece published in *The New York Times* and the *Toronto Star*, K'naan reflected that his "truest voice" is the one that evokes Africa's angst in a personal story. He described reaching out for a broad American audience with songs such as "Is Anybody Out There?," which focuses on the evils of drugs, and compared that with singing about how his mother, when she fled war-torn Somalia, had to choose a family member to leave behind. "I come with all the baggage of Somalia," he wrote, "of my grandfather's poetry, of pounding rhythms, of the war, of being an immigrant, of being an artist, of needing to explain a few things. Even in the friendliest of melodies, something in my voice stirs up a well of history—of dark history, of loss's victory."

42

SARAH BURKE AND HAYLEY WICKENHEISER

Elite athletes open doors for women

Women world-champion skier Sarah Burke lay in a coma following a terrible skiing accident, an anonymous, twenty-three-
year-old woman from Burnaby went online and spoke of the sadness
she felt and how it was shared by thousands around the world. But
then she added a word of thanks: "I have all these types of women
(Sarah Burke, Hayley Wickenheiser, etc.) to thank for crusading on
behalf of female pro athletes. It's because of them that I get to play
sports without being looked down upon, and it'll be because of them
that my daughter (if I ever have a daughter) will get to do the sport of
her choice and not just the ones that are considered 'girly.'"

That captured it precisely: these elite women athletes changed
the world of sports for other women. Sarah Burke passed away a few
days after her accident. But like Wickenheiser, and as the anonymous
young woman noted, she had already opened doors on behalf of
female athletes. As Olympic moguls champion Jennifer Heil put it,
Burke "paved a new path for her sport as a whole and for women in
sport." To Wickenheiser we shall return.

Born September 3, 1982, in Barrie, Ontario, Sarah Burke grew up
in the town of Midland, 55 kilometres northeast, on Georgian Bay.
She started skiing at nearby Collingwood as a child, and after excelling as a teenage mogul skier, began sneaking onto the snowboard-

ing half-pipe. This semicircular ditch, frequented by male daredevils, finds competitors performing tricks while sliding from side to side and soaring into the air. Judges score the sport, considering execution, variety, difficulty, pipe use, and amplitude (height).

Having fallen in love with half-pipe, the irrepressible Burke moved to Squamish, British Columbia, to be near the ski slopes at Whistler, where she could devote more time to her sport. In 2001, at eighteen, she won first place at the U.S. Freeskiing Open in the half-pipe, and finished second in slopestyle. These victories earned her ESPN's award for female skier of the year. Four years later, when half-pipe made its debut at the Freestyle World Ski Championships, Burke emerged as the first world champion. She also became a four-time Winter X Games gold medalist in freestyle skiing, and was the first woman to land a jump that featured three complete revolutions in competition (a 1080-degree rotation: 360 degrees x 3). In 2007, at the ESPY Awards, she was voted Best Female Action Sports Athlete.

The photogenic, effervescent young woman began turning up in skiing films. These included *Propaganda*, in which Burke threw backflips and spun 540 degrees (one and a half circles) in the pipe. She began promoting the superpipe skiing event, leading the drive to add it to the Winter Olympics program. Superpipe happens in an especially large half-pipe built of snow, with near-vertical walls about 6 metres in height. The superpipe is wider than the walls are high and requires special grooming equipment. In the X Games, between 2005 and 2011, Burke won the gold medal in superpipe four times and the silver medal once. She led a lobby to add the event to the 2010 Olympic Games in Vancouver, without success. She persevered and convinced the International Olympic Committee to add the event for the 2014 Games in Sochi, where she was favoured to win the gold medal.

Admired mainly for her on-slope exploits, Burke also became a mentor, serving in coaching camps and working with young kids. She ran the 2011 Nautica South Beach Triathlon as a fundraising effort for St. Jude's Children's Research Hospital in Memphis, Tennessee. In a Ski Channel video clip of unique poignancy, Burke and her husband, fellow skier Rory Bushfield, raved about their life in winter sports. "That's where we're the happiest," Burke said. "Whether it's an X Games contest, out snowmobiling together . . . it's what our lives are, being on the hill. And there's a reason for that, it's amazing, it's where we met, it's where we play, we live—" At this point, Bushfield interjected, "And hopefully where we'll die." Burke grinned and nodded: "And where we'll die."

On January 10, 2012, while training in Park City, Utah, Burke took a tumble as she finished a routine trick. The fall looked innocuous, but she landed on her head, sustained a critical injury, and suffered cardiac arrest. She was airlifted to Salt Lake City, went into a coma, and underwent neurosurgery to repair a tear in a vertebral artery. She never came out of her coma and, on January 19, succumbed to her injury.

Peter Judge, chief executive of the Canadian Freestyle Ski Association, lauded Burke as "someone who lived life to the fullest and in doing so was a significant example to our community and far beyond." She was "involved since the very, very early days as one of the first people to bring skis into the pipe." She sought "to define her sport but not define herself by winning," he said. "She took on her athletic role and saw it as a larger responsibility and lived that all the way through."

Hundreds of people posted condolences online. Silken Laumann, an Olympic rowing legend, said, "Sarah did so much for women in sport and her accident and death is absolutely tragic. She was a game changer in the sport of freestyle skiing, taking down barrier after barrier to ensure access and opportunity in a sport she loved." And another elite athlete, hockey great Hayley Wickenheiser, wrote, "A tragic loss for the sporting community. My thoughts are with the friends and family of Sarah Burke today."

Born four years before Burke, on August 12, 1978, Hayley Wickenheiser is to women's hockey what Sarah Burke was becoming in women's superpipe skiing—not just the best in the world at her sport, but also a superlative role model. Over the years, at the Women's World Hockey Championships, Wickenheiser has led Canada's national team to six gold and one silver medal. At the Winter Olympics, she has earned three gold medals and one silver, the latest gold coming at the Vancouver 2010 Winter Olympics. In both 2002 and 2006, she was named most valuable player in the tournament.

Not long ago, *Sports Illustrated* included Wickenheiser among the top twenty-five toughest athletes in the world (at number twenty, one of only two women). What makes her tough? According to the magazine, "No player in women's hockey drives to the net with such purpose and fury. Wickenheiser has grown from teen phenom to grande dame of Canadian hockey, carrying the weight of her country and game every time on the ice."

Wickenheiser was twice a finalist for the Women's Sports Foundation's Sportswoman of the Year Award (Team Sports), and was recently included, for the second time, among *The Globe and Mail's* Power 50 influencers in sport. In 2011, the QMI Agency named Wickenheiser one of the ten greatest female athletes in the history of sports, and in 2012, she became an Officer of the Order of Canada "for her achievements as an athlete and for her contribution to the growth of women's hockey."

Wickenheiser grew up 350 kilometres west of Regina in the town of Shaunavon, Saskatchewan, where she started playing hockey on an outdoor rink at age five. "I watched my dad play hockey a lot at the rink with the senior players," she told CBC Sports, "and that's why I wanted to play. Watching it on TV and watching my dad play senior hockey, it made me want to play." She played on boys' teams until 1991. That year, at thirteen, she led Team Alberta to the gold medal at the Canada

Winter Games: she scored the game-winning goal and was named the final game's most valuable player. Two years later, Hockey Canada's National Women's Team came calling, and at fifteen, Wickenheiser became the youngest member of a gold-medal team.

Excelling as an all-round athlete, Wickenheiser went to the Canadian Midget Softball Championships, where she won awards as All-Canadian Shortstop and Top Batter. She would continue to shine in both softball and fastball, even playing with the Canadian softball team in the 2000 Summer Olympics. This made her only the second woman to compete in both Summer and Winter Games, and the first to do so in team sports. At the 1998 Winter Olympics, when women's hockey was introduced as a medal event, Wickenheiser played with Team Canada. The team won a silver medal. Wickenheiser was named to the tournament all-star team, and ended up participating in the Philadelphia Flyers rookie camps for the next two years.

In 2002, she led Team Canada to the gold medal at the Winter Olympics in Salt Lake City, incidentally winning the most valuable player award. "We lost to the U.S. all along," she said later, "and then we came back to beat them in the final game, the game that mattered most. It was a great moment, and probably my most memorable." At those Olympics, Wickenheiser shared the scoring crown, with ten points. Four years later, while leading Team Canada to another gold at the Torino Games, she won that crown again, racking up seventeen points and earning top forward honours.

By that time, Wickenheiser had made hockey history by playing a season with a professional men's team—the first woman to do so in a position other than goalie. On January 31, 2003, while playing for a Finnish team, she became the first woman to score a goal in a men's professional league, a feat that became one of the top 100 international hockey stories of the past 100 years. That same year, *The Hockey*

News named Wickenheiser one of the top 100 most influential people in hockey.

During the past decade, the honours and awards have continued to accumulate. In 2007, Wickenheiser was named Canadian Press Female Athlete of the Year. That May, she travelled to Rwanda with Right to Play, an athlete-driven humanitarian organization, and in 2011 she returned to Africa, this time to Ghana, on a similar goodwill mission. She has also been active internationally through KidSport and Dreams Take Flight.

Over the years, Wickenheiser has led numerous projects around the world to raise the profile of women's hockey, and also established the Wickenheiser International Women's Hockey Festival. Now in her thirties, she is studying kinesiology at the University of Calgary, hoping to attend medical school, while also playing with the Dinos women's hockey team. In 2010, despite playing in only fifteen of the team's twenty-four regular-season games, she finished tied for the conference scoring title with forty points (seventeen goals and twenty-three assists). She scored four short-handed goals and five game-winners, and was named the Canada West Most Valuable Player.

At the Olympics in February of that year, during a hockey game against Sweden, Wickenheiser became the top Olympic goal scorer of all time. She then notched a couple more goals against other teams to set an Olympics career total record of sixteen goals. Later in 2010, Wickenheiser published a book about her experience at the Vancouver Games. In *Gold Medal Diary: Inside the World's Greatest Sports Event,* she writes that women's hockey is improving internationally, and Canada is showing the way. "If Russia, Sweden, or Finland inject more resources into their female hockey," she writes, "I'd consider going over and helping them when I finish my playing days. Why not? It would be a great challenge. Ideally, I'd like to work with the International Ice Hockey Federation to help with women's hockey around the world."

Like the late Sarah Burke, Haley Wickenheiser has a global perspective. These two elite athletes opened doors for women internationally. They also showed that, when it comes to transforming any given sport, this polite, accommodating country produces fiercely competitive leaders.

Part VI

Scientists and Inventors

They extend our knowledge of the physical world

More than 16,000 people had gathered in a rainforest 290 kilometres north of Vancouver to express their support for the wilderness that encircled them, a rich and varied ecosystem that is home to at least fifty species of animals. As the evening wore on, environmentalist David Suzuki took to the stage and gave an inspirational twenty-seven-minute speech calling for action on climate change. The date was August 6, 1989. The landmark occasion: the Stein Valley Festival. Today, you can go online and watch Suzuki's fiery performance, which galvanized not just Canadians, but Americans and Australians.

The previous year, Suzuki had created a series of five CBC Radio shows on climate, entitled *It's a Matter of Survival.* He had travelled to conferences in North and South America, Europe and Asia, and interviewed more than 150 scientists and experts. That experience infused him with a sense of urgency, he writes in *David Suzuki: The Autobiography*, "that has only increased over the years." Suzuki's radio series elicited more than 17,000 letters, most of them ending, "What can I do?"

The celebrated environmentalist offered a first response at Stein Valley, where he illustrated the sentiment expressed two years before he was born, in 1934, by Lewis Mumford: "However far modern science and technics have fallen short of their inherent possibilities, they have taught mankind at least one lesson: Nothing is impossible."

That sentiment drives the work not only of Suzuki, to whom we shall return, but the work of those scientists who turn up here in Part VI. These include the pioneer who laid the foundations of neuroscience, the geneticist battling rare diseases, and the astrophysicist leading the search for life on other planets. But now we come up against a corollary view expressed by science fiction writer Isaac Asimov. "Science can amuse and fascinate us all," he wrote, "but it is engineering that changes the world." Those who agree with Asimov will be keen to encounter the Nobel Prize winner who pointed the way to lasers, the electrical engineer who sparked a communications revolution, and the Canadarm, which changed exploration.

Three centuries ago, Isaac Newton captured a universal truth about science and technology: "If I have been able to see farther than others, it was because I stood on the shoulders of giants."

43

BRENDA MILNER

A memory pioneer lays the foundations of neuroscience

In the Hollywood movie *50 First Dates*, actress Drew Barrymore plays an art teacher who, as a result of a serious car accident, suffers from "Goldfield syndrome." Her character awakens each morning with her short-term memory wiped clean. She remembers everything that happened until the morning of the accident, but nothing since. The 2004 film sparked controversy. One clinical neuropsychologist, Dr. Sallie Baxendale, wrote that *50 First Dates* "maintains a venerable movie tradition of portraying an amnesic syndrome that bears no relation to any known neurological or psychiatric condition." But a neuroscientist at Cambridge University, Dr. Peter Nestor, said in 2010 that "it is reasonably rare to have this kind of amnesia but it does exist." Nestor cited the example of a British woman who, after two car accidents, could not remember anything before 1994. In addition, although she functioned normally each day, overnight she forgot everything that had happened the previous day. Researchers determined that she did show some improvement at tasks she had previously performed, though she had no memory of having done them.

Scientists are able to have this discussion, according to Nobel Prize winner Eric Kandel, thanks only to the work of Canadian Brenda Milner. The American neuropsychiatrist credits Milner with creating the field of cognitive neuroscience. The Montreal-based Milner modestly demurs: "We shouldn't quite say I created a field, but I certainly played a significant part." Her work in brain science laid the foundations, for example, for the later explorations of Norman Doidge, who in 2007 published *The Brain That Changes Itself.*

The pioneering scientist was born Brenda Langford in Manchester, England, in July 1918. Her father, the music critic for the *Manchester Guardian,* died of tuberculosis when she was eight. He had given her an excellent grounding in several core subjects and, to allow her to skip a grade at school, her mother spent a summer teaching her French grammar. This not only gave the girl "enough French for the next three years," she wrote later, but led her to develop a love for French language and literature that "would stand me in good stead when I came to live and work in Montreal."

At fifteen, the student had to choose between science and the humanities. If the school had offered Greek, she wrote in an autobiographical essay, she would have opted for the classics—and a completely different life. Instead, she turned to mathematics and physics, largely because she believed, as she still does, that "it is possible to develop one's knowledge and enjoyment of foreign languages and literature on one's own, but that once you give up science you abandon it forever." In 1936, the young woman won a scholarship to attend Newnham College at the University of Cambridge. By the end of her first year, having realized that she would never distinguish herself in mathematics, she considered switching to philosophy. Professors warned that this was a subject "strictly for people of independent means," and she turned finally to experimental psychology, a discipline little known in England.

Biologically oriented, the psychology department shared a building with a physiological laboratory. The brilliant student worked with Oliver Zangwill, who taught her that one could gain insight into the normal brain by analyzing defective or damaged specimens. She won a post-graduate studentship to do research at Cambridge, but this was 1939: the Second World War erupted and she was redirected to the British war effort. She developed and administered tests for air crews, and then became one of three women officers at a radar centre on the south coast. While evaluating methods of display and control for radar operators, she met an electrical engineer named Peter Milner. In 1942, she moved with the rest of the radar research establishment to a country town in the West Midlands "that took on the atmosphere of a college campus." After two years, as the war finally wound down, she planned to resume researching at Cambridge.

But then Milner was invited to help launch atomic energy research in Canada. She married Milner and, two weeks later, the two were crossing the Atlantic, along with a bevy of war brides. In Montreal, Brenda Milner landed a job at the francophone Université de Montréal. Initially, she found teaching in a second language difficult. But she polished her French, lectured on memory, and taught laboratory courses in experimental and comparative psychology. By 1949, across town at McGill University, a newly appointed chair had established a department of physiological psychology. Milner enrolled in a doctoral program. She created experiments to explore thought processes. At age thirty-two, she began working with Wilder Penfield at the Montreal Neurological Institute (MNI), where patients were undergoing brain surgery to relieve epileptic seizures. "I knew immediately that this was the kind of work I wished to pursue," she would write, "whatever the practical difficulties."

Over the next few years, Milner pursued her research in English while working full-time *en français* at the Université de Montréal. Penfield suggested that "somewhere in the brain of each of us, there is a continuous, ongoing record of the stream of consciousness . . . extending from birth to death." Milner rejected this "tape-recorder notion of memory" as highly implausible: "I had been trained to think of remembering as a reconstructive rather than a reproductive process." At this stage, Milner concentrated not on memory but on complex perceptual tasks. But then two post-operative patients in succession complained of severe memory loss. "Memory was not a fashionable topic when I started working on it," she said later. "I only started working on it because the patients complained of poor memory. And if a patient complains of memory, you don't say, 'No, no, I'm interested in perception,' and then forget about memory. You study memory or you take a different job."

In 1955, a neurosurgeon in Hartford, Connecticut, read an article Milner wrote about these two cases. He called Montreal to say that, after operating on a patient to control seizures, he had seen a similar memory disturbance. Milner travelled south to work with this patient, who would eventually become the most famous in cognitive neuroscience, known by the initials H.M. Two years before, epileptic seizures had left him unable to work or live a normal life. Near-toxic doses of medication had proved ineffective, and the twenty-seven-year-old H.M. had undergone "a radical bilateral temporal-lobe resection." This experimental brain operation, Milner writes, did control the epilepsy, "but at far too high a price." H.M. could no longer remember what he had eaten for breakfast. His earlier memories remained intact "and his social behaviour entirely appropriate." Milner discovered that his I.Q. had risen, and that he could retain a three-digit number for fifteen minutes by continuous rehearsal: "Yet the moment his attention was diverted by a new topic, the whole event was forgotten."

Subsequent studies enabled Milner, acutely sensitive to human tragedy, to make extraordinary advances in understanding memory. Over the ensuing years, she and her graduate students distinguished between "a primary memory process with a rapid decay and an overlapping secondary process (impaired in H.M.) by which the long-term storage of information is achieved." Milner's pioneering work with H.M. led to neurological breakthroughs in the 1970s and '80s, when researchers undertook behavioural studies with monkeys. Neuropsychology flourished at the Montreal Neurological Institute, and spawned extensive collaborations with doctors in Britain, the United States, Italy, and Japan. In the 1980s, Milner served as director of neuropsychology at MNI, and continued to lead research teams until she was well into her eighties. After fifty years in the field, Milner reflected that she had had "a lot of luck in being in the right place at the right time, but also enough tenacity of purpose not to be discouraged when the going got rough." At this stage, she added, her greatest satisfaction "comes from seeing behavioural neuroscience so firmly established."

Brenda Milner changed the world by laying the foundations of neuroscience. In 2004, when she was made a Companion of the Order of Canada, she was said to be known "around the world for revolutionizing the study of memory," and for using advanced technology "to broaden our understanding of cognitive learning, language, sensations and emotions." Five years later, when at age ninety she was still directing MNI research as Dorothy J. Killam Professor, Milner won the Balzan Prize for Cognitive Neuroscience. That Europe-based international award is worth $1 million, half of which must go to research by young scientists—an arrangement Milner welcomed joyfully as both challenging and "very rejuvenating."

In November 2012, Milner was named to the Canadian Science and Engineering Hall of Fame—the ninth woman and fifty-fourth researcher to be so honoured. After her acceptance speech, according to a story in *The Globe and Mail*, female scientists crowded around, anxious to be photographed with her. Milner accepted their kudos gracefully, though she prefers to see herself as a scientist among scientists. Thanks to the Balzan Prize, she recently began to oversee two new post-doctoral fellowships, making her, almost certainly, the oldest supervisory scientist in the world.

44

JOHN POLANYI

A Nobel Prize winner points the way to lasers

"Modern science has totally transformed our world," Canadian scientist John Polanyi wrote in an article called "The Power of Ideas." "We can, today, be alive under circumstances that would previously have spelled death. We can be transported speedily wherever on earth we wish and see what we wish. We can mass-produce most things, including, appallingly, death." As a result, the Nobel Prize winner added, "we can no longer wall ourselves off from one another, nor therefore have nations as we used to, nor make war as we did, nor squander resources, nor litter the globe or neglect the oppressed, as has so long been our custom."

Polanyi changed the world by doing research that led to chemical lasers, and to an industry worth more than $1 billion. In his 1997 article, writing of what he called "fundamental science," he insisted that "by far the greater part of this [scientific] transformation has been for the good." But he warned that scientific ideas "will overpower us unless we *continue* to value them, rejecting mindless materialism and fanaticism." A couple of years later, Polanyi—widely regarded as a spokesperson for scientists globally—reiterated this warning: "Some would wish us [scientists] only to discover things that can be used for good. We should not even pretend to do that, because we cannot. What basic science gives us is a powerful vocabulary, and it is impossible to produce a vocabulary that can be used only to say nice things."

Polanyi's message is more timely than ever. Late in 2012, nearly 100 scientists and researchers at the National Research Council received layoff notices as part of a shift from purely scientific to industry-driven research—a shift that one critic described as short-sighted: "Industry hits singles and science hits home runs."

In 1933, when Berlin-born John Polanyi was four years old, his father, a prominent chemist of Hungarian Jewish background, moved the family from Germany to Manchester, England. This he did in response to the rise of Adolf Hitler and the persecution of Jews. In 1940, when the boy was eleven and Manchester became a bombing target during the Second World War, his father sent him to Toronto to live with a Canadian family. At school, he dabbled in sociology and literature, and in science class, instead of following instructions to obtain a particular result, he would try different approaches to see what would happen. His teachers complained that he lacked discipline, but his intuitive curiosity would one day pay dividends.

When the war ended, the youth returned to Manchester, finished high school, and attended university. Although he dabbled in poetry, Polanyi completed his Ph.D. in chemistry in 1952. "Chemistry was the field in which I felt at home," he wrote later. "My father was a chemist for a major part of his career, so the sight and smell of a chemistry laboratory was lodged in my subconscious." After graduating, Polanyi spent two years doing post-doctoral research at the National Research Council in Ottawa, working on the energy states of molecules. He moved to Princeton University as a research assistant, and in 1956, he took a job as a lecturer at the University of Toronto, which provided him with a glorified broom closet in which to do research.

One autumn evening, with the assistance of a graduate student, Polanyi created an experiment to determine what happens in a particular chemical reaction. He set up an apparatus involving hydrogen, chlorine, a vacuum pump and an electrical discharge unit from an old neon sign. He threw a switch, jolted the gas with 6,000 volts of electricity and, for the first time in history, recorded the tiny bit of light emitted when hydrogen reacts with chlorine. This "chemi-luminescence" enabled him to predict the amount of energy needed to create a given chemical reaction. Nine years later, American scientists would use Polanyi's findings to create a chemical laser that emitted infrared light.

Polanyi won the 1986 Nobel Prize as a result of asking a new question about what happens when molecules collide: What types of forces lead to a chemical reaction and the making of a new molecule? His experiment measured the feeble infrared emission in a newly formed molecule of hydrogen chloride. This explained, he wrote, "how the newborn molecules vibrate and rotate, and hence what forces are operating when they are born." This new understanding led to the creation of "a large category of lasers based on vibrating molecules . . . the most powerful sources of infrared radiation in existence." In other words, he added, as a result of an attempt to understand molecular reactions, "one of the world's most significant technologies was born. And that is the power of fundamental science."

During the years before he won the Nobel, at the University of Toronto, Polanyi advanced briskly. He became a full professor in 1962. Down through the decades, he would publish 250 scientific articles aimed at his peers, and another 100 geared to a broad general audience, focusing on science policy and armaments control. In these, he repeatedly stressed the importance of scientific research. Having given the world lasers, Polanyi co-edited a book whose title said much: *The Dangers of Nuclear War*.

Meanwhile, he achieved recognition not just in Canada but globally, from such organizations as the Faraday Society, the British Chemical Society, and the Royal Society of London. Awarded two dozen honorary degrees, he was also welcomed into the U.S. National Academy of

Sciences, the Pontifical Academy of Sciences, and the Royal Society of Edinburgh. When he received the Nobel, along with two American scientists who had built on his work, Polanyi was cited for developing "a new field of research in chemistry—reaction dynamics—[which] has provided a much more detailed understanding of how chemical reactions take place." Even more specifically, Polanyi was cited for pioneering "the method of infrared chemi-luminescence, in which the extremely weak infrared emission from a newly formed molecule is measured and analysed. He has used this method to elucidate the detailed energy disposal during chemical reactions."

Eight years after he won the Nobel Prize, eleven fellow laureates gathered at the University of Toronto to honour Polanyi at the inauguration of the John C. Polanyi Chair in Chemistry. At the gala festivities, Polanyi returned to an old favourite theme. "For one of the wealthiest and most favoured nations in the world to turn its back on the sort of research represented by those gathered here today," he said, "would be a betrayal of the hope that has brought so many to this country. It would be as if the early settlers, complaining of the peril of their existence, declined to map the land. The prosperity that we owe to those pioneers affords us a dazzling opportunity today to explore the vast new land of science. By exploring with daring, we shall leave a legacy that matches the one that is ours."

45

STEM CELL RESEARCHERS

An "accidental" discovery transforms human biology

In the summer of 1960, eight years before Pierre Elliott Trudeau became prime minister of Canada, and around the time that Brenda Milner was laying the foundations of neuroscience, two young scientists working at the Ontario Cancer Institute in Toronto were studying radiation sensitivity by injecting bone marrow cells into irradiated mice. Ernest McCulloch, a hematologist (blood specialist), and James Till, a biophysicist, were surprised to discover that the number of visible nodules in the spleens of the mice matched the number of bone marrow cells with which they had been injected. The two called the nodules "spleen colonies" and speculated that each arose from a single marrow cell, a "colony forming unit." Their hypothesis, which emerged in a scientific paper they wrote in July and published in *Radiation Research* in February 1961, proved correct. McCulloch and Till had discovered stem cells.

That discovery, which they called "accidental," and for which they won the 1969 Gairdner Foundation International Award, changed the world by laying the foundation for bone marrow transplants. Not incidentally, it turned Toronto into a global leader in stem cell research. According to Christopher Paige, vice-president of research at the University Health Network, "It's impossible to overstate the enormity of Till's and McCulloch's discovery and long-time collaboration. Their work changed the course of cancer research and lit the way to what we now call regenerative medicine—the use of stem cells for bone marrow transplants and many other types of disease research."

Paige, marking the fiftieth anniversary of the discovery, added, "Toronto is truly the city where stem cell science was born, thanks to Till and McCulloch." In March 2012, Alan Bernstein, president of the Canadian Institute for Advanced Research, reiterated this in *The Globe and Mail*, explaining that the discovery "transformed the understanding of human biology" and led to the creation of "the entire field of stem-cell science." Toronto-based scientists "have done much of the heavy lifting for decades," Bernstein added, "discovering neural stem cells, skin stem cells and cancer stem cells. If hockey is Canada's game, stem-cell science is Canada's science. Not knowing about Dr. Till and Dr. McCulloch is not knowing about Maurice Richard and Wayne Gretzky." In 2004, McCulloch (1926–2011) and Till (1931–) were made Officers of the Order of Canada and inducted into the Canadian Medical Hall of Fame. The following year, they received the Albert Lasker Award, considered the most prestigious medical science award in the United States.

Meanwhile, in 2002, the Canadian Institutes of Health Research developed guidelines for stem cell research that, Bernstein tells us, "have become the gold standard for other countries, including the United States." The following year, thanks to a donation from business leaders Robert and Cheryl McEwen, the McEwen Centre for Regenerative Medicine was established at Toronto's University Health Network. It focuses on harnessing the power of stem cells to treat such conditions as heart disease, diabetes, respiratory disease, and spinal cord injury.

The McEwen Centre has solidified Canada's reputation as a global leader in stem cell research. It stands behind a bone marrow transplant program at Princess Margaret Hospital, for example, that alone has saved thousands of lives. And it has become a hub for leading specialists and researchers. In 2007, Saskatchewan-born scientist Gordon

Keller returned home to Canada from New York to direct the McEwen Centre. Keller (b. 1950) had spent more than two decades working in Europe and the United States, and had become director of a stem cell institute at the Mount Sinai School of Medicine.

New York Magazine had recently profiled him as one of "Six Doctors New York Can't Lose." But Keller, named by *The Globe and Mail* in 2010 as one of twenty-five "transformational Canadians," felt drawn to the McEwan Centre because "Canada, and Toronto in particular, has a very strong scientific community, but also a very strong stem cell biology community." As a Canadian, he also appreciated the chance "to return home and spend part of my career here." Keller has been amazed by the speed at which stem cell research has progressed: "What I find most remarkable is the evolution of the field and seeing it change almost on a weekly basis." The greatest challenge, he said, "is to find a way to get the cells that we make in a dish to integrate into adult tissue and function."

Another McEwen researcher, Andras Nagy, was named to the *Scientific American* Top 10 Honor Roll in 2011. He was the only Canadian on a list that included U.S. President Barack Obama and businessman-philanthropist Bill Gates. Born and raised in Hungary, Nagy came to Canada in 1988 on a three-month trip as a visiting scientist and settled here the following year. He has explained that times were tough in Hungary and he saw little scope for funded research. This country, on the other hand, had made an official policy of multiculturalism. It offered an atmosphere conducive to discovery and innovation: "Science is a unifying field. What I loved about Canada was the openness and the enthusiasm to innovate."

The first thing he did on arriving was to take evening classes in English. "It was a daunting time because of my heavy work schedule," he said in 2011, but he needed language skills to succeed and "I enjoyed it thoroughly." The hard work paid off. Today, Nagy is senior investigator at the Samuel Lunenfeld Research Institute at Toronto's Mount Sinai Hospital. Scientists in that laboratory are of eighteen different ethnicities. Nagy noted, "My lab reflects the multicultural flavour of Canada."

That lab also gets results. *Scientific American* recognized Nagy for "demonstrating exceptional leadership and accomplishment in guaranteeing that new technologies and biomedical discoveries are applied to the benefit of humanity." In 2009, Nagy discovered a new method of creating stem cells from adult cells. He was building on recent advances made by Japanese and American scientists who created stem cells from a patient's skin. Their technique relied on viruses, which risks creating cancerous cells. Nagy's approach avoided this problem. Also, by using a patient's skin cells, it circumvented the ethical concerns of those who question the morality of using stem cells.

Keller and Nagy signify what is happening in Toronto, where in 2012, between forty and fifty early-phase clinical trials, as yet unfunded, were ready to roll using transplanted cells. These are under the guidance of figures such as Janet Rossant, the developmental biologist who invited Nagy to Toronto. Today, she is chief of research at Toronto's Hospital for Sick Children Research Institute. Her research has produced major findings on how genetically identical cells adopt distinct characteristics during embryo development. This is crucial to understanding diseases caused by abnormal development processes, as well as birth defects and genetic predispositions to various diseases, such as cancer.

Another award-winning scientist, John E. Dick, based at the Toronto General Research Institute, was the first to identify cancer stem cells in certain types of human leukemia. His findings highlighted the importance of understanding that not all cancer cells are the same, and so opened up a new direction in cancer research. Meanwhile, at McMaster University in Hamilton, Mick Bhatia has led the way in determining how to make human blood from adult human skin. This discovery, published in November 2011 in the science journal *Nature*, could mean that those in need of blood for any number of reasons could have it created from a patch of their own skin.

Bhatia, director of McMaster's Cancer and Stem Cell Biology Research Institute, has found a way to make the conversion directly, without any intermediate step. "We have shown this works using human skin," Bhatia said in the *McMaster Daily News*. "We know how it works and believe we can even improve on the process. We'll now go on to work on developing other types of human cell types from skin, as we already have encouraging evidence." Bhatia's research was funded by the Canadian Institutes of Health Research, the Canadian Cancer Society Research Institute, the Stem Cell Network, and the Ontario Ministry of Research and Innovation. And it derives directly, as does all of the work outlined above, from the 1960 discovery of stem cells by two young Canadian scientists.

46

DAVID SUZUKI

An environmental warrior awakens the world to climate change

At the Stein Valley Festival in the British Columbia rainforest (see the introduction to this section on page 275), David Suzuki began answering the question that more than 17,000 people had asked in letters. "We want to help protect the earth. What can we do?" Suzuki spoke for half an hour, arguing that the earth comprises a single eco-system and must be treated as such. "If you care about this planet," he said, "if you care about your children's future, you must support native land claims with all your strength and all your passion because there lies the way out of this mess we're in. If native peoples win, everyone wins."

Three months after speaking at Stein Valley, Suzuki began elaborating. He organized a gathering of environmentalists on Pender Island, one of the Gulf Islands off the west coast of British Columbia. The ensuing brainstorming session, which included scientists, lawyers, professors, writers, and First Nations administrators, decided to create a science-based organization to bring information to the public. The group insisted, despite Suzuki's protracted opposition, on calling it the David Suzuki Foundation. After all, Suzuki had not only brought the foundation into existence, but had become prominent enough to attract attention and resources. David Suzuki changed the world by awakening people to climate change.

In 1942, when Vancouver-born Suzuki was six years old, he and his family were uprooted and brought to a Japanese Canadian internment camp in the interior of British Columbia. The previous December, with a surprise attack on Pearl Harbor, Japan had entered the Second World War. But Suzuki, one of the few children who spoke almost no Japanese, felt himself an outsider whichever way he turned. Later, he would write that his life as an adult, and notably his drive to succeed, "has been motivated by the desire to demonstrate to my fellow Canadians that my family and I had not deserved to be treated as we were."

When the war ended, as we have learned from Joy Kogawa, Japanese Canadians were ordered to relocate east of the Rockies. Suzuki and his family moved to southwestern Ontario, where his father joined his uncles in a construction business. Encouraged by his parents, young David shone as a student in both elementary and high school. In his last year at London Central Secondary School, trained as a public speaker by his father, Suzuki was elected president of the students' council.

Yet still he felt an outsider. Throughout high school, like the Scottish Canadian Farley Mowat, he took refuge in nature: "My main solace was a large swamp a ten-minute bike ride from our house." The boy was fascinated by plant and animal life, especially insects: "Anyone who spotted me in that swamp would have had confirmation of my absolute nerdiness as I waded in fully clothed, my eyes at water level, peering beneath the surface, a net and jar in my hands behind my back."

Suzuki worked summers for Suzuki Brothers Construction, and was stunned when he learned that many of his classmates did not work at all during the holiday. "The alienation that began with our evacuation from the coast of B.C. and continued through high school," he writes, "has remained a fundamental part of who I am."

Thanks to his strong academic record and the recommendation of a well-connected former classmate, Suzuki received a scholarship to attend the prestigious Amherst College in Massachusetts. Despite his loneliness as seemingly the only Asian at Amherst, he adjusted to the high expectations and excelled, earning his bachelor of science degree in 1958. He had been accepted into medical school at the University of Western Ontario in London, but opted to study genetics instead, and headed for the University of Chicago (U of C): "My mother was disconsolate for weeks after I told her I was not going to become a doctor, and that I would study fruit flies instead."

In 1961, at twenty-five, Suzuki received his doctorate in zoology from U of C. He found work as a researcher at Oak Ridge National Laboratory in Tennessee, which he describes as "an oasis of liberalism" in a southern American state that showed "overt signs of racism." Suzuki identified strongly with the black community and felt deeply estranged from American mainstream culture. After one year in Tennessee, he landed a job in Edmonton, taking a pay cut to join the University of Alberta as an assistant professor. "Even though Canada had invoked the War Measures Act against Japanese Canadians," he writes, "the country was smaller, and I believed there was more of a chance to work for a better society. The opportunities for a scientist in the United States were much greater at that time, but I have never regretted my decision to return home."

From Edmonton, Suzuki landed a job in Vancouver at the University of British Columbia (UBC). He remained linked to that institution throughout his career, becoming a tenured and then an emeritus professor, while evolving into a world leader on environmental issues. He recalls that, not long after he arrived at UBC, he heard a colleague boasting that the university had one of the best zoology departments in Canada and felt upset: "I was only interested in being among the best in the world."

In 1972, Suzuki received the E.W.R. Steacie Memorial Fellowship as Canada's outstanding research scientist under the age of thirty-five. Four years later, he co-authored *An Introduction to Genetic Analysis*, which has been translated into seven languages and remains the most widely used genetics textbook in the United States. Suzuki then began writing for a broader audience. He has written or co-authored more than fifty books, including nineteen for children.

Internationally, Suzuki has made his greatest impact through television. He began dabbling in broadcasting in the 1960s, hosting science programs for CBC Radio. He never dreamed, he writes, that broadcasting "would occupy most of my life and make me a celebrity in Canada." But Suzuki proved wonderfully effective on both radio and television, and projects overlapped and multiplied. In 1971, he launched *Suzuki on Science* on CBC-TV, a program aimed at children. Three years later, he began hosting *Quirks & Quarks* on CBC Radio. He then developed two acclaimed radio series on the environment, *It's a Matter of Survival* and *From Naked Ape to Superspecies*. The same year he launched *Quirks & Quarks*, he began a five-year stint hosting *Science Magazine* on CBC-TV. In 1979, he kicked off *The Nature of Things with David Suzuki*, an award-winning series that aired in nearly fifty countries, changing public opinion on everything from renewable energy to wildlife habitat conservation.

His achievements have not gone unrecognized. Here in Canada, Suzuki has been adopted into three First Nations clans. He was elected to the Royal Society of Canada and is a Companion of the Order of Canada. Suzuki has won four Gemini Awards as best host of a TV series, and in 2002 he received the John Drainie Award for broadcasting excellence. In 2004, when the CBC held a vote to choose the all-time greatest Canadian, David Suzuki placed fifth—but since all those ahead of him had already died, he had in fact been voted the greatest living Canadian.

Nor has he lacked international recognition. In 1985, his eight-part series *A Planet for the Taking* attracted a world audience of almost two million viewers per episode. Another eight-part series, *The Secret of Life*

(BBC/PBS), drew international acclaim, and so did a five-part Discovery Channel series called *The Brain*. Suzuki has received twenty-five honorary degrees around the world. He is the recipient of UNESCO's Kalinga Prize for the Popularization of Science and a United Nations Environment Programme Medal. In 2009, he won the Right Livelihood Award, which is considered the "Alternative Nobel Prize."

But let's go back to the result of the Stein Valley Festival. In 1989, having launched the David Suzuki Foundation, the man himself went to work giving lectures to raise operational funds. His wife, Tara Cullis, organized volunteers and sent out 25,000 letters. Before long, they had raised enough money to begin hiring staff, starting with ex-politician Jim Fulton, who took a drastic pay cut to become the foundation's executive director. Fulton jumped into the job with both feet, Suzuki writes, launching projects "as if we already had the money. I'm still hostage to my early years of poverty, but he had faith that we would raise the necessary funds. And he was right, but in the beginning, I was very nervous about all the spending."

With every author, some books are more significant than others. And in 1997, when Suzuki published *The Sacred Balance: Rediscovering Our Place in Nature*, he channelled the royalties—worth well over $200,000 and counting—to the foundation that bears his name. That book, which also became a five-hour miniseries, explores the impact of humankind on the natural world and warns against toxic pollution and global warming. These concerns are central to the David Suzuki Foundation. Many of its early projects were international in scope, and involved working with indigenous peoples not only on Vancouver Island, but in Australia, Japan, Columbia, and Brazil. The foundation has also inspired copycat environmental organizations around the world. Together, they have driven climate change onto the international agenda. The work is not finished. But thanks to Suzuki, it is well begun.

47

MICHAEL R. HAYDEN

An immigrant geneticist battles rare diseases

When Michael Hayden was a twenty-six-year-old medical student at the University of Cape Town in South Africa, just beginning to work on a Ph.D. in genetics, he came across a patient suffering from Huntington's chorea. This devastating disease, which strikes about one person in 10,000, causes uncontrollable movements and progresses to dementia. Medical orthodoxy held that it did not exist in Africa. And when Hayden reported his discovery to his favourite "crazy professor," Peter Beighton, the older scientist responded with pointed whimsy: "H is for Hayden, H is for Huntington's. Why don't you spend your time on Huntington's?"

This casual suggestion would change not only Hayden's life, but the lives of tens of thousands of people around the world. As he worked on his doctorate, Hayden met hundreds of families affected by Huntington's disease. By 1978, well on his way to becoming an authority on this little-known disease, he attended a conference in San Diego. There he met the influential widow of the folksinger Woody Guthrie, who had died of Huntington's. She had just succeeded in getting the American Congress to set up a commission to control the disease, and she invited Hayden to continue his work in the United States.

According to a story by Claudia Cornwall in *BCBusiness*, Hayden was open to emigrating from apartheid South Africa because he had begun attracting police attention: "My phone was tapped and I had been taken in a few times." Hayden went to work at Boston Children's Hospital and did post-doctoral research at Harvard Medical School. In 1983, when he accepted an offer from the University of British Columbia (UBC), his Harvard colleagues thought he was crazy, that he was moving to the back of beyond to become irrelevant. The last three decades have proven them farcically wrong. Now a Killam Professor of Medical Genetics at UBC, holder of a Canada Research Chair in Human Genetics and Molecular Medicine, and the most cited author in his field, Michael Hayden has changed the world by transforming our understanding of Huntington's disease.

His numerous honours include the Order of Canada, and in 2011, he received the Canada Gairdner Wightman Award, frequently a predictor of Nobel Prize winners. Hayden is also founder and director of the Centre for Molecular Medicine and Therapeutics at UBC. And he has founded three biotechnology companies, enabling him to find treatments for patients with rare diseases who are often ignored by the pharmaceutical industry. In a video available online, Hayden declares that UBC and Vancouver have provided "an environment that has given life support to my dreams." He cites "the incredible students, who have come here from every country in the world; the faculty who have crossed traditional boundaries from arts, science and medicine; and the community in which we live."

Born in Cape Town, South Africa, on November 21, 1951, Hayden saw his parents divorce when he was eight. He grew up with his strong-minded mother, who scooted around town on a Vespa and risked persecution by illegally allowing black people into her home. Hayden originally planned to become a lawyer but worried that he would end up defending the South African legal system and shifted to medicine.

In his thirties, while based at UBC, he published the results of his genetics research in such leading journals as *Nature*, *The Lancet*, and the *New England Journal of Medicine*. Some of his findings showed significant potential for treating patients, and when drug companies declined to pursue those leads, Hayden grew frustrated. In 1992, he founded the Centre for Molecular Medicine and Therapeutics, an interdisciplinary research institute. He won the support of the Montreal-based pharmaceutical company Merck Frosst Canada, which provided $15 million, no strings attached.

With various colleagues, Hayden founded two companies, one that produced drugs to treat a rare form of brain cancer (glioblastoma), and another, called Xenon, that addressed the problems of osteoporosis and low bone density, especially prevalent in South Africa. Proceeding on the premise that understanding the genetics of rare diseases generates insights into more common ones, Hayden identified a gene, ABCA1, that has improved the treatment of cardiovascular disease. Hayden gained the support of major pharmaceutical companies, including Pfizer (U.S.), Novartis (Switzerland), and Takeda Pharmaceutical (Japan). In 1997, he discovered that a drug used to treat epilepsy alleviated the suffering of patients with Huntington's. But to Hayden's dismay, decision-makers at the company that produced the drug refused to underwrite the relatively cheap clinical trial needed to expand usage: they could not make enough profit.

An infuriated Hayden identified two like-minded medical researchers and with them founded another company, Aspreva. Their research suggested that CellCept, used to prevent rejection in organ transplants, might also work with lupus and other autoimmune disorders. The three men approached the maker of CellCept, the Swiss corporation F. Hoffmann-La Roche, and signed a deal. In 2005, when Aspreva offered shares to the public, it raised $100 million overnight. Within two years, Aspreva became the second most profitable biotech company in Canada. Another Swiss pharmaceutical giant, Galenica Group, bought it for $915 million. As chief scientific director of Xenon,

Hayden remains bent on developing a Vancouver-based cutting-edge genetics and pharmaceutical company with a global reach. Already, Xenon's innovative methods have attracted the support of a world-wide clinical network. Recently, it has been studying those rare individuals who do not perceive pain, with a view to developing drugs that will treat common forms of pain.

For Michael Hayden, author of more than 600 peer-reviewed publications, the accolades keep coming. In 2006, he received five entrepreneurial awards, including one for career achievement from the BC Innovation Council. Two years later, he was named Canada's Health Researcher of the Year and was one of the five finalists in *The Globe and Mail*'s nation-builder competition. The Gairdner Foundation may have summarized his achievements best when it presented Hayden with the $100,000 Wightman Award, citing his "outstanding national and international leadership for medical genetics, entrepreneurship, and humanitarianism." That just about covers it.

48

Mike Lazaridis

An electrical engineer sparks a communications revolution

Walk down any main street at rush hour in any major city in the world. How far will you travel before you spot someone using a smartphone? Twenty metres? Thirty? Five? Certainly you will not get far before you see a mobile user talking on the phone, sending a text message, browsing the Web, playing a game, catching up on Facebook, or using an app to check the news on the far side of the world.

You can get some idea of the answer without even leaving home. Just flip open your smartphone and do a Google search: "How many people have smartphones?" This will turn up millions of links—no exaggeration. Click around and you will find a few credible sources. You might discover, for example, that mobile Web users around the world number more than 1.2 billion, with Asia leading the way in saturation. Many "mobile handset" users, 25 percent in the United States, rarely access the Web using any other device, such as a desktop, laptop, or tablet computers. More than twenty million Canadians have a mobile device, including eight million smartphones (40 percent and soaring). Put it this way: from Glasgow to Buenos Aires, Frankfurt to Seoul, and Calgary to Kuala Lumpur, people are using mobile phones to trade text messages, shoot photographs, download music, watch videos, check Twitter, play games, and buy goods and services.

It is staggering to realize that, just twenty years ago, having a mobile phone meant you could make or receive a telephone call, period. To do anything else you needed a different device, a pager or personal data assistant (PDA) that would enable you to connect to the Internet. Today, consumers buy about three million stand-alone PDAs each year, compared with more than 150 million smartphones. The communications revolution is all around us. And the man who launched it, who made it happen with the help of others, is a Greek Canadian engineer and businessman whose parents brought him to Canada from Turkey when he was five. Mihalis "Mike" Lazaridis changed the world by inventing the BlackBerry, the wireless handheld device that turned the cellphone into a smartphone.

Born in Istanbul on March 14, 1961, to a Greek Christian family in a world of Turkish Muslims, Mike Lazaridis arrived in Windsor, Ontario, late in 1966. His father worked at a tool-and-die shop and then on the assembly line for Chrysler, while his mother worked as a waitress and a seamstress. Before arriving in Canada, the boy had played obsessively with an electric train. At eleven, he conducted experiments with walkie-talkies. Before he turned twelve, he had received a special prize from the Windsor Public Library for having read all the science books on the shelves.

Attending a well-equipped high school, he took both academic subjects and shop, which included hands-on work in automotive mechanics and electronics. In *BlackBerry: The Inside Story of Research in Motion*, author Rod McQueen describes Lazaridis as a precocious student. His shop teacher would recall that, when other students were finishing a first module on lighting, Lazaridis would be using the next three or four modules to test out some theory. When a fire disabled the system that powered individual workbenches, the teacher assigned Lazaridis to fix it. "In the end I got it working," he told McQueen, "but it took me a long time."

Still in his teens, Lazaridis built an oscilloscope, an electronic test instrument that measures voltages. He became keenly interested in computers, read several books on microprocessors, and decided to build his own computer. With the help of a long-time friend, Doug Fregin, he scrounged parts from the high school lab, built a rudimentary computer, and programmed it to play a game that entertained even his mother.

After graduating from high school, Lazaridis decided to attend the University of Waterloo, already a leader in engineering, mathematics, and computer science. It also ran a unique co-op program that mixed work and study so that he could earn much needed money as he progressed. While studying, he worked for Control Data Corporation at a major research and manufacturing site. He saved the company time and money by devising an automated process to identify failed circuit boards. This got him assigned to a team developing an air-cooled mini-computer. Internal office politics derailed that project, but Lazaridis remembered the experience as special because he was working on "brand-new integrated technology, new packaging, a new physics. . . . We're not talking about a satellite office here, we built and designed our own stuff."

By late 1983, when Pierre Elliott Trudeau was nearing the end of his political career, Mike Lazaridis was in his final year at Waterloo. He knew not only that he wanted to create something transformative, but that he needed to be his own boss. With Fregin, who was also studying electrical engineering, Lazaridis built a computerized device that allowed users to display messages on a series of pages that showed up on a screen. It was designed as an in-store advertising device, and Lazaridis called it a Budgie. After devising a controller for a hot-water tank and a program to allow pharmacists to keep track of medications, he decided to start his own company.

Nearing graduation, the impatient Lazaridis quit university, brought aboard his detail-man, Fregin, and rented a basement apartment to use as headquarters. While casting about for a company name involving "research," he caught a television show that used the phrase "poetry in motion." On March 7, 1984, he incorporated Research in Motion (RIM). His parents lent him $15,000 to launch the business, and the Ontario government provided a matching loan. With Fregin, he rented a two-room office in a strip mall, and there put the finishing touches on the Budgie. It sold poorly, but did lead to a major sign-building contract and then to further projects.

In 1987, Lazaridis attended a conference where a speaker described a wireless system in Japan that monitored vending machines. When supplies ran low, the machine would relay that news to a truck driver. North America had nothing like it, though Rogers Communications had begun investigating wireless data systems. These used a cellular infrastructure called Mobitex, a wireless network for two-way paging and mobile messaging originally developed so dispatchers could direct firemen and policemen. Unlike telephones, which use circuit switching, Mobitex relied on packet switching, which breaks down content into tiny segments and allows more data to travel in a smaller transmission space, or band.

Rogers had this network capability, but its only receivers were giant boxes that cost thousands of dollars. A Rogers executive got wind of RIM and late in 1989 contacted Lazaridis, who immediately accepted the challenge. RIM set out to link the Mobitex hardware with software and to create applications. By autumn 1990, Lazaridis and his team had created Mobi-Talk, a wireless chat program with a split screen so participants could see their messages in real time. A year later, when Rogers changed direction, RIM continued working on Mobitex.

The company had grown to twelve employees. Lazaridis, like Guy Laliberté before him, realized he could not do everything alone and showed an uncanny ability to attract key people. He had hired outstanding hardware engineers and software developers, but a recent attempt to bring aboard a business expert had collapsed. Then, in August 1992, Lazaridis got the chance to hire a savvy businessman with whom he had previously negotiated—a man five weeks older than himself who came from Peterborough, Ontario, and whose track record in business shone as bright as his own in electrical engineering.

While still in his twenties, Jim Balsillie had taken an MBA at Harvard Business School and worked as a chief financial officer. He joined RIM in August 1992. He invested $125,000, drawing on severance pay and an increased mortgage, and became a one-third owner (later to be increased). By now RIM was selling a lot of radio modems to people in field services and transportation. But Lazaridis and Balsillie both saw real possibilities in messaging devices and email. Cellphones had been growing in popularity, but wireless email had been languishing.

Lazaridis made the unusual move to go "two in a box" with Balsillie. He became co-CEO in charge of research, development, and production, while Balsillie handled business development and finance. In 1993, with this arrangement in place, RIM made its first big wireless sale for 2,500 Mobitex modems that would relay messages between corporate computers and paging networks. This generated $3 million in revenue. Lazaridis decided to focus exclusively on the wireless business. As one engineer put it, "That was the moment that changed RIM."

The strategy paid off with more deals. In 1994, with email growing in popularity, Lazaridis fixed his attention on inventing and manufacturing a portable, user-friendly device that would allow people to send and receive email. At this point, they could use cellphones for voice and pagers to receive simple messages such as "Call the office." Lazaridis wanted to create a portable wireless device—"email on a belt"—that could send and receive longer messages. He had seen the PalmPilot, with a touch screen and flawed handwriting recognition, and wanted no part of that. He wanted RIM to develop a device with a keyboard.

The technological challenge was massive. But Intel was designing computer chips that were ever smaller, and Lazaridis specified his goals for the first wireless handheld device. It had to last a long time on a single small battery, take the rough form of a one-way pager, and be workable with one hand. In mid-1996, RIM received the parts from Intel that enabled it to build its first portable two-way wireless messaging device, the Inter@ctive Pager 900. It featured a full keyboard, a four-line display screen, and four rubber buttons for navigation, and it ran on two batteries. Because of its bulbous shape, people nicknamed it Bullfrog.

RIM made a sleeker version, the 950, known as the Leapfrog. And as Intel produced smaller chips, RIM put them to use. Faced with critics and doubters, Lazaridis produced a vision document he called "Success Lies in Paradox," elaborating a strategy for turning an existing wireless data network into a two-way network using devices (Leapfrogs) that look and feel like pagers but with far greater capability. Balsillie turned that document into a glowing PowerPoint presentation, and in 1997 closed a deal with BellSouth for $70 million worth of Leapfrogs, so driving total orders to $100 million.

The Leapfrog was the precursor of the next mobile device, which would not only send and receive emails and have an address book and calendar, but would be able to access mailboxes on desktop computers back at the office. In 1998, RIM hired a specialist firm, Lexicon Branding, to come up with a name for this device. Before long, they had settled on the BlackBerry. Lazaridis and Balsillie launched the BlackBerry on January 19, 1999. Early adopters included Intel, IBM, Dell, Oracle, and the American armed forces. By February 2000, there were 25,000 subscribers. A decade later, RIM had sold over 75 million BlackBerries.

By 2010, with annual revenues of about $15 billion, RIM topped the list of 100 Fastest-Growing Companies in the World. The BlackBerry continued to evolve and, inevitably, spawned fierce competition. In recent years, competitors have cut into its market share, and the company has run into well-publicized troubles. Lazaridis and Balsillie both stepped back to let RIM find its own way. In January 2013, the company launched an array of BlackBerry 10 devices. It also rebranded itself, changing its name from RIM to BlackBerry in a move widely interpreted as signalling a new era.

Whatever happens next with the corporation, these facts remain: the BlackBerry was the first smartphone, the original device, the one that revolutionized global communications. And Mike Lazaridis invented it.

49

SARA SEAGER

An astrophysicist leads the search for life on other planets

When she was twenty-four years old and beginning work on her doctoral thesis at Harvard University, physicist Sara Seager learned of the discovery of several extrasolar planets orbiting distant Sun-like stars. These "exoplanets" were larger than Earth and nearer their respective stars, but they raised the question: Would scientists soon find planets that resemble our own? Planets that support life? Fascinated, Seager faced a difficult choice. The subject of a doctoral thesis lays the foundation for any career in science. Having become a specialist, Seager would get hired or not on the basis of her particular expertise. But would exoplanets become a legitimate field of study? Some physicists called them a flash in the pan.

The year was 1995. Only four exoplanets had been confirmed. None resembled Earth, or even the giant planets in our solar system, Jupiter and Saturn. If the field proved irrelevant, or unable to support and reward extensive study, it would wither and die. But Seager, who had become a math and physics specialist at the University of Toronto, decided to follow her instincts: she turned away from theoretical physics to pursue astronomy, her "first love." The gamble paid off. Since the mid-1990s, scientists have identified more than 500 exoplanets, using instruments to measure a star's "wobble" in relation to a planet's gravitational pull, or its temporary drop in starlight as an orbiting planet passes in front of the star.

In 2011, scientists confirmed the existence of twenty-eight exoplanets and another 1,235 candidates. Those confirmed included one exoplanet, Kepler-20f, that is very slightly larger than Earth and inside the "habitable zone" of its star. Already, a 2006 textbook called *The Earth and the Moon* had declared the field "fascinating, fruitful, and relevant." It also profiled Seager, now an astronomer at the Massachusetts Institute of Technology who works with the most advanced telescope in the world, as "one of its first and most prominent researchers." Seager is changing the world by leading the search for life on other planets.

Born in Toronto on July 21, 1971, Sara Seager remembers being five or six years old, sitting in the back of a station wagon with several other girls on the way home from her suburban school, and realizing she had nothing in common with them. "But it wasn't a sad thought," she told a *Globe and Mail* reporter in 2011. "Because if you don't fit in, you don't have to do normal things." Her father, a general practitioner who would become a hair transplant specialist, encouraged her to pursue her passions, including astronomy. One of her earliest memories is of her father taking her to a "star party" to look at the moon through a telescope. "He was constantly doing things to make me uncomfortable," Seager said, "to push my boundaries, then push them again."

Seager attended Jarvis Collegiate Institute, the oldest high school in Toronto, renowned for its science program. She was surprised to learn that someone could earn a living as an astrophysicist, but entered the University of Toronto, focusing on math and physics. Then came Harvard and the Ph.D. turnaround. In a book called *Talking About Life: Conversations on Astrobiology*, edited by Chris Impey, Seager says she was "working on recombination in the early universe. But that problem was becoming a dead end, so I wrapped up my calculations. The basic physics had been worked out by other people, and I was just dotting I's and crossing T's."

The discovery of four extrasolar planets opened up a possible new field. "It was exciting," Seager says. "The whole paradigm of planets established by our Solar System—the Jupiters far from the star and the terrestrial planets closer—was shot. There was a new class of giant planets close to the star." Many scientists were sceptical of exoplanets, insisting that they might be "some kind of stellar variation." But as she studied the newly discovered "hot-Jupiters," Seager realized with increasing excitement that she was onto something. Her thesis, *Extrasolar Giant Planets Under Strong Stellar Irradiation*, has long since been vindicated.

After receiving her Ph.D. in 1999, Seager did post-doctoral work at the Institute for Advanced Study in Princeton, New Jersey, where Albert Einstein was once a faculty member. There she found a mentor in the late John Bahcall, an astrophysicist who helped develop the Hubble Space Telescope. From Princeton, Seager went to the Carnegie Institution for Science in Washington, and then to the Massachusetts Institute of Technology, where she became a professor of physics and planetary science. Her academic honours include the Helen B. Warner Prize for Astronomy from the American Astronomical Society and the Bok Prize from Harvard's Department of Astronomy. *Discover* magazine named her one of the "20 Best Brains Under 40," and *Nature* magazine one of its "Ten People Who Mattered" in 2011.

Seager is a member of the Kepler Mission, sponsored by NASA, whose long-term objective is to prove that life exists beyond Earth. According to *Nature* magazine, Seager predicts that, centuries from now, "people will look back at us, and they won't remember me or you. They'll remember us as the generation of people who first found the Earth-like worlds" outside our solar system. But getting there won't be a cakewalk, as Seager is the first to admit. "Finding an Earth twin around a sun-like star," she told one reporter, "is like trying to see a firefly fluttering less than a foot from a huge searchlight—when the searchlight is 2,600 miles away."

Our galaxy is home to 50 billion planets, including 500 million in the zone where life could exist. The Kepler telescope can determine their size and orbital radius, but to identify an Earth-like planet with oxygen or other biological activity in its atmosphere, astronomers need a spectrum of the parent star's light to pass through or bounce off the atmosphere. The stars in Kepler's field of view are too far away, and so too dim, to allow for proper analysis. Seager is hunting Earth-like planets within 30 parsecs (98 light years). These she proposes to study with tiny space telescopes, 30-centimetre-long "ExoplanetSats," designed to watch a single star for a planetary transit. To analyze the data, she would need a large orbiting telescope such as the Terrestrial Planet Finder, a project which NASA put on hold in 2006.

But a fleet of ExoplanetSats could show the planet finder where to look. Each would cost less than $1 million, and dozens could piggyback cheaply on other missions. Her MIT group has raised roughly $3 million. Seager is studying the requisite engineering, and is hoping to launch some ExoplanetSats in 2013: "I'm trying to do new things." A Kepler colleague, astronomer Geoffrey Marcy, says Seager is taking a unique approach. She has already "pioneered several entirely new areas of planetary science," he says, "including the detection of Earth-like planets around other stars and the assessment of their chemical composition as gleaned from the light coming from their atmospheres." Seager herself says she hopes to change the way people see their place in the universe. She would like "to take people and point at a star you can see with the naked eye in a really dark sky and say, 'That star has a planet like Earth.'"

In December 2011, scientists did discover a rocky planet roughly the same size as Earth, and also orbiting a star like our sun. Kepler-20f, which is 945 light years away, may have a water-vapour atmosphere. But with a boiling-hot surface temperature of 426 degrees centigrade, it is probably too hot for life. Even so, one of

Seager's colleagues, astronomer Francois Fressin, says "this could be an important milestone. I think ten years or maybe even 100 years from now, people will look back and ask when the first Earth-sized planet was found. It is very exciting." Sara Seager concurs. "Even if they don't like science in general," she says in *Talking About Life*, "most people on the street are interested in whether there are other Earths out there, and whether we're alone. It speaks to people from all walks of life."

50

THE CANADARM

Yesterday's robot is tomorrow's ancestor

Science fiction writers, and even some scientists, tell us that advances in robotics and artificial intelligence will soon create a new kind of human being. You've seen movies featuring cyborgs? Superhuman creatures that combine biological and artificial parts? Think Arnold Schwarzenegger as *The Terminator*, a robotic assassin designed by a supercomputer to exterminate the human race. Eventually, he becomes a defender of same, and not a moment too soon. The Terminator is, of course, a fiction. He springs from the same lineage as Frankenstein's monster, dreamed up by Mary Shelley two centuries ago. Artificial beings appear even in Greek mythology, where we find the golden robots of Hephaestus and Pygmalion's Galatea. More recently, they have turned up in movies such as *I Robot*, *Blade Runner*, *Matrix*, and *A.I.: Artificial Intelligence*.

In the real world, we can identify two landmark dates in the evolution of artificial intelligence (AI). In 1997, a computer chess-playing system called Deep Blue defeated a reigning world chess champion; and in 2011, in a *Jeopardy!* quiz show contest, an IBM system called Watson annihilated the two greatest-ever human players. As for robotics, in 2005, a Stanford University robot that incorporated AI was able to drive unassisted for more than 200 kilometres along an unfamiliar desert trail. Two years after that, during a university competition, six teams managed to develop robot vehicles that were able, unassisted, to complete a 96-kilometre course featuring red lights, stop signs, obstacles, and even merging traffic.

Today, advances in AI and robotics are coming so quickly that some people dream of prolonging their lives through biotechnology, by adding artificial parts, or else by uploading their consciousnesses into artificial bodies. Even serious scientists, among them Jeffrey Grossman at the Massachusetts Institute of Technology, are predicting the evolution and emergence of some form of humanoid robot. A prototypical cyborg may soon be upon us—one that, inevitably, will draw on Canadian robotics.

The key date is November 13, 1981. That's when the Canadarm, Canada's robotic spacearm, first went into space aboard the American space shuttle *Columbia*. MacDonald, Dettwiler and Associates (MDA), a Canadian company based in Richmond, British Columbia, developed and built the Canadarm at a cost of $108 million. Before retiring at age thirty, the Canadarm served on ninety space shuttle missions and travelled more than 624 million kilometres. It changed the world by preparing the way and doing the requisite groundwork for the emergence of a whole new order of being.

The original robotic arm, 15 metres long, was attached to the shuttle. An astronaut would operate it mainly to pick up and move free-floating cargo, but also to repair satellites in space and to fix broken toilets. MDA improved on the initial design with the seven-jointed Canadarm2. Unlike its predecessor, which flew back and forth, this robotic arm remained at the International Space Station, where it specialized in assembly and repair. Then came Dextre, a two-armed, $200 million robot that still maintains the exterior of the International Space Station.

Working in conjunction with the Canadian Space Agency, MDA is developing yet another generation of Canadarms for use on landing craft or rovers sent to explore Mars or the moon. Just 2.5 metres long, these robotic arms are much more sophisticated than the original. According to a Capital News Online video, the arms will be sent out on a rover to collect rock or ore samples. Where the Canadarm required a human operator, these enhanced robots can act on a simple order and deduce what to do next based on past experience. MDA president Andrew Goldenberg, who worked on the original Canadarm, says these latest models will be smart enough to learn from their mistakes and perform operations without human involvement.

MDA has developed smaller robotic arms capable of performing brain surgery, and also a two-armed system, called neuroArm, that performs surgery inside a Magnetic Resonance Imaging (MRI) machine that presents detailed images of internal structures. NeuroArm has already been used to augment human capabilities in operations at Calgary's Foothills Hospital. Yet another descendant of the Canadarm is KidsArm, which surgeons have used at Toronto's Hospital for Sick Children to perform operations on small children and babies, notably to reconnect tiny veins, arteries and intestines. MDA is also developing robotic systems to detect and treat breast cancer, and to inspect nuclear power plants.

Kevin Shortt, the head of the Canadian Space Society, has gone on record warning that several other countries, among them Germany, Japan, and the United States, are creating robotic arms of their own. A prototype American "robonaut," for example, is more humanoid than anything Canada has yet developed. But that robot must remain fixed in place. Canada's new robotic rovers—able to learn from mistakes, make choices, and perform without human agency—will be mobile. And they will be ready to leave Earth in 2013.

One century from now, having evolved through many more generations, these AI-enhanced robots will be self-directing. As such, according to the experts, they will constitute a new order of being. And if, at that point, a cyborg named Adamoid goes looking for antecedents the way family historians and genealogists seek out human forebears, then he, she or it will light upon 1981 as a pivotal year. Adamoid will discover that, on the robotics branch of its family tree, one of its progenitors was born that year in Richmond, British Columbia. Yesterday's Canadarm is tomorrow's ancestor.

RUNNING ON A ROOF

Choosing 50 world-changing Canadians proved harder than I anticipated, even after dividing them into groups and stipulating that they be born in the twentieth century. Activists, visionaries, artists, humanitarians, performers, scientists, and inventors: while astounded by the transformative individuals who turn up in these pages, I find myself yearning to add to their number. How does that old Swahili proverb go? "Running on a roof finishes at the edge." I have run out of roof without exhausting my nominees. Perhaps I should produce a sequel, *50 More Canadians Who Changed the World.*

Activists worth considering include John Ralston Saul, the public intellectual who challenged corporatism and, as president of PEN International, campaigned globally to protect endangered languages and cultures. And I wonder about three visionaries: Joseph-Armand Bombardier founded Bombardier, a Fortune 500 company, and invented the snowmobile; Northrop Frye wrote *Anatomy of Criticism,* a profoundly influential work of literary theory; and Mark Carney, governor first of the Bank of Canada and now of the Bank of England, and also chair of the G20's Financial Stability Board, shows signs of becoming a transformative figure in global finance.

Turning to artists, Norval Morrisseau has been hailed in France as the "Picasso of the North," and ethnologist Basil Johnston produced *The Manitous,* which is akin to a bible for the Objiwa nation.

Humanitarians worthy of more research include Jean Vanier, who spearheaded Faith and Light, an international movement that serves people with developmental disabilities, and also Flora MacDonald, a former Tory cabinet minister who founded Future Generations Canada and has been rebuilding civil society in Afghanistan. Then there is Jeffrey Skoll, the first president of eBay, the only Canadian among eighty-one billionaires to sign the Giving Pledge, organized by Bill Gates and Warren Buffet: Skoll is tackling water scarcity and nuclear proliferation.

Among performers, I think of Ethel Stark, who founded the Montreal Women's Symphony Orchestra, the first Canadian orchestra to play Carnegie Hall; and of Buffy Sainte-Marie, a Canadian Cree singer-songwriter who has drawn attention to issues involving the Native peoples; and also of Robert Lepage, the theatre impresario recognized internationally as a multimedia artist and performance art visionary. And what about Bryan Adams, the singer-songwriter who has won dozens of awards for his music, and has also created a foundation that improves education for people around the globe?

Scientists and inventors might include Roger Tomlinson, who introduced geographic information system (GIS) technology in the 1960s, so laying the foundation for Google Maps and GPS receivers in cars. Turning to theoretical physics, we find John Moffat, whose "variable speed of light" theory refined the work of Albert Einstein; and also Robert Orr, lead investigator of the Canadian team that helped snare the elusive Higgs boson particle. Sylvia Asa, a pioneering figure in pathology, advanced our knowledge of thyroid cancers, and Tom Chau is a biomedical engineer inventing life-changing devices for children with physical challenges. Ronald Deibert, founder of the Citizen Lab at the Munk School of Global Affairs, is a world leader in uncovering cyber espionage networks.

That makes nineteen candidates. Surely, together, they constitute the edge of a whole different roof? *Another 50 Canadians Who Changed the World.* Yes, as a title, that works better. Keep an eye out for it.

ACKNOWLEDGMENTS

In a book about twentieth-century Canadians who changed the world, obviously I could not include Vincent Massey. First, he was born in 1887. Second, Massey did not change the world, though he did change Canada by spearheading the creation, in 1957, of the Canada Council for the Arts. That arms-length granting agency has provided crucial assistance to Canadian writers and artists of all kinds. It also inspired the creation of several similar arts institutions. I am happy to report that one of them, the Toronto Arts Council, gave me some support for *50 Canadians Who Changed the World*.

Five individuals who turned up in my last book, *How the Scots Invented Canada*, could not be excluded from this one. And three figures I treated initially in columns for *Canada's History* magazine also demanded recognition. This is my sixth book with the team at HarperCollins Canada, a team that is second to none in Canadian publishing. With *50 Canadians*, I had the privilege of working with two of the finest editors in the country: Phyllis Bruce and Patrick Crean. Both contributed so much to this book that when I hear writers talk about self-publishing and not needing an editor, I can only shake my head. Crucial contributions came from Noelle Zitzer, Allegra Robinson, Alan Jones, and freelance copy editor Sue Sumeraj, while those who led the charge outward included Leo MacDonald,

Rob Firing, Colleen Simpson, Michael Guy-Haddock, Cory Beatty, Bridget Haines, and, in the West, Terry Toews. My literary agent, Beverley Slopen, showed yet again why she is renowned as one of the best in the business.

On the home front, I owe thanks to Carlin, Keriann, Sylwia, and Travis. Finally, without Sheena Fraser McGoogan, my life partner and fellow traveller, this book would not exist.

SELECT REFERENCES

Books

Alexiou, Alice Sparberg. *Jane Jacobs: Urban Visionary*. Toronto: HarperCollins Canada, 2006.

Babinski, Tony. Art by Kristian Manchester. *Cirque du Soleil: 20 Years under the Sun—An Authorized History*. New York: Harry N. Abrams, 2004.

Barlow, Maude. *Blue Covenant: The Global Water Crisis and the Coming Battle for the Right to Water*. Toronto: McClelland & Stewart, 2007.

Barris, Alex. *Oscar Peterson: A Musical Biography*. Toronto: HarperCollins Canada, 2002.

Beard, William, and Jerry White, eds. *North of Everything: English-Canadian Cinema Since 1980*. Edmonton: University of Alberta Press, 2002.

Bego, Mark. *Joni Mitchell*. Lanham, MD: Taylor Trade Publishing, 2005.

Bell, John. *Invaders from the North: How Canada Conquered the Comic Book Universe*. Toronto: Dundurn, 2006.

Blodgett, Jean. *Kenojuak*. Toronto: Firefly Books, 1985.

Boddy, Trevor. *The Architecture of Douglas Cardinal*. Edmonton: NeWest Press, 1989.

Brown, Chester. *Paying for It: A Comic-Strip Memoir About Being a John*. Montreal: Drawn & Quarterly, 2011.

Brunt, Stephen. *Gretzky's Tears: Hockey, Canada, and the Day Everything Changed*. Toronto: Knopf Canada, 2009.

Cohen, Andrew. *While Canada Slept: How We Lost Our Place in the World.* Toronto: McClelland & Stewart, 2003.

Cole, Janis, and Holly Dale. *Calling the Shots: Profiles of Women Filmmakers.* Kingston: Quarry Press, 1993.

Dallaire, Roméo. *Shake Hands with the Devil: The Failure of Humanity in Rwanda.* Toronto: Random House Canada, 2003.

Dallaire, Roméo. *They Fight Like Soldiers, They Die Like Children: The Global Quest to Eradicate the Use of Child Soldiers.* Toronto: Random House Canada, 2010.

Davis, Wade. *The Wayfinders: Why Ancient Wisdom Matters in the Modern World.* Toronto: House of Anansi Press, 2009.

Denault, Todd. *Jacques Plante: The Man Who Changed the Face of Hockey.* Toronto: McClelland & Stewart, 2009.

Dion, Celine, with George-Hébert Germain. *Celine Dion: My Story, My Dream.* Translated by Bruce Benderson. New York: William Morrow, 2000.

Elkins-Tanton, Linda T. *The Earth and the Moon.* New York: Chelsea House, 2006.

Everett, Deborah, and Elayne Zorn. *Encyclopedia of Native American Artists: Artists of the American Mosaic.* Westport, CT: Greenwood Press, 2008.

Fox, Michael J. *Always Looking Up: The Adventures of an Incurable Optimist.* New York: Hyperion, 2009.

Galbraith, John Kenneth. *The Scotch.* Cambridge, MA: Riverside Press, 1964.

Graham, Ron. *The Last Act: Pierre Trudeau, the Gang of Eight and the Fight for Canada.* The History of Canada series. Toronto: Allen Lane, 2011.

Gretzky, Wayne, with Rick Reilly. *Gretzky: An Autobiography.* Toronto: HarperCollins Canada, 1990.

Halperin, Ian. *Guy Laliberté: The Fabulous Story of the Creator of Cirque du Soleil.* Montreal: Transit Publishing, 2009.

Hansen, Rick, and Jim Taylor. *Rick Hansen: Man in Motion.* Vancouver: Douglas & McIntyre. 1987.

Harris, Mason. *Joy Kogawa and Her Works.* Canadian Author Studies series. Toronto: ECW Press, 1996.

Hinton, Brian. *Joni Mitchell: Both Sides Now—The Biography*, 2nd ed. London: Sanctuary Publishing, 2000.

Holbrook, Kate, Ann S. Kim, Brian Palmer, and Anna Portnoy, eds. *Global Values 101: A Short Course*. Boston: Beacon Press, 2006.

Impey, Chris, ed. *Talking About Life: Conversations on Astrobiology*. Cambridge: Cambridge University Press, 2010.

Isenberg, Barbara. *Conversations with Frank Gehry*. New York: Alfred A. Knopf, 2009.

Jacobs, Jane. *The Death and Life of Great American Cities*. New York: Random House, 1961.

Klein, Naomi. *No Logo: Taking Aim at the Brand Bullies*. Toronto: Vintage Canada, 2000.

Klein, Naomi. *The Shock Doctrine: The Rise of Disaster Capitalism*. Toronto: Knopf Canada, 2007.

Kogawa, Joy. *Obasan*. Toronto: Lester & Orpen Dennys, 1981.

Konieczny, Vladimir. *Glenn Gould: A Musical Force*. Toronto: Dundurn Press, 2009.

Lazo, Caroline Evensen. *Frank Gehry*. Minneapolis: Twenty-First Century Books, 2006.

Lees, Gene. *Oscar Peterson: The Will to Swing*. Toronto: Key Porter, 1988, 2000.

Lester, Malcolm. *Glenn Gould: A Life in Pictures*. Foreword by Yo-Yo Ma. Introduction by Tim Page. Toronto: Doubleday Canada, 2002.

Levitin, Jacqueline. "Deepa Mehta as Transnational Filmmaker, or You Can't Go Home Again," in *North of Everything: English Canadian Cinema Since 1980*, edited by William Beard and Jerry White. Edmonton: University of Alberta Press, 2002.

Lewis, Stephen. *Race Against Time*. Toronto: House of Anansi Press, 2005.

MacKay, Gillian. "Frank Gehry: The Early Years," in *Frank Gehry: Toronto*. Toronto: Art Gallery of Ontario, 2006.

Margoshes, Dave. *Tommy Douglas: Building the New Society*. Toronto: XYZ Publishing, 1999.

Martin, Lawrence. *Harperland: The Politics of Control.* Toronto: Viking Canada, 2010.

McQueen, Rod. *BlackBerry: The Inside Story of Research in Motion.* Toronto: Key Porter, 2010.

Monk, Katherine. *Joni: The Creative Odyssey of Joni Mitchell.* Vancouver: Greystone Books, 2012.

Moskovits, Martin, ed. *Science and Society: The John C. Polanyi Nobel Laureates Lectures.* Toronto: House of Anansi Press, 1995.

Nadel, Ira B. *Various Positions: A Life of Leonard Cohen.* New York: Random House, 1996.

Parker, Richard. *John Kenneth Galbraith: His Life, His Politics, His Economics.* Toronto: HarperCollins Canada, 2005.

Peters, Russell. *Call Me Russell.* Toronto: Doubleday Canada, 2010.

Saltzman, Devyani. *Shooting Water: A Memoir of Second Chances, Family and Filmmaking.* Toronto: Key Porter, 2005.

Scrivener, Leslie. *Terry Fox: His Story.* Toronto: McClelland & Stewart, 1981.

Shapiro, Marc. *James Cameron: An Unauthorized Biography of the Filmmaker.* Los Angeles: Renaissance Books, 2000.

Simmons, Sylvie. *I'm Your Man: The Life of Leonard Cohen.* Toronto: McClelland & Stewart, 2012.

Squire, Larry R., ed. *The History of Neuroscience in Autobiography,* vol. 2. London: Academic Press, 1998.

Sullivan, Rosemary. *The Red Shoes: Margaret Atwood—Starting Out.* Toronto: HarperCollins Canada, 1998.

Tapscott, Don. *Grown Up Digital: How the Net Generation Is Changing Your World.* New York: McGraw-Hill, 2008.

Tapscott, Don, and Anthony D. Williams. *Macrowikinomics: Rebooting Business and the World.* Toronto: Penguin Group, 2010.

Tapscott, Don, and Anthony D. Williams. *Wikinomics: How Mass Collaboration Changes Everything.* New York: Portfolio, 2006.

Walk, Ansgar. *Kenojuak: The Life Story of an Inuit Artist.* Toronto: Penumbra Press, 1999.

Watson, Patrick. *The Canadians: Biographies of a Nation,* Omnibus edition. Toronto: McArthur, 2003.

Wickenheiser, Hayley. *Gold Medal Diary: Inside the World's Greatest Sports Event.* Vancouver: Greystone Books, 2010.

Wilson, Carl. *Let's Talk About Love: A Journey to the End of Taste.* New York: Continuum, 2007.

Wojna, Lisa. "Louise Arbour/Lady Justice," in *Great Canadian Women: Nineteen Portraits of Extraordinary Women.* Great Canadian Stories series. Edmonton: Folklore Publishing, 2005.

Yoe, Craig. *Secret Identity: The Fetish Art of Superman's Co-creator Joe Shuster.* New York: Abrams ComicArts, 2009.

Films and Television Episodes

Findley, Peter. *Immovable Maude: The Life and Times of Maude Barlow.* Directed by Peter Findley. Toronto: CBC-TV, 2001.

Garvey, Bruce. *Oscar Peterson: The Life of a Legend.* Directed by William R. Cunningham and Sylvia Sweeny. Toronto: NFB/CBC, 1995.

Jackson, Judy. "Stephen Lewis: The Man Who Couldn't Sleep." *The Nature of Things,* episode 56. Directed by Judy Jackson. Toronto: CBC, 2006.

Pollock, Sydney. "Sketches of Frank Gehry." *American Masters,* season 20, episode 7. Directed by Sydney Pollock. Culver City, CA: Sony Pictures, 2006.

Reece, PJ. *Radical Attitudes: The Architecture of Douglas Cardinal.* Directed by Jim Hamm. Vancouver: Jim Hamm Productions, 1994.

Shuster, Frank. *The Wayne & Shuster Years.* Directed by Trevor Evans. Toronto: CBC Home Video, 2000.

INDEX